D0648884

Land Economics Monographs
Number 6

University of Wisconsin Sea Grant College Program
Technical Report No. 239

# BUYING A BETTER ENVIRONMENT

# BUYING A BETTER ENVIRONMENT

## Cost-Effective Regulation through Permit Trading

### Erhard F. Joeres & Martin H. David, Editors

The Proceedings of a National Conference on

"Regulatory Reform, Transferable Permits
and Enhancement of Environmental Quality"

Sponsored by the
University of Wisconsin Sea Grant Institute
June 23–25, 1982
Madison, Wis.

Published for
the Journal of LAND ECONOMICS
in cooperation with the
UNIVERSITY OF WISCONSIN SEA GRANT INSTITUTE

The University of Wisconsin Press 1983

LAND ECONOMICS Monographs • Number 6

A quarterly journal devoted to studies in natural resources, urban and public policy issues.

U.W. SEA GRANT Technical Report • Number 239

The "Regulatory Reform, Transferable Permits and Enhancement of Environmental Quality" conference and the preparation of this manuscript for publication was funded by the University of Wisconsin Sea Grant Institute under grants from the Office of Sea Grant, National Oceanic and Atmospheric Administration, U.S. Department of Commerce, and from the State of Wisconsin.

Federal grant NA80AA-D-00086
Projects R/PS-28 and A/AS-2/Tech. Rpt. WIS-SG-83-239

Copyediting • Stephen Wittman
Design & Cover • Christine Kohler
Production assistance • Linda Campbell

Cover photo • Michael Brisson

# Contents

INSTITUTIONS & MARKETS (cont'd.)

WATER

DISCUSSION

APPENDICES

# List of Figures

# List of Tables

# Foreword

This conference on transferable discharge permits marked another important milestone in an exciting and, I hope, environmentally and economically beneficial program. Our own TDP work at Wisconsin has become a model of university-industry-government cooperation. It involves research and outreach on an important common problem. What started out as a rather esoteric University of Wisconsin Sea Grant research project has moved quite rapidly to the stage where it could become a part of national resource management policy. The State of Wisconsin has now accepted the idea of transferable discharge permits for water and has begun to use it as a technique for dealing with the Fox River industrial complex.

I am pleased that this conference was convened here in Wisconsin, in a Great Lakes setting. The Great Lakes, as a system, are probably as intensively used as any marine region in the nation. Because the region has a high population density and high level of industrialization, and because the Great Lakes are a closed system of water with a flushing time measured in decades or centuries, the need to manage the lakes, to protect them, has become more acute than for coastal regions. As a result -- and fortunately so -- the Great Lakes are now being viewed as a single system, and the philosophy for managing them is being based more and more on maintaining the overall quality of the water and the ecosystem as opposed to regulating single point sources of pollution or individual coastal developments. This is the thesis of the transferable discharge permit idea, and this is why Sea Grant could offer and sustain its support of research on the TDP idea over a number of years. Whether the TDP model can or should be expanded to the larger Great Lakes "bubble" remains to be seen, but the basic TDP model will in any case help to move our thinking ahead.

Several of the papers in this monograph deal with the question of the size of this "bubble." For example, can it be expanded to very large dimensions to deal with acid rain? Theoretically it can, but whether the necessary scientific and technical base can be developed is much less certain.

In dealing with these and other very difficult but important questions, it is crucial that all points of view be examined. In this regard, I was glad to see that this conference brought together industry scientists and managers and government resource managers as

well as university scientists. Obviously, the invention of such a
technique for pollution control will be of little value without the
understanding and cooperation of all three groups. This conference
provided a crucial forum for communicating these various points of
view and improving our understanding of how the TDP idea can be used
to accelerate the improvement of the Great Lakes and their bays and
tributaries.

**Robert A. Ragotzkie**
**Director, Sea Grant Institute**
**University of Wisconsin**

# Preface

The literature on the application of market mechanisms to environmental regulation is a recent one. It resulted from the realization in the late 1960s and early 1970s that a concerted national effort would be required to achieve harmony between the various forces affecting environmental management. Once this imperative was understood, the difficult next phase of determining ways to translate this fundamental understanding into environmental policy brought forth a variety of suggestions and approaches. A principal one among them is that the assimilative carrying capacity of the environment, once legally defined, quite naturally becomes a property right, and consequently social welfare can best be achieved through creating markets in these rights.

Recent economic pressures have quickly pushed research on alternative regulatory mechanisms towards policy implementation. The work we carried out on the efficacy of marketable pollution rights -- termed by us Transferable Discharge Permits (TDPs) -- very quickly moved from academic conception to policy design when planners in the Wisconsin Department of Natural Resources, charged with developing new water pollution permit systems, asked for our help. As we proceeded with our research, we discovered a variety of related efforts underway elsewhere, both in relation to air and to water pollution control. By 1981, Wisconsin had written the option of permit trading into the administrative code regulating the discharge of wastewater into its rivers. We noted strong interest in other states to emulate Wisconsin's experience, along with significant progress in some locales to implement transferable permit systems for air pollution control. Clearly, the consideration of market mechanisms for environmental pollution control had taken on national dimensions. The danger of such widespread activity becoming fragmented presented the concomitant need to highlight the complex economic, technical and institutional issues involved and to identify common ground in the application of a market system.

With the sponsorship of the University of Wisconsin Sea Grant Institute, we invited a select group to a conference entitled "Regulatory Reform, Transferable Permits and Enhancement of Environmental Quality," held June 23-25, 1982, at Madison, Wis. The conference involved policy planners, agency administrators, economists, engineers, attorneys and institutional experts, and practitioners representing industrial dischargers and regulators as well.

Our agenda was to define the domain and dimensions of market structures for the environmental applications currently being contemplated.  Issues addressed include the definition of pollution rights;
their spatial variability; distributional matters relating to permit
issuance, trading and benefit accounting; and stochastic quantities to
be considered in demand for the use and response of the environment.
Questions of market participation, permit pricing, institutional
behavior and political perceptions were also considered in varying
degrees.  One significant issue only parenthetically touched upon but
which deserves future scrutiny is the impetus for technological
innovation inherent in TDP systems.

An examination of the papers in this book will reveal an extraordinary
range of creative endeavor.  Such a catholic view of new ideas about
market structures applied to environmental regulation is not available
from any other single source, and it is for this reason that we have
published this volume.

We offer our thanks to the University of Wisconsin Sea Grant
Institute, without whose unfailing vision of the need for creative and
unfettered inquiry neither our work nor this volume would have come to
pass.

E.F.J./M.H.D.
Madison, Wis.
November 1982

# BUYING A BETTER ENVIRONMENT

## Cost-Effective Regulation through Permit Trading

# Achieving Environmental Quality in the Face of Social, Economic and Political Constraints

**Anthony S. Earl\***

**Governor
State of Wisconsin**

It was a pleasure for me to accept the invitation to address the "Regulatory Reform, Transferable Permits and Enhancement of Environmental Quality" conference and comment on its timely and thought-provoking theme. It has become readily apparent that if we are to flourish as a society, we must be able to enhance our environmental quality while also maintaining an economic system that allows men and women to earn a viable living. Any attempt to fulfill these dual objectives usually causes a certain amount of tension, but our experience in Wisconsin indicates that it is not an impossible task to meet both objectives.

Inevitably, efforts to clean up our environment meet resistance in the form of certain social, economic and political constraints. This is not surprising, because such efforts usually challenge the status quo. I wish to share with you one example of how we in Wisconsin successfully overcame these constraints by adopting and implementing innovative management strategies, regulations and technologies to clean up the Lower Fox River.

But before I discuss the components of our achievement in the Fox River Valley, I think it is important to place this success story in perspective by providing some background on our state's history and traditions.

## THE WISCONSIN IDEA

Over the years, Wisconsin has led the nation in adopting creative ideas for ensuring the continued wise use of our natural resources and in solving certain resource management problems. The reasons for this are inextricably tied to our state's enlightened citizenry and progressive political traditions. We have long recognized the unique beauty of Wisconsin and the imperative of protecting its bountiful but fragile resource base for the sake of our economic and mental well-being.

---

\*Mr. Earl was Secretary of the Wisconsin Department of Natural Resources during the years 1975-80.

The basis of our strong commitment to protecting our natural resources comes as no surprise to anyone who has had the wonderful opportunity of viewing firsthand the majesty of Lakes Superior and Michigan and the Mississippi River, the beauty of our many inland lakes and streams, the splendor of our North Woods and the Apostle Islands, and the unique land forms in the southern part of the state.

The uniqueness that is Wisconsin has been deeply appreciated by the vast majority of our citizens, whether farmers or city dwellers. It has deeply influenced the writings and philosophy of John Muir and Aldo Leopold, and it has had a major impact on the farsighted policies of notable governors like Gaylord Nelson. The appreciation of our rich legacy and the commitment to maintaining it for later generations is also manifested in our ardent defense of the Public Trust Doctrine and our pioneering efforts in legislation and programs designed to ensure that each new generation of citizens will have unfettered access to clean lakes and streams and that our renewable resources will be used wisely.

Of equal importance to this commitment is the practical dimension of bringing together the relevant actors of the public and private sectors and our great university system to build the requisite consensus to solve the emergencies of a particular period. Time and again, Wisconsin has forged the appropriate coalitions for solving the complicated problems of each era. Our state's present dairy and forest industries are examples of the success of past coalitions in developing, refining and implementing innovative solutions to specific resource management and economic development problems. The effort to clean up our rivers, lakes and streams continues in this fine tradition. So often have we been successful in forming partnerships between the public and private sectors and seeking innovative approaches to new problems that we have taken to describing this process as "the Wisconsin Idea."

In this context, I will now turn to our experience in the Fox River Valley, where we have made considerable progress in cleaning up a very polluted river by adopting some of the innovative techniques that were the center of attention at this conference. My comments focus on the practical dimensions of the constraints we faced and how they were overcome.


THE FOX RIVER EXPERIENCE


The Fox is a relatively small, winding river about 40 miles west of Lake Michigan in east-central Wisconsin. It is a river broken up by numerous dams and lakes, and in its valley is the second-largest concentration of people in the state. Among the industrial dis-chargers along its banks are 14 paper mills -- the largest concentra-tion of paper and pulp mills in the United States. The river has experienced very heavy BOD loadings over the years, and the levels of dissolved oxygen were near or at zero in many stretches of the river.

## Constraints on the Clean-up Effort
The State of Wisconsin's goal for the Fox River was to bring its water quality up to federal/state standards. We recognized at the outset that there were significant social, economic and political constraints to reaching this goal. One of the most notable obstacles was the resignation of many people in the valley that the river was beyond help and that any attempt to clean it up would be a waste of public and private funds.

We also knew that there was considerable reluctance to spend any dollars on "end-of-pipe" technologies; in particular, there were very strongly held beliefs that "best practical technologies" would never get us to the federal/state water quality standards. We were also confronted with a great deal of wariness on the part of industry and municipalities that they would be asked to pick up an unfair share of the clean-up costs.

Finally, there was enormous resistance -- built on years of distrust -- to any role for the Wisconsin Department of Natural Resources in the clean-up effort. In Wisconsin the DNR has the lead responsibility for implementing federal and state antipollution laws. As such it has substantial regulatory power, and for this reason the state agency is not welcomed by local officials and interest groups.

## Overcoming the Constraints
Recognizing the nature and extent of the constraints on any effort to significantly improve the quality of the Fox River, we set out to turn this situation around on a variety of fronts.

To start, we presented a convincing case that certain technological innovations and management/regulatory strategies would provide the opportunity to avoid or minimize the traditional cost centers associated with "end-of-pipe" methods. We did this by demonstrating that through the combination of a variety of technologies -- such as issuing permits based on river flow and temperature rates, setting rolling averages, encouraging aeration processes, and establishing a transfer of discharge permits processes -- the goal of the water quality standards would be met.

To deal with the skepticism about the fairness with which the the costs and responsibilities for the clean-up would be distributed, we developed a waste allocation system for dischargers along the entire length of the river. The specifics of the allocation system were extensively publicized and discussed, and ultimately it was accepted by all the principal actors. In addition, it was decided -- and it was an important decision -- that the primary monitoring responsibility for ensuring compliance with the allocation system would be placed at the local level rather than with the WDNR.

In a broader context, the role of the WDNR in the entire process of cleaning up the Fox River became one of a facilitator among many diverse groups rather than that of the enforcer or regulator. Intensive efforts were directed at involving local government officials and other elected officials, regional planning groups,

industry, active citizen groups and the news media. Involvement of
the general public was never very successful, due in part I think to
the complexity of the subject matter.

## The Results

After extensive efforts spanning several years, we were able to gain
broad acceptance of the goals and methods of achieving the federal-
state clean water standards. We did so without confrontation -- a
major accomplishment in and of itself. Biologically, the river has
experienced a remarkable comeback, and fish have returned to the river
as the clean up has progressed. Significant portions of the river are
now available for use by outdoor enthusiasts, and property values
along the river are on the rise.


## THE NEED FOR INNOVATION

Are any of the experiences that we gained from employing innovative
technologies in achieving improved water quality in the Fox River
suitable for replication elsewhere? Most definitely!

The need for innovation and for accepting innovation in achieving
environmental quality has never been greater. Our industry and
municipalities especially need assistance in finding the most
cost-effective methods and processes for reaching the ultimate goal of
environmental quality. The fact is that we are a long way from
exhausting the supply of ideas for attaining that goal. In addition,
we must fully anticipate the needs and skepticism of those groups and
individuals who ultimately have the responsibility for attaining a
better environment. The skeptics' views typically cover a wide
spectrum -- that we have gone far enough, or that some new concepts
like TDPs are merely selling "rights to pollute," or that the
"tried-and-tested" methods for solving pollution problems are the only
way to proceed.

Our experiences in the Fox River Valley and elsewhere in Wisconsin
have taught us that new techniques for achieving environmental quality
like those discussed at this conference will be accepted and can be
effectively utilized if:

1.  We have accurate information (e.g., about waste loadings and
    assimilative capacity) and that the information is kept current;

2.  We have involved all of the right actors (decision-makers) from
    the onset;

3.  We ensure that strong and effective monitoring and enforcement
    procedures are in place and being carried out;

4.  We establish some identifiable standards and benchmarks from
    which we can measure progress -- mere maintenance of the status
    quo will not be enough, nor will the release of a string of
    numbers that provide no real means by which to judge the extent
    to which progress is being made in achieving water quality
    standards;

5.   We describe the techniques that are eventually chosen for the
     clean-up effort (TDPs, banking, offsets, public-private-mixed) in
     terms that are understandable to the general public;

6.   We update the techniques for pollution clean up on a regular
     basis -- clean-up timetables, wasteload allocations and so on
     must be changed in a timely manner to reflect changing
     circumstances.


CONCLUSIONS

Our experience in Wisconsin indicates that achieving environmental
quality is possible even when significant social, economic and
political constraints exist.  In fact, if many of these constraints
are handled adroitly, they may be turned into opportunities for
gaining a new perspectives on problems and an acceptance of innovation.  But ultimately, to be successful, each of us -- as public
administrators, economists, academicians, engineers and politicians --
must participate in the process of persuading the appropriate groups
and individuals that the ideas and concepts discussed at this
conference are workable and worthwhile.

# On Marketable Air Pollution Permits:
# The Case for a System of Pollution Offsets

**Alan J. Krupnick**

**Wallace E. Oates**

**Eric Van De Verg**

Resources for the Future
Washington, D.C.

Department of Economics
University of Maryland

Maryland Dept. of Economic
and Community Development

For most air and water pollutants, the extent and spatial pattern of the damages to the environment depend not only on the level of emissions, but on the locations and the dispersion characteristics of the sources. This implies an inherently spatial problem in the design of a system to control these pollutants. A regulatory system that ignores the spatial problem can pass up potentially large cost savings in the achievement of objectives for environmental quality.

This paper explores alternative techniques for incorporating spatial elements into a system of marketable air pollution permits. There exist several such alternatives, and they have fundamentally different implications for the structure and functioning of a permits market. We shall contend that, among the alternatives, a system of "pollution offsets" offers the most promising approach to the design of an effective market in pollution permits.

The seminal paper on this issue is Montgomery (1972). The Montgomery paper analyzes two systems of marketable pollution permits: a system of "pollution licenses" that define allowable emissions in terms of pollutant concentrations at a set of receptor points, and a system of "emission licenses" that confer directly the right to emit pollutants up to a specified rate. Montgomery demonstrates that the former system satisfies the important condition that a market equilibrium coincides with the least-cost solution for attaining any predetermined level of environmental quality and does so for <u>any</u> initial allocation of licenses among polluters.

However, as we discuss, the transactions costs for polluting firms associated with Montgomery's system of pollution licenses are likely to be quite high. His alternative system of emissions licenses promises considerable savings in transactions costs. Unfortunately, however, the Montgomery paper also demonstrates that an extremely restrictive (and, in fact, a generally unattainable) condition is required for an initial allocation of rights to ensure that the market equilibrium is the least-cost solution. This finding is particularly disturbing on two counts. First, the environmental authority may not be able to find an initial allocation of permits that ensures an

efficient outcome. And second, should such an allocation even exist,
a substantial degree of flexibility in the choice of this initial
allocation is lost; such flexibility may be extremely important in
designing a system that is politically feasible (as well as efficient).

We show in this paper that this shortcoming of Montgomery's system of
emission licenses is the result of an unnecessarily restrictive
condition that he imposes on the trading of the licenses. By suitable
(and quite straightforward) modifications to this condition, we find
that an efficiency property similar to the one that characterizes his
system of pollution licenses also characterizes our modified schemes
of "pollution offsets": a "trading equilibrium" exists that coincides
with the least-cost pattern of emissions for any initial allocation of
emissions permits. We show also that the pollution offsets approach
offers some important advantages over other techniques in terms of
minimizing the total of abatement and transactions costs.

In the early part of this paper, we go back over some familiar terrain
to put the problem and Montgomery's analysis in its proper perspective.[1] We then proceed to an analysis and assessment of the
alternative approaches to the design of a system of marketable
pollution permits.


A FORMAL STATEMENT OF THE PROBLEM:  A BENCHMARK CASE

It will clarify the analysis somewhat and allow us to establish one of
the baseline cases if we set forth, at this point, a more formal
statement of the spatial problem.[2] Assume that we have a specific
region, an airshed, in which there are $\underline{m}$ sources of pollution, each of
which is fixed in location. Air quality in terms of a particular
pollutant is defined by concentrations at $\underline{n}$ "receptor points" in the
region; we thus describe air quality by a vector $Q = (q_1,\ldots,q_n)$
where $q_j$ is the concentration of the pollutant at point (receptor)
$\underline{j}$. The dispersion characteristics of the problem are described in
terms of a diffusion model, which we represent by an $\underline{m}$ x $\underline{n}$ matrix of
unit diffusion, or transfer coefficients:

$$D = \begin{bmatrix} & \vdots & \\ \cdots & d_{ij} & \cdots \\ & \vdots & \end{bmatrix}$$

In this matrix, the element $d_{ij}$ indicates the contribution that one
unit of emissions from source $\underline{i}$ makes to the pollution concentration
at point $\underline{j}$.[3]

The environmental objective is to attain some predetermined level(s)
of pollutant concentrations within the region; we denote these
standards a $Q^* = (q_1^*,\ldots,q_n^*)$. Note that the standard need not
be the same at each point; the environmental authority could, for

example, prescribe lower concentrations as the target in densely populated areas.

The problem thus becomes one of attaining a set of predetermined levels of pollutant concentrations at the minimum aggregate abatement cost. Or, in other words, we are looking for a vector of emissions from our $\underline{m}$ sources, $E = (e_1,\ldots,e_m)$, that will minimize abatement costs subject to the constraint that the prescribed standards are met at each of the $\underline{n}$ locations in the region. The abatement costs of the $\underline{i}^{th}$ source are a function of its level of emissions: $c_i(e_i)$. So our problem, in formal terms, is to:

$$\text{Minimize} \quad \sum_i c_i(e_i)$$

$$\text{s.t.} \quad ED \leq Q^*$$
$$E \geq 0$$

Montgomery (1972) has shown that such a vector of emissions exists, and that if the sources of pollution are cost-minimizing agents, the emission vector and shadow prices that emerge from the minimization problem satisfy the same set of conditions as do the vectors of emissions and permit prices for a competitive equilibrium in an air permits market. In short, if the environmental authority were simply to issue $q_j^*$ permits (defined in terms of pollutant concentrations) for each of the $\underline{n}$ receptor points, competitive bidding for these permits would generate an equilibrium solution that satisfies the conditions for the minimization of total abatement costs.

These results establish a benchmark case for a control system that minimizes abatement costs. Two properties of this outcome are noteworthy. First is the utter simplicity of the system from the perspective of the environmental agency. In particular, officials need have no information whatsoever regarding abatement costs; they simply issue the prescribed number of permits at each receptor point, and competitive bidding takes care of matters from there. Alternatively, the environmental authority could make an initial allocation of these permits to existing polluters. Subsequent transactions in a competitive setting would then establish the cost-minimizing solution. As Montgomery (1972) proves formally, the least-cost outcome is independent of the initial allocation of the permits.

Second, in contrast to the modest burden it places on administrators, this system can be extremely cumbersome for polluters. Note that a firm emitting wastes must assemble a "portfolio" of permits from each of the receptor points that is affected by its emissions: a source at point $\underline{i}$ will have to acquire permits at each receptor $\underline{j}$ in the amount $(d_{ij}e_i)$. There will, therefore, exist $\underline{n}$ different markets for permits, one for each receptor point, and each polluter will participate in the subset of these markets corresponding to the receptor points affected by his emissions. It would appear that the transactions costs for polluters are likely to be substantial under our benchmark system, although this expense may be justified, under certain circumstances, by the savings in abatement costs.

THE DESIGN OF A MARKETABLE PERMIT SYSTEM:   AN ALTERNATIVE APPROACH

The scheme examined in the preceding section is a kind of prototype of
an _ambient-based_ permit system (APS) of pollution permits:   the
permits are defined in terms of pollutant concentrations at the
receptor points.   An alternative approach in the literature is an
_emission-based_ permit system (EPS), under which the permits are
defined in terms of levels of emissions rather than in terms of the
effects of these emissions on ambient air quality.[4]   This latter
approach typically makes use of a set of emission zones within which
emissions of a particular pollutant are treated as equivalent.   The
environmental authority determines an allocation of permits to each
zone, and polluters within a zone trade permits on a one-to-one
basis.   There are no trades across zones:   each zone is a self-
contained market with its own price for permits determined by the
polluters' demand for permits and the supply as determined by the
authority.[5]

From this perspective, we can envision at one extreme for EPS
(following Tietenberg 1980) a system in which the entire region is a
single market.   The environmental authority issues a fixed number of
permits into the region as a whole, and the subsequent bids and offers
of participants generate a single market-clearing price.   As we move
away from this special case, we encounter continually more finely
divided systems of zones designed to account for the spatial character
of the airshed.   However, regardless of the total number of zones,
each pollution source will be in only a single zone and will consequently operate in only one permit market for a given pollutant.

It is this last feature of the EPS that constitutes its basic appeal.
Recall that under APS the polluter must operate in a number of markets
for each pollutant (in the benchmark case, one for each receptor site
that his emissions affect) and is subject to a different "weighting
parameter" (i.e., diffusion coefficient) in each market.   The
assembling of the requisite portfolio of permits could get quite
complicated for firms; they might even find themselves, in some
instances, buying in one market while selling in another (Russell
1980).   It is not altogether clear just how large these "transactions
costs" are likely to be (more on this shortly); some well-organized
brokerage operations could conceivably facilitate greatly the transfer
of permits.   But it would appear, nonetheless, that from the perspective of the polluter, EPS offers a major attraction by requiring
polluters to buy and sell permits within a single market and with no
system of source-specific weights attached to individual firms.

However, while the EPS approach may simplify life for polluters, it is
a potential nightmare for the administrators of the system.   Recall
that under APS the environmental authority need only establish the
number of permits to be offered for sale at each receptor site (so as
to meet the prescribed air quality standard) and specify the diffusion
or transfer coefficients for each source of pollution.   Market forces
take over from there and, under competitive conditions, generate the
least-cost pattern of waste emissions.[6]

In contrast, EPS makes enormous demands on the administering agency: it requires much more information than APS; it will not, in general, achieve the least-cost outcome, and it necessitates continuing readjustments among zonal stocks of permits. The rationale for the failure to achieve the least-cost solution is straightforward: since polluters with somewhat varying dispersion coefficients are aggregated into the same zone, one-for-one trades of pollution rights will not reflect the differences in concentrations from their respective emissions. The price of emissions to each polluter will not, in short, reflect accurately the shadow price of the binding pollution constraint. This objection to EPS need not be a serious one if the dispersion characteristics for emissions within zones are not very different (Hahn and Noll 1981). This suggests that increasing the number of zones can reduce the "excess abatement costs" associated with EPS. However, increasing the number of zones will tend to reduce the number of participants in each market, with the undesirable repercussions of less competitive markets for permits and increased uncertainty of permit prices.

A more troublesome issue is that even were there no differences in the dispersion characteristics of emissions within each zone, the environmental authority must still determine an allocation of permits to each zone. And this requires, for the attainment of the least-cost outcome under EPS, the complete solution by the administrator of the cost-minimization problem. This implies that the administering agency must have not only an air quality model (to provide the $d_{ij}$) and a complete emissions inventory, but source-specific abatement cost functions. With this information, the agency would solve the cost-minimization problem from which it could determine the least-cost pattern of permit allotments to each zone.[7] In the absence of the requisite models or with less-than-perfect information, the outcome may easily miss the mark of the ambient air quality targets. If pollution were excessive, the authority would have to re-enter the market (in at least some of the zones, where again the pattern of zonal purchases would require a fairly sophisticated analysis) and purchase or confiscate permits. Such an iterative procedure is not only cumbersome for the administrator of the system, but may create considerable uncertainty for firms as to the future course of permit prices.

We stress, moreover, that this is not just a matter of groping once and for all toward an unchanging equilibrium. Altered patterns of emissions resulting from the growth (or contraction) of existing firms, the entry of new firms and changing abatement technology will generate a continually shifting least-cost pattern of emissions across zones. The environmental authority under EPS faces a dynamic problem that will require periodic adjustments to the supplies of permits in each zone.


A HYBRID APPROACH:  A MARKET FOR POLLUTION OFFSETS

From the last two sections, we find that both the ambient-based and emission-based permit systems for pollution control have some

troublesome properties. There is an alternative, however, that
combines certain characteristics of both the APS and EPS approaches
and possesses some quite attractive properties. The basic idea is to
define permits in terms of emissions and to allow their sale among
polluters, but not on a one-to-one basis. More specifically,
transfers of emission permits are subject to the restriction that the
transfer does not result in a violation of the air quality standard at
any receptor point. The source of new emissions (or of expanded
emissions) must purchase a sufficient number of emission permits from
existing sources to "offset" the effects of the new emissions on
pollutant concentrations in such a way that the pollution constraint
is everywhere satisfied. For this reason, we prefer to call this
general approach to a system of marketable permits one of "pollution
offsets."

The hybrid character of the offset approach is apparent. Like EPS, it
involves the purchase and sale of emission permits; yet the permits
are not associated explicitly with a particular receptor market as
under APS. At the same time, however, it captures the spirit of the
ambient-based permit system in that the ratio at which permits
exchange for one another depends on the relative effects of the
associated emissions on ambient air quality at the receptor points.

The Montgomery system of "emission licenses" is, in fact, a special
case of the offset approach. Montgomery places as a constraint on the
transfer of emission permits a "nondegradation condition": he
effectively requires that any transactions among polluters result in
no increase in pollutant concentrations at any receptor point. As we
shall see shortly, this condition is unnecessarily restrictive.
Moreover, it generates an outcome that, for most initial allocations
of permits, will not coincide with the least-cost solution.

By relaxing Montgomery's overly stringent constraint on the trading of
emissions permits, we can show that an equilibrium outcome under an
appropriately designed system of pollution offsets coincides with the
least-cost solution irrespective of the initial allocation of emission
permits. We develop the argument in terms of Figure 1: the horizontal
and vertical axes measure, respectively, the levels of emissions of
firms 1 and 2 (i.e., $e_1$ and $e_2$).[8] The curves $C_1$ and $C_2$ are
iso-cost curves for pollution abatement costs.[9] Note that higher
curves correspond to lower total abatement costs ($C_1 < C_2$). The
line FG indicates the pollution constraint associated with Receptor
a. Points on FG denote combinations of $e_1$ and $e_2$ for which
$q_a = q_a^*$; the slope of the line equals the ratio of the transfer
coefficients (i.e., the rate at which emissions from Firm 2 can
substitute for emissions from Firm 1 with no change in pollution
concentrations at Receptor a). Similarly LM depicts the pollution
constraint for Receptor b. The combinations of emissions from firms 1
and 2 that satisfy the pollution constraint at both receptors is thus
the set of points OLAG. We see immediately that the least-cost
solution occurs at E*, at which point the ratio of marginal abatement
costs equals the ratio of the transfer coefficients. E* is therefore
the optimum; our problem is to determine the circumstances under which

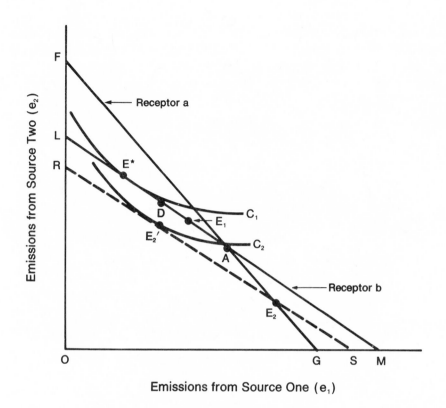

FIGURE 1
Spatially Differentiated Permit Systems

E* will also be the market equilibrium. Under Montgomery's system of "emission licenses," the environmental authority makes an initial allocation of permits to polluting firms, after which firms are free to buy and sell the permits subject to a kind of "nondegradation" condition. More formally each firm faces the constraints:

$$d_{ij}e_i \leq \sum_k d_{kj}l_{ik} \qquad\qquad j = 1,\ldots m$$

where $l_{ik}$ is the emission permits that Firm $\underline{i}$ purchases from Firm $\underline{k}$. This restriction implies that a transfer of emission permits from one polluter to another must take place in such a way that there is no increase in the level of pollution at <u>any</u> receptor point.

Returning to Figure 1, suppose that the environmental authority established an initial allocation of emission permits indicated by $E_1$. Firm 2 would then find it profitable to purchase permits from

Firm 1.[10]  The effective rate of exchange of permits would be the
slope of the line LM, since the constraint at receptor $\underline{b}$ is, in this
instance, the binding constraint.  The gains from trade would be
exhausted at E*.  For the initial allocation of rights indicated by
$E_1$, we thus find that the market equilibrium coincides with the
optimum.

Suppose, however, that instead of $E_1$, the environmental authority
had selected $E_2$ as the initial allocation of permits.  Once again
Firm 2 would find it profitable to purchase permits from Firm 1, but
Montgomery's nondegradation constraint would now limit the feasible
set of outcomes to $ORE_2G$.  The market equilibrium would, in this
instance, be $E_2'$, which does not coincide with the optimal outcome.
The solution at $E_2'$ entails an excessive level of expenditure on
abatement resulting, in a sense, from an "excessive" level of
environmental quality.  The nondegradation constraint prevents a
movement from $E_2'$ to E*.  We thus find that attainment of the
least-cost solution is not independent of the initial allocation of
emission permits.

The problem confronting the environmental authority is that it must
know which segment of the frontier contains E* before it can determine
an initial allocation of permits that makes the market solution
coincident with E*.  There is one qualification:  if the initial
allocation is that represented by point A, market transactions will
move the outcome to E* irrespective of whether E* happens to lie on
line segment LA or segment AG.  This is Montgomery's restriction on
the initial allocation of permits:  the initial allocation must be
such that the pollution constraint is binding at all receptor points
in order to ensure that the market equilibrium coincides with the
least-cost solution.[11]

While this condition seems reasonable enough in terms of our example
in Figure 1 with only two receptor points, the severity of the problem
becomes clear when we introduce additional receptors.  A third line in
Figure 1 indicating the pollution constraint for yet another receptor
point would pass through point A only by coincidence.  This implies
that, in general, with three or more receptor points there will not
exist a vector of emissions for which all the pollution constraints
are binding!  In short, the environmental authority will not, in
general, be able to find an initial allocation of permits that will
ensure the least-cost outcome without a complete solution of the
programming problem.  Under Montgomery's system, the agency must
determine E* (which requires knowledge of firms' abatement cost
functions as well as the transfer coefficients) before it can specify
an initial allocation of permits that will generate E* as the market
equilibrium.  Even if this can be done, it removes most of the
flexibility in setting the initial permit allocation -- a flexibility
that may be extremely important for rendering such a system politically feasible.

However, as the analysis suggests, Montgomery's constraint on the
market behavior of polluters is unnecessarily restrictive.  In the
case, for example, where the initial allocation of permits was $E_2$ in

Figure 1, we saw that trades took place along the dotted line RS instead of the actual constraint LM implied by our predetermined standards of air quality. Montgomery's restriction on market trades of permits is sufficient to ensure that $q \leq q^*$ for all receptors, but it is not necessary. By relaxing this restriction, we can describe a modification of Montgomery's system for which the only point representing an equilibrium is the least-cost outcome.

Suppose that we amend Montgomery's nondegradation condition on trades of permits with the following provision: Firms can always obtain from the environmental authority additional permits so long as the air-quality standard is not violated at any receptor point. We note immediately in Figure 1 that this disqualifies $E_2'$ as a point of market equilibrium; since the pollution constraint is not binding at either receptor point, firms will obtain additional permits from the environmental agency.[12] Suppose, for example, that Firm 2 obtained LR of additional permits, thereby moving the vector of emissions from $E_2'$ to point D. At D, there exists the potential for mutually profitable sales of emission permits by Firm 1 to Firm 2 until $E^*$ is attained. In short, $E^*$ would be a "trading equililbrium" (and the only such equilibrium).[13]

More generally, we can see that our amendment to Montgomery's condition on the issuance and trades of permits gives the modified system two important properties:

1.  No point inside the frontier of feasible points established by the air quality standards can be an equilibrium (since polluters will seek and obtain additional permits).

2.  No point on this frontier other than the least-cost solution can be an equilibrium (since at any other point mutually profitable transfers of permits exist).

We conclude that the trading equilibrium under our offset system coincides with the least-cost solution irrespective of the initial allocation of emission permits; like APS, a suitably designed offset system can achieve the predetermined standards for air quality at the least cost for any initial allocation of emission permits.[14]

Moreover, from the perspective of polluters, the offset system would appear a good deal simpler than APS: a polluting firm need not procure a portfolio of permits from all the receptor points affected by its emissions; it need only purchase permits from other firms sufficient to prevent any violations of the air quality standards.[15] We would surmise that this will often involve a transaction with a single other firm or perhaps a few firms. The pollution offset system should typically reduce transactions costs relative to APS. In contrast, it is probably a bit more complicated for polluters than EPS with zones; under the latter, the polluter simply purchases emission rights on a one-for-one basis from sources within its zone. The extent, however, of the additional complications (or "transactions costs") would be modest. Moreover, the offset system could conceivably extend the geographical range of transactions and thereby increase the number of participants in the market, since a firm will not be limited in its purchases or sales of emissions rights to polluters in its own zone.[16]

## THE CHOICE AMONG ALTERNATIVE SYSTEMS:  SOME FURTHER THOUGHTS

Our search is for the system that promises to minimize the sum of abatement and transactions costs for the attainment of predetermined levels of ambient air quality.[17]  As we noted earlier, the object of our quest depends in fundamental ways on the characteristics of the particular pollutant and the geographical setting.  Consider, for example, a polar case of perfect mixing, where a unit of emissions from any point within the airshed has the same effect on concentrations at all points in the area.  For this special case, all three of our systems essentially degenerate into one.  Since there is a need only for a single receptor point and the dispersion coefficients of all sources are identical, the APS system will involve only a single market in which permits trade on a one-for-one basis.  This is obviously identical to an EPS system with a single zone encompassing the entire airshed or to an offset system in which sources will find that, to increase emissions by one unit, they must induce another source (any source in the airshed) to reduce its emissions by one unit.

The simplicity of this special case is a great attraction:  it implies substantial savings in transactions costs for both polluters and administrators.  Under APS, for example, polluting firms need operate in only a single permit market.  Under EPS, the large single zone means more potential buyers and sellers and a much simplified planning problem for the environmental regulatory agency.  Likewise, under the offset approach, the increased scope for trades at a single "rate of exchange" should facilitate the functioning of the permit market.

An interesting case of (at least virtually) perfect mixing involves the emission of chlorofluorocarbons (CFCs), which are thought to affect adversely the stratospheric ozone layer.  The location of emissions is, as we understand it, irrelevant; CFCs and the ozone problem seem to involve a truly global public good, so there is no need to differentiate the incentives for abatement by the location of the source.  For cases like CFCs, the permit market can take a very simple structure and, other things equal, should work quite well.  In fact, the USEPA is considering a national permit market for CFC emissions.

The potential savings in transactions costs suggest that even for cases that deviate somewhat from perfect mixing, it may, on net, be beneficial to maintain the fiction of our polar case.  For hydrocarbon emissions in certain airsheds, for instance, it may make sense to ignore the spatial issue and treat it as a case of perfect mixing.  In such circumstances, the savings in transactions costs will exceed the "excess" abatement costs from the failure to make finer spatial distinctions.  In an intriguing study of water pollution involving BOD emissions into the Willamette River, Eheart (1980) has found that there is only a very small increase in total abatement costs from simply allowing all sources to trade permits on a one-for-one basis. Hahn and Noll (1981) suggest a similar result for sulfate pollution of the atmosphere in Southern California. For such cases (and even where the abatement cost differential is somewhat larger), the optimal system will likely be our polar case.

The more general point is that the attempt to introduce finer spatial differentiation, while reducing total abatement cost, results in increased transactions costs for both polluters and administrators. There is, in short, a tradeoff between the savings in abatement costs and the reduced transactions costs associated with finer spatial distinctions. As we move farther away from our case of perfect mixing, the excess abatement costs from ignoring spatial differences tend to grow. For air pollutants like particulate matter and nitrous oxides, for example, the spatial pattern of emissions seems typically to be quite important.[18] For such cases, our problem becomes that of choosing among our three general approaches to the design of a system of marketable permits.

While it is impossible to reach any completely general conclusions, we feel that our treatment establishes a strong presumption in favor of our modified systems of pollution offsets. The APS approach has the attractive property of minimization of aggregate abatement costs. But, as we have shown, so does the offset approach. Moreover, the offset system should entail large savings in transactions costs relative to APS, since under the latter a polluter will typically have to operate in a multiplicity of different permit markets.[19]

The EPS approach with a system of emission zones in which permits are traded on a one-for-one basis promises some savings in transactions costs for polluters (but not for the environmental authority); this must certainly be true in comparison to APS and probably in most instances relative to an offset system. However, as we discussed earlier, the EPS approach will not in general result in the least-cost pattern of emissions. The planning problem for the environmental agency is a very formidable one -- and one for which the solution is continually changing over time.

In addition, the assumption under EPS that a unit of emissions from one source in a zone is precisely equivalent in its effects on air quality to a unit of emissions from any other source in the zone may, under certain circumstances, do serious violence to reality. The ambient effects of emissions do not depend solely on the geographical location of the source; they depend in important ways on such things as stack height and diameter, and on gas temperature and exit velocity. Variations in these parameters among polluters can be accommodated under the offset system through their effects on the source's vector of transfer coefficients. In contrast, EPS cannot readily incorporate such elements without losing the basic simplicity of one-for-one transfers of emission rights. EPS has some potentially quite troublesome problems that do not plague the pollution offset scheme.

## POLLUTION OFFSETS AND U.S.E.P.A. REGULATORY REFORM

It is important to distinguish our conception of a pollution offset system from the existing program of regulatory reform at the USEPA known as Emissions Trading (see USEPA 1979). Under the Emissions Trading program, trades of emission rights are permitted under the "bubble," "offset," and "banking" provisions. Under the bubble provision, existing firms were initially permitted to make intraplant "swaps" of emissions of a particular pollutant to effect savings in abatement costs; this provision has subsequently been extended to encompass emission swaps across existing plants and even across existing firms so long as air pollution is not made worse. In a similar spirit, the USEPA offset provision allows trades of emissions between old and new sources in nonattainment areas. In addition, under the banking provision, firms can accumulate credit for past emission reductions that can then be used in bubble or offset transactions.

The Emissions Trading program is a reform that gives states the option to circumvent some of the older USEPA technological requirements (such as those specifying retrofit equipment to reduce emissions from exisitng sources). At the same time, we stress that Emissions Trading is circumscribed by a number of procedural and technological constraints that differentiate the program in important ways from our model of pollution offsets. The USEPA requires, for example, that new sources emitting more than a prescribed tonnage of a pollutant incorporate the most advanced emission control technology available. These constraints interfere with cost-reducing trades of emissions rights; the USEPA could greatly reduce the costs of pollution abatement by relaxing them. Finally, we note that each state must decide the exact form of its Emissions Trading regulations. Emissions Trading defines only a framework, not a single system.[20]

## TOWARD IMPLEMENTATION

We have not been very specific about the market structure or institutions under which the trading of permits takes place. We have proposed simply to supplement Montgomery's nondegradation condition on transfers of permits with the provision that polluters can obtain additional permits from the environmental authority as long as the resulting emissions do not cause any violations of the air quality standards.[21] And we showed that, under this modified system, potential gains from trading exist for any vector of emissions other than the least-cost one.

There is an alternative version of the pollution offset approach that is more straightforward and that can attain the same end: we can dispense altogether with the nondegradation condition and simply require the source of new emissions to induce existing polluters to reduce their emissions by amounts sufficient to prevent violations at any receptor point. Suppose, for example, that in Figure 2 our initial point was $E_1$, where $E_1 = (e_1', e_2')$ and $E^* = e_1^*$, $e_2^*$) are the emissions vectors corresponding to $E_1$ and $E^*$,

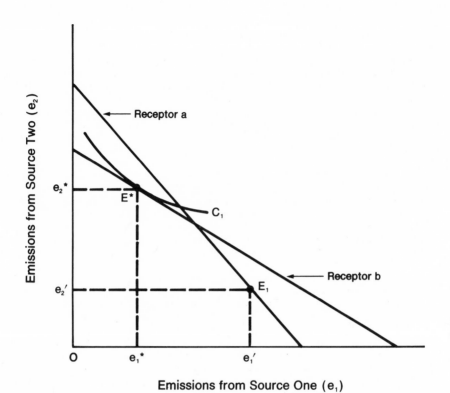

FIGURE 2
An Alternative Pollution Offset System

respectively. Firm 2 would pay Firm 1 to reduce its emissions from
$e_1'$ to $e_1*$, which would enable Firm 2 to increase its emissions
from $e_2'$ to $e_2*$. This transaction would, at the same time, move
the system directly from $E_1$ to $E*$ and exhaust the potential gains
from trading.

A system of this general sort has recently been proposed in Maryland.
Under the Maryland approach, a polluting firm proposes a package of
emissions reductions by existing polluters (for which it presumably
makes payment to the latter) and an increase in its own emissions
subject to the restriction that the resulting pattern of pollutant
concentrations does not violate the air quality standards at any
receptor point.

It is our sense that the Maryland approach to the implementation of
the pollution offset strategy offers the more feasible and promising
alternative. Such a system promises to encourage an efficient pattern
of emissions consistent with the attainment of air quality standards
and to do so with relatively modest transactions costs.

ACKNOWLEDGEMENTS

We are grateful to William Baumol, Charles Bausell, Martin David, Matthew Gelfand, Allan Gruchy, Jr., and Henry Peskin for their helpful comments; to Padraic Frucht, director of the Division of Research of the Maryland Department of Economic and Community Development, for his direction of a program of research on economic incentives to control air pollution in the State of Maryland, and to the National Science Foundation, the Appalachian Regional Commission and the Sloan Foundation for their support of parts of this work.

FOOTNOTES

[1]    Such a restatement is needed in part to clear up some confusion in the literature. Tietenberg (1980), for example, has mis-interpreted the Montgomery proposal for "emission licenses" to refer to a system of zones within which permits trade on a one-for-one basis (pp. 405-06). Montgomery's system of emission licenses is, however, quite different from a system of permit zones.

[2]    We follow closely here Montgomery (1972). Although we have framed the discussion in terms of air pollution, the analysis has obvious relevance to the regulation of water pollution as well.

[3]    We should note that the $d_{ij}$ are, in fact, dependent on stack height and diameter, gas temperature and exit velocities, as well as on a host of meteorological conditions; we will consider some of these complications later.

[4]    For reasons that will become clear, our choice of terminology to describe alternative systems of marketable permits differs from that of Montgomery. Our ambient-based approach (APS) is in the spirit of his system of "pollution licenses." However, we shall distinguish among several types of emission-based systems that are quite different from Montgomery's system of emission licenses.

[5]    Under a varient of this approach, trading may take place across zones at "exchange rates" set by the administering agency to reflect the damage attributable to emissions from the various zones. More on this later.

[6]    This may be something of an oversimplification for the reason that changes in emission levels can be associated with changes in dispersion coefficients. A polluter may reduce his emissions by the installation of new equipment, of baghouses, precipitators or scrubbers, or by the addition of afterburners to stacks in such ways as to alter the source's emission parameters. Trades involving such changes may thus require a recalculation of dispersion coefficients.

[7]    Of course, with all this information a market would hardly be necessary. After solving the cost-minimization problem the environmental authority could simply distribute the optimal number of permits to each polluter.

8    This diagram is a modification of Figure 2 in Montgomery (1974, p. 30).

9    A sufficient (but not necessary) condition for the iso-cost curves to have the desired curvature in Figure 1 is that both firms face a schedule of rising marginal abatement costs.

10   The potential gains-from-trade from sales of emission rights by Firm 1 to Firm 2 follow from the fact that the linear pollution constraint at $E_1$ is steeper than the iso-cost curve passing through that point. In the case, for example, where the slope of the constraint LM is -1 (indicating that emissions from Firm 1 and Firm 2 have equivalent effects on pollutant concentrations at Receptor b), Firm 2 has a higher marginal abatement cost at $E_1$ than does Firm 1, so transfers of permits from 1 to 2 can be mutually profitable.

11   The intuition of this condition is clear in terms of our discussion of the initial allocation of permits, $E_2$, in Figure 1. More generally, suppose that the least-cost solution entails a binding constraint at some particular receptor point j (i.e., the least-cost solution implies that $q_j = q_j*$). Assume, however, that the initial allocation of emission rights selected by the environmental authority results in pollutant concentrations at receptor j that are less than the allowable level so that the constraint at j is not binding. Under Montgomery's nondegradation restriction on subsequent trades of permits, it is clear that these trades cannot generate the least-cost outcome, because the restriction implies that ambient air quality at j cannot be less than that under the initial allocation. Thus, the constraint at j can never become binding. One way to circumvent this problem is to establish an initial allocation of permits such that $q_j = q_j*$ for all j. However, as we note in the text, such an allocation will, in general, not even exist.

12   This requires that, over the relevant range, the marginal product of waste emissions for polluting firms is strictly positive.

13   We refer to our equilibrium under the offset approach as a "trading" equilibrium rather than a "market" equilibrium, since we have not shown formally that there exists a specific set of prices that will sustain an equilibrium among buyers and sellers corresponding to the efficient allocation of permits among polluters. We show instead that the only allocation of permits for which there exist no potential gains from trade (our definition of a "trading equilibrium") is the efficient one.

14   We note, however, that the least-cost outcome involves, in general, higher (although "legal") levels of pollution than those under Montgomery's version of the pollution offset system. Relative to Montgomery's scheme, our version of the pollution offset system effectively realizes lower abatement costs by allowing more emissions where it can be accomplished without violations of the prescribed standards for pollutant concentrations.

15  This determination, incidentally, would involve a fairly
    straightforward procedure making use of an air quality model.
    One would simply enter a new emissions vector (incorporating the
    proposed addition to emissions and deleting the offsetting
    rights) and examine through a simulation exercise the projected
    effects on pollutant concentrations at each of the receptor
    points.  The proposed transaction would be approved as long as
    there is no violation of standards at any receptor point.

16  One might expect, however, that polluters will tend to purchase
    emissions rights from neighboring sources, since these should be
    available at more favorable "exchange rates."  To offset the
    effects of the emissions on a nearby receptor, a polluting firm
    might well have to purchase quite large quantities of rights from
    a distant source.

17  We define transactions costs broadly to include both the costs to
    polluters and the costs to the environmental authority of
    managing the system.

18  See, for example, the Atkinson and Lewis (1974) study of
    particulate emissions in the St. Louis AQCR and the studies of
    nitrous oxide emissions by Anderson et al. (1979) and USEPA
    (1980) in the Chicago AQCR and by Krupnick (1981) for the
    Baltimore AQCR.  All these studies produce large estimates of the
    potential cost-savings from a spatially sensitive policy.

19  Based on a given set of dispersion coefficients, the APS approach
    also encounters problems where (as noted earlier) trades entail
    changes in dispersion coefficients.  The offset approach
    accommodates such changes more routinely by incorporating them
    into the calculations of the net effects on air quality of a
    proposed trade.

20  Van De Verg and Frucht (1981) examine some of the pitfalls that
    states may encounter as they prepare Emissions Trading regula-
    tions.

21  Allan Gruchy (1980) has recently developed a conceptual
    alternative to Montgomery's system of "emission licenses."
    Gruchy's scheme effectively makes the initial allocation of
    rights endogenous; each polluter, in a sense, defines his own
    rights in the course of determining his level of emissions.
    Gruchy shows that his version of the offset system, in contrast
    to Montgomery's, generates the least-cost solution.  While the
    Gruchy system is of considerable interest at a conceptual level,
    we have been unable to translate it into a workable proposal for
    a system of marketable pollution rights.

REFERENCES

Anderson, R., et al. 1979. An Analysis of Alternative Policies for
    Attaining    and    Maintaining    a    Short-term    $NO_2$    Standard.
    Princeton, N.J.: Math-Tech, Inc.

Atkinson, S., and Lewis, D. 1974. A cost-effectiveness analysis of
    alternative air quality control strategies. Journal of Environ-
    mental Economics and Management 1:237-50.

Eheart, J.W. 1980. Cost-effectiveness of transferable discharge
    permits for the control of BOD discharges. (Unpublished).

Gruchy, A. 1980. Market systems for pollution control — another
    view. (Unpublished).

Hahn, R., and Noll, R. 1981. Designing a market for tradable
    emission permits. (Unpublished).

Krupnick, A. 1981. Simulating alternative policies for controlling
    $NO_x$ emissions. Draft report for the Maryland Department of
    Economic and Community Development.

Montgomery, W.D. 1974. Artificial markets and the theory of games.
    Public Choice 18(Summer):25-40.

Montgomery, W.D. 1972. Markets in licenses and efficient pollution
    control programs. Journal of Economic Theory 5:395-418.

Russell, C. 1980. The Delaware model in the sloan project:
    alternative instruments and model structure. (Unpublished).

Tietenberg, T. 1980. Transferable discharge permits and the control
    of stationary source air pollution: a survey and synthesis.
    Land Economics 56(Nov.):391-416.

U.S. Environmental Protection Agency. 1980. An analysis of market
    incentives to control stationary source $NO_x$ emissions.
    (Unpublished).

U.S. Environmental Protection Agency. 1979. Regulatory Reform
    Initiative: Progress Report. Washington: USEPA Office of
    Planning and Management.

Van De Verg, E., and Frucht, P. 1981. On trying to be first:
    Maryland's efforts to implement the USEPA's "emissions trading"
    policy. (Unpublished).

# Emission Transfer Markets:
# How Large Should Each Market Be?

**Robert Mendelsohn**

**Department of Economics**
**University of Washington**

## INTRODUCTION

In an effort to improve the efficiency of emission control laws,
regulators are exploring the possibility of establishing markets for
emissions. Unlike typical markets for goods and services, the true
beneficiaries of an "emissions market" (the victims of pollution) are
prevented from participating in the market because of unusually high
transaction costs. The role of government in this case is to simulate
the demand side of the market if it can be done at reasonable expense.

The basic model of an emissions market envisions the government's role
as defining a market area and establishing a limit on aggregate
emissions. Potential emitters would then buy the "right to pollute"
from existing polluters. Firms with high marginal abatement costs
would buy away emissions from firms with low abatement costs. For
each market, the aggregate level of emissions would be produced
efficiently. The government simply has to define the market area
appropriately and choose an aggregate level of emissions that equate
marginal cost to marginal damages.

An important complication to this basic emission market concept is
that not all emissions are alike. With heterogeneous goods, typical
markets often differentiate among goods. For example, though all
motorized vehicles provide transportation, the market for station
wagons remains distinct from the market for sports cars. The
simulated emissions market probably should also differentiate among at
least some emissions. There are two important dimensions that
separate emissions — the nature of the emission, and the location of
the emitter. The purpose of this paper is to discuss how to treat
unique products in a regulatory environment. How large should each
market ("bubble") be?

In the next section, a simple model of how to classify heterogeneous
goods is developed. In the following sections, this model is applied
to heterogeneous emissions and spatially varying emitters.

Though the principles of market segmentation are demonstrated with air pollution examples, the model clearly applies to all forms of pollution.


## THEORY OF CLASSIFICATION

Suppose we wish to regulate a population of emissions that are not all alike. Let us, for now, represent the differences among the emissions in terms of a single variable, X. For example, the $X_i$ of the $i^{th}$ emission could be the level of marginal damage a pollutant causes because of its particular toxicity and proximity to a sensitive environment. Suppose the distribution of X in the population is known with a probability density function $f(X)$. Let us examine whether the regulator should treat each unit alike or fully discriminate each pollutant. Suppose the regulator acts as if all units had a value of $\overline{X}$. Let $L(X_i - \overline{X})$ be the economic loss associated with treating an emission of marginal damage $X_i$ as if it caused damage $\overline{X}$. That is, $L(X_i - \overline{X})$ is the welfare cost of uniformity. The expected economic loss of treating dissimilar units alike is:

$$E[L(X_i - \overline{X})] = \int_{-\infty}^{\infty} L(X_i - \overline{X}) f(X) \, dX \qquad (1)$$

and is equivalent to the benefits of differentiating between heterogeneous units. Units should be differentiated only if the benefits of reducing the economic loss exceed the organizational costs, H, of differentiation. Let us begin with a discussion of the cost of uniformity and conclude with some observations on the cost of differentiation.

In general, one can describe any loss function in terms of a unique polyomial:

$$L(X_i - \overline{X}) = B_0 + B_1(X_i - \overline{X}) + B_2(X_i - \overline{X})^2 + \ldots B_n(X_i - \overline{X})^n$$

$$i = 1, \ldots, m.$$

Expected losses can then be described in terms of the moments ($\alpha_k$) of the probability density function $f(X)$ about the regulated level of X, $\overline{X}$:

$$E[L(X_i - \overline{X})] = B_0 + B_1 \alpha_1 + B_2 \alpha_2 +, \ldots, B_n \alpha_n \qquad (2)$$

where $\alpha_i = F[(X_i - \overline{X})^i]$.

Let us now apply this general apparatus to study a specific model of pollution abatement. We begin with a number of simplifying assumptions. First, we suppose that the marginal benefits of abatement are solely a function of the abatement of each pollutant. That is, we ignore possible cross-elasticities of demand for abatement across pollutants. Second, we model the total benefits and costs of abatement as quadratic functions of the level of abatement. In most examples, the quadratic functional form is adequately close to what we believe is the true form, at least within the parameters' range of interest. Third, we begin with a model where only the level of the marginal benefit of abatement varies across pollutants. At least in this initial case, the marginal cost function of abatement is assumed to be identical. Variations in the curvature of the marginal benefit curve are ignored partially because the curvature effects clutter the model, hiding insights, and partially because the curvature effects frequently have only slight quantitative effects.[2] The total benefit and cost curves in the initial model are:

$$B(Q) = A_0 + (A_1 + X)Q - A_2Q^2 \qquad\qquad (3)$$

$$C(Q) = C_0 + C_1Q + C_2Q^2$$

where $A_0$, $A_1$, $A_2$, $C_0$, $C_1$ and $C_2$ are nonnegative constants, $Q$ is the level of abatement, and $X$ is a random variable with probability density function $f(X)$. Without loss of generality, we assume:

$$E[X] = 0$$

$$E[X^2] = \sigma_x^2$$

where $E[\ ]$ is the expected value operator.

To maximize the net benefits of abatement, one must differentiate equation (3) and equate actual marginal benefits with marginal costs:

$$MB(Q) \equiv A_1 + X_i - 2A_2Q = MC(Q) \equiv C_1 + 2C_2Q.$$

Solving for the optimal $Q^*$ for each emission:

$$Q^*(X_i) = \frac{A_1 + X_i - C_1}{2(A_2 + C_2)}$$

The rule $Q^*(X_i)$ minimizes the total costs and damages associated with emission $X_i$.

Suppose the regulator chooses to treat all emissions alike. His best policy, in this case, is to equate the marginal cost curve with expected marginal benefits:

$$C_1 + 2C_2Q = E[A_1 + X_i - 2A_2Q].$$

The optimal uniform rule $Q$ is to treat all emissions as though they produce the expected or mean level of marginal damage:

$$\overline{Q} = \frac{A_1 - C_1}{2(A_2 + C_2)}$$

The economic welfare loss of treating the $X_i$th emission with regulation $\overline{Q}$ is:

$$L(Q^* - \overline{Q}) = D(Q^*) - C(Q^*) - \left(D(\overline{Q_i}) - C(\overline{Q_i})\right) \tag{4}$$

Substituting in equation (3) and simplifying yields:

$$L(Q^* - \overline{Q}) = \frac{1}{4(A_2 + C_2)} (X_i)^2 \tag{5}$$

The loss function in this model is a quadratic function of X. Since $E[X_i^2] = \sigma_X^2$, the expected loss function of a uniform rule implemented over the entire population is:

$$E[L(Q^* - \overline{Q})] = \frac{\sigma_X^2}{4(A_2 + C_2)} \tag{6}$$

where $\sigma_X^2$ is simply the variance of the distribution. The expected loss function increases along with the second central moment of the probability distribution of $f(X)$. As the slopes of the marginal cost or benefit curves increase, the expected loss of treating units alike declines.

Equation (6) describes the cost of uniformity, the welfare loss of permitting dissimilar units to be traded equally in a market. For example, suppose a market were composed of a dangerous $X_H$ and a harmless $X_L$ pollutant. If the pollutants were differentiated, far less of the harmful emissions would be permitted than the harmless pollutants. However, if firms are permitted to trade harmful and harmless pollutants as though they were alike, emission levels for both pollutants would equilibrate. Too much abatement costs would be spent on harmless pollutants, and too little abatement would be spent on the more dangerous pollutant. The greater the difference between the pollutants, the greater the population variance, and the greater the economic loss.

Let us now complicate the model further by permitting the marginal cost of abatement also to vary across firms. Again we introduce this variation solely as vertical shifts in the marginal cost curve. Though this assumption may not be appropriate in all cases, we adopt it here as a pedagogical device. The total cost and benefit functions for abatement become:

$$B(Q) = A_0 + (X + A_1)Q - A_2Q^2$$
$$C(Q) = C_0 + (Z + C_1)Q + C_2Q^2 \tag{7}$$

where $A_0$, $A_1$, $A_2$, $C_0$, $C_1$ and $C_2$ are nonnegative constants, Q is the level of abatement, and X and Z are random variables with a joint probability density function of $f(X,Z)$.

Without loss of generality, it is assumed that:

$$E[X] = 0$$

$$E[Z] = 0$$

$$E[X^2] = \sigma_X^2$$

$$E[Z^2] = \sigma_Z^2$$

$$E[XZ] = \gamma_{XZ}$$

Equating the true marginal cost and marginal damage function for each emission gives the optimal fully differentiated rule for each emission $(X_i Z_i)$:

$$Q^*(X_i, Z_i) = \frac{A_1 - C_1 + X_i - Z_i}{2(A_2 + C_2)}$$

If, instead of the fully differentiated rule, the regulator chose a single quantity rule, his best strategy is to equate expected marginal cost to expected marginal damage. Solving for the optimal uniform rule Q:

$$\overline{Q}(X, Z) = \frac{A_1 - C_1}{2(A_2 + C_2)}$$

The market permit system, however, does not assign quantity limitations to specific firms. Instead, the quantity limitation is set for the aggregate market only. Clearly the optimal aggregate quantity limit maximizes the expected net benefits of abatement. Correspondingly, the aggregate limit is established so that prices equate with expected marginal cost and expected marginal damage. Thus, the optimal price of a permit for the entire population is:

$$\overline{P} = E[MC] = E[MD].$$

Differentiating equation (7) and substituting above yields:

$$\overline{P} = \frac{A_2 C_1 + A_1 C_2}{A_2 + C_2}$$

In contrast, if each emission was treated as a separate market, the optimal fully differentiated price would be:

$$P^*(X_i, Z_i) = \frac{A_2(C_1 + Z_i) + (A_1 + X_i)C_2}{A_2 + C_2}$$

The economic loss of mixing heterogeneous emissions into the same market $L(P* - P)$ depends upon the abatement outputs generated by each rule. The rule $P*(X_i, Z_i)$ generates the optimal levels of output for each pollutant $Q*(X_i, Z_i)$. Because each firm in a market permit system equates its actual marginal cost of abatement with the market price, the level of abatement in the permit system can be found by solving the following equation:

$$\overline{P} = MC_i(Q) = Z_i + C_1 + 2C_2 Q_p.$$

Solving for $Q_p$ reveals:

$$Q_p = \frac{A_1 - C_1}{2(A_2 + C_2)} - \frac{Z_i}{2C_2}$$

Substituting $Q_p$ and $Q*$ in equations (7) and (4) and solving yields:

$$L(Q* - \overline{Q}) = \frac{1}{4(A_2 + C_2)} \left(X^2 + \frac{A_2^2}{C_2^2} + 2\frac{A_2}{C_2} XZ\right) \qquad (8)$$

The expected welfare loss associated with a uniform price regulation applied over the entire population is:

$$E[L(P* - \overline{P})] = \frac{1}{4(A_2 + C_2)} \left(\sigma_X^2 + \left(\frac{A_2^2}{C_2^2}\right)\sigma_Z^2 + 2\frac{A_2}{C_2}\gamma_{XZ}\right) \qquad (9)$$

The market permit system permits firms to equate their marginal cost of abatement, so one may have thought variations in the marginal cost of abatement would not matter in a permit system. However, as long as $A_2$ is nonzero, the variance of the marginal cost curves do decrease the efficiency of the market permit system. As the cost curves move about, the desired level of marginal benefits changes across firms, adding to the cost of uniformity.

Positive covariances between the marginal cost and damage functions across firms also reduce the efficiency of a permit system. When shifts in the marginal benefit function positively correspond to shifts in the marginal cost function, the two effects offset each other. The desired output consequently remains relatively unaffected by the shifts. The permit system, utilizing prices, tends to react solely to the shifts in the marginal cost curve, producing undesired variation in the regulated output. Negative covariances, in contrast, have just the opposite effect, enhancing the efficiency of uniform price rules. When upward shifts in the marginal benefit curve are met by downward shifts in the marginal cost curve, the result is to leave the price relatively unchanged. A uniform price works well in this type of population.

Given the tools in our model, we can examine how a uniform market permit system across a population compares with a uniform quantity rule (firm-specific emission limits). Substituting $\overline{Q}$ and $Q_p$ into equation (4) and solving for the welfare advantage of prices reveals:

$$L(\overline{Q} - Q_p) = \frac{1}{4c_2^2}\left((C_2 - A_2)Z - 2(C_2XZ)\right)$$

Taking the expected value of $L(Q - Q_p)$ over a sample population yields:

$$E[L(\overline{Q} - Q_p)] = \frac{C_2 - A_2}{4c_2^2}\,\sigma_Z^2 - \frac{\gamma_{XZ}}{2C_2} \tag{10}$$

Equation (10) resembles the findings of Weitzman (1974) concerning price and quantity rules under uncertainty. A market permit system improves relative to quantity rules as the slope of the marginal cost of abatement exceeds the slope of the marginal benefit function.[3] The effect of variation in the benefits of abatement do not enter equation (10); both rules are affected by marginal damage variance the same way. Negative covariances favor price rules, and positive covariances between costs and damages favor quantity rules.

Up to this point, the analysis has been concerned with either complete uniformity or complete differentiation. In practice, one may be able to classify emission into a finite number of categories.[4] Taking the bubble concept as captured in (1) and adapting it to $\underline{n}$ finite classes yields the following expected loss function:

$$E[L(X - \overline{X}_i)] = \int_{-\infty}^{a_1} L(X - \overline{X}_1)f(X)dX + \int_{a_1}^{a_2} L(X - \overline{X}_2)f(X)dX \tag{11}$$

$$+ \ldots + \int_{a_n}^{\infty} L(X - \overline{X}_n)f(X)dX \ .$$

The number of categories, $\underline{n}$ (markets), and the subpopulations within the boundaries $a_k$ of each category are endogenous to this system. The $X_i$ are the means of the subsamples of the population. Individual pollutants of firms should always be allocated to the nearest sample mean where distance is measured by the loss function.

For example, suppose we have a uniform distribution of points from 0 to 10, and we are trying to minimize the square of distance (variance) between points. If all the points are treated alike, the variance of this line is 50. If a single division is made at the expected value of the distribution (5), the sum of the variances of the two subsamples drops to 12.5. A third subdivision drops the total variance to 8.33, and a fourth to 6.25. Expected losses continue to decline as the number of categories increase, and the decline is at a decreasing rate. In this example, the second order conditions are well-behaved with respect to the number of categories. The optimal number of categories can be determined by simply equating the marginal reduced loss (marginal benefit) with the marginal administrative cost of an additional category.

In addition to the expected loss of uniformity, it is also important
to examine the structure of the organizational costs of differentiating units H(n). These costs can be broken down into two major
categories: measurement and administrative costs. In most cases, the
high costs of determining the unique qualities of a unit is the
primary reason for treating units alike, of having a single market.
In some circumstances, however, it is difficult to act on detectable
differences; a downtown plant may cause more harm than a suburban
plant, for example. Fixing a distinct boundary between the two plants
may violate notions of equity and add to administrative complexities.
Furthermore, treating individual units in a unique manner can require
extensive resources. In general, the more categories (markets) that
units are divided into, the greater the administrative costs.

The structure of information is another important consideration with
respect to the cost of additional categories (markets). Some random
variables may have inexpensive proxies that make them easy to
identify. For example, if one is trying to approximate the population
exposure that will result from an emission, knowledge of spatial
population densities and prevailing wind patterns may be adequate. On
the other hand, if precise estimates are needed, sophisticated
meteorological models that incorporate wind patterns, inversions and
topography would be needed. In this case, rough calculations are
relatively inexpensive, but exact calculations would be very costly.
How administrative costs will vary with increased categorization (more
markets) depends heavily on the structure of information.


HETEROGENEOUS POLLUTANTS

Current emission regulations do make distinctions among pollutants.
Nitrogen dioxide, carbon monoxide and sulfur dioxide are all dis-
tinguished by air pollution regulations. Particulates, which are a
collection of over 100 different molecules, however, are treated as a
class. If a bubble concept is implemented, should there be separate
bubbles for each pollutant, or should firms be permitted to trade one
pollutant for another?

The key to an efficient bubble program is for the government to
simulate demand. For example, if the marginal benefits associated
with any two pollutants are similar, consumers would be willing to
substitute one for the other. All pollutants with similar marginal
damages can be combined in a single bubble. The waste or loss
associated with combining pollutants with dissimilar marginal benefits
is described in equation (6).

Though the precise contribution of individual pollutants is still a
subject of debate, enough evidence exists to suggest that the marginal
damages caused by different types of pollutants vary. For example,
Mendelsohn (1979) calculates the effect of various emissions on
health, visibility, vegetation and materials. Though the vegetation
and material damages are easy to quantify in dollar terms, health and
visibility losses are more controversial. Suppose that a day of
health is worth $50 and that visibility is valued at 50 cents per

kilometer per person per year.  An emission of one ton of each of the following pollutants in a moderately dense urban environment will induce the following marginal damages:

| | | |
|---|---|---|
| Sulfur dioxide | -- | $254 per ton |
| Particulates | -- | 41 per ton |
| Nitrogen dioxide | -- | 13 per ton |
| Carbon monoxide | -- | 1 per ton |
| Sulfate | -- | $1,384 per ton |

Using these estimates, examine whether any of these pollutants should be mixed in a single market.  Suppose we ask whether the emission for particulates and sulfur dioxide ought to be combined in a single market.  Suppose we have 200 identical markets, each of which emit about 100,000 tons of each pollutant.  Let us assume that evidence supports the following marginal damage and cost curves:

$$MD = X_i$$

$$MC = 100,000 - .2Q.$$

Equating marginal cost and damage reveals that about 100,000 tons of each pollutant are produced.  The expected marginal damage level

$$E[X_i] = \frac{\sum_i X_i}{N} = \$147 \text{ per ton.}$$

The welfare loss of treating both pollutants alike from (6) is:

$$E[L(X - \overline{X})] = \frac{\sigma_X^2}{2(A_2 + C_2)} = \frac{\Sigma(X_i - \overline{X})^2}{2(A_2 + C_2)} = \$114,490.$$

The welfare cost of treating sulfur dioxide and particulates alike in this model amounts to more than $100,000 per year per market.  Adding across markets to account for the national level of emissions yields a total figure of $229 million.  If the assumptions are reasonable, the welfare cost of equating particulates and sulfur dioxide appear to be prohibitive.


HETEROGENEOUS ENVIRONMENTS

It is clear that one of the more difficult decisions that needs to be made with respect to a bubble concept is deciding what the physical boundaries of each bubble should be.  Figure 1 indicates that treating all areas alike is costly because they are not alike.  On the other hand, creating multiple submarkets is also costly.  Markets need to be sufficiently large to encourage competition or efficient trading of emittants.  Boundaries will always be contested because firms may obtain substantial benefits from just small changes in boundary lines, the fewer boundaries the better.  Finally, if there are too many markets, it will be difficult to administer each effectively.

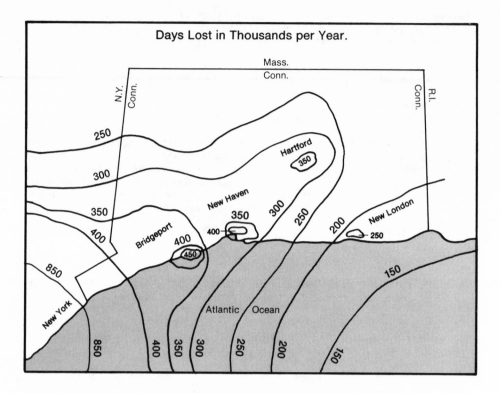

FIGURE 1
Health Days Lost from the Uncontrolled Emission
of a Coal-Fired Power Plant at Any Given Location in Connecticut

(Effective height of emissions:   100 meters.)


To shed some light on the magnitude of the costs of differentiating
pollution rules by marginal damage curves, an analysis is made of
uniform national sulfur dioxide emission regulations.  The results may
apply to other pollutants as well, though the magnitude of benefits of
differentiation are probably less for other pollutants.  Though sulfur
dioxide emissions have many possible effects on our ecosystem, a large
fraction of the harmful consequences appear to be related to population density (see Mendelsohn 1979).

As a rough approximation, the marginal damage of a unit of emissions
is assumed to be proportional to the population density of the Census
county group from which it is emitted.[5]  The useful life lost to
sensitive materials is converted to dollars via their market price.
We continue to assume that a health day is worth an average of $50 and
that visibility is worth 50 cents per kilometer.   Given these
assumptions, a ton of sulfur dioxide produces about 250 dollars of

marginal damage if emitted in a county group of 100 persons per square mile. The slope of the marginal cost of abatement is assumed to be $4 per 1,000 tons, and the slope of the marginal damage curve is assumed to be zero. [6] Suppose, for simplicity, that emissions are uniformly distributed across county groups.

Figure 2 shows a histogram of the densities of the nation's county groups. The minimum of the distribution is .67 and the maximum is 6,692 persons per square mile. While an area with density of 100 persons results in marginal damages of $250, an emission in an area of just .67 persons would produce about $2 worth of damages. The densest area, Manhattan, increases marginal damages to $16,730. Combining $16,730 with the probable $250 average of the suburbs yields an expected damage per ton of about $8,500. The variance of X is $1.36 million. Utilizing (6), the expected loss per ton of sulfur emissions for combining Manhattan with the New York suburbs is about $85 million per year. Clearly this is not a good idea.

How many markets should exist across the United States, and which counties can be lumped together? One interesting aspect of the answer to this question is that symmetric divisions of asymmetric distributions are not optimal.

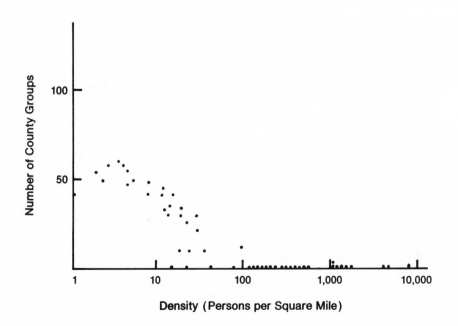

FIGURE 2
Distribution of County Groups by Density

For example, suppose we divide the national distribution pictured in
Figure 2 at the mean. Referring back to equation (11), the expected
loss function would become:

$$E[L(X_i - \bar{X})] = \int_{-\infty}^{E[X]} L(X_i - \bar{X}_1)f(X)dX + \int_{E[X]}^{\infty} L(X_i - \bar{X}_2)f(X)dX$$

where $E[X]$ is the mean of the entire sample, and $X_1$ and $X_2$ are the
means of their respective subpopulations. The division of the sample
by the mean reduces the welfare loss from 8,560 to 6,230. On the
other hand, just separating the three densest county groups (all in
New York City) from the rest of the country reduces the efficiency
loss to 2,320. Because this sample is skewed with a few dense county
groups, removing the tail of the distribution from the rest of the
sample is the most effective division of the sample. Table 1 displays
the optimal division of county groups across 1 to 6 markets. Even
with six separate categories, three-fourths of the sample is still
grouped together (the 334 lower-density county groups). The differences among suburban and rural counties is not as great as the
difference between suburban and central cities. Consequently, most of
the divisions focus on treating dense central cities differently from
the rest of the country.

TABLE 1

The Optimal Division of Firms by the Marginal Damage
of a Ton of Sulfur Dioxide[a]

| Number of Categories | Marginal Improvement of Additional Category[b] | Configuration of Firms Within Each Category |
|---|---|---|
| 1 | -- | 1-404 |
| 2 | 6234 | 1-3/4-404 |
| 3 | 1220 | 1-3/4-12/13-404 |
| 4 | 615 | 1/2,3/4-12/13-404 |
| 5 | 325 | 1/2,3/4-10/11-22/23-404 |
| 6 | 72 | 1/2,3/4-10/11-22/23-70/71-404 |

[a]The marginal damage of each firm is proportional to the population
density of the county group in which it is located. The distribution of marginal damage across firms is assumed to be equivalent to
the distribution of county groups shown in Figure 1.

[b]The economic cost is measured in arbitrary units.

[c]The 404 areas are numbered from highest population density (1) to
lowest (404). The first three areas are in New York City, and the
next 40 are mostly in central cities.

The marginal benefit of differentiation noticeably drops as the categories become finer. Whereas the first division saves 6,230, the fifth division of the sample saves only an additional 72. The calculation of the optimal division point also becomes more complicated as the number of categories increase because more boundaries need to be drawn (there are more potential combinations) and more combinations are nearly equally effective. It is entirely plausible that one may want no more than six, and possibly only five, bubbles (markets) for sulfur dioxide emissions in the United States.

Dense central cities should probably each be a single market, or at least only be combined with other dense central cities. On the other hand, vast areas of rural and suburban country can be safely combined into a single market because the local marginal damages per emission do not vary enough to warrant separating the areas.

FOOTNOTES

[1]    This assertion is contingent upon the existence of the necessary moments of the probability distribution. This limitation should generally be of no practical consequence. The moments are central if they are distributed around the expected value of the distribution.

[2]    Mendelsohn and Orcutt (1979) and others have found no evidence to suggest any curvature in human mortality dose-response curves to air pollution. In this case, any uncertainty about the exact size of the curvature of the benefit function would have little impact upon the analysis.

[3]    If the emission in one area tends to enhance the marginal benefit curve of abating an emission in another area, this positive covariance among pollutants tends to favor a permit or price system. See Weitzman's (1974) analysis of the behavior of multiple firms under price and quantity rules for an illustration of this principle.

[4]    Choosing optimal categories is identical to choosing the optimal number of cities and their boundaries in a metropolitan area. Product differentiation by a manufacturer in $\underline{n}$-dimensional quality space is also a problem of optimal categorization. Econometricians have also studied the problem when analyzing the information lost by discrete characterization of continuous variables.

[5]    Population exposures can be calculated by weighting the populations around an emission source by the concentration of the pollutant in their area. The greater the density of population is near the emission source, the greater the population exposed. Whereas it is not clear that the county group is the appropriate single area to measure density, the measure at least proxies the important interaction between dispersion and the population distribution.

[6]    The slope of the marginal cost curve varies from 30 cents to $8
       per thousand tons of sulfur across industries (see Bingham et al.
       1974).   Mendelsohn and Orcutt (1979) and others have found
       evidence that the sulfur mortality dose-response curve is linear
       within the relevant range of doses.   Thus an additional ton of
       sulfur has about the same effect regardless of the background
       levels.


BIBLIOGRAPHY

Bingham, T.; Cowley, P.; Fugel, M.; Johnston, D., and Le Sourd, D.
     1974.   The Cost-Effectiveness of Uniform National Sulfur Emission
     Taxes.   EPA 600/5-74-009 (February).

Mendelsohn, R.   1979.   "Towards efficient regulation of air pollution
     from  coal - fired  power  plants."    Ph.D.  dissertation,  Yale
     University.   Published  in  Outstanding  Economics  Dissertation
     Series.   New York: Garland Press.

Mendelsohn, R., and Orcutt, G.   1979.   An empirical analysis of air
     pollution  dose  response  curves.    Journal  of  Environmental
     Economics and Management 6(June).

Weitzman, M.   1974.   Prices vs. quantities.   Review of Economic
     Studies 41:477-91.

# Distributive Consequences and Political Concerns: On the Design of Feasible Market Mechanisms for Environmental Control

**Timothy H. Quinn**

**The Rand Corporation**
**Santa Monica, Calif.**

## INTRODUCTION

Economists and other policy analysts have long recognized that the use of economic incentives for environmental control poses serious implementation problems. One of the most important implementation issues reflects how the design of economic incentive strategies affects the distribution of wealth. While economic incentives can minimize the aggregate costs of regulation, they portend potentially serious wealth losses for some specific groups -- namely, the consumers, workers and owners in the regulated industries. This tradeoff between the aggregate costs of regulation and how the cost is distributed within society poses an important challenge for the policy analyst.

This paper explores the difficulties of designing environmental policies that retain, to the extent possible, the allocative effi- ciency properties of market-oriented policies and yet actually attempt to compensate the members of society who bear the brunt of regulatory losses under simple pollution taxes or auctions.

This analysis is divided into two parts. First, we address the rationale for compensating (at least partially) the victims of environmental regulation in the first place, arguing that only policies that do so can claim to be Pareto superior to other policies. Moreover, given the view of the political process adopted in the next section, policies that compensate regulatory losses reasonably accurately are also far more likely to be politically successful. The second part of the paper considers some important distributional challenges to the design of pricing mechanisms by examining the implications of alternative forms of implementing marketable or transferable discharge permits (TDPs). These latter arguments are illustrated with numerical examples from an analysis of potential regulations on chlorofluorocarbons (CFCs), which are suspected by the U.S. Environmental Protection Agency of depleting the earth's protective ozone layer.

Ultimately, this paper only scratches the surface of some analytical issues that have important implications for understanding how the policymaking process functions and the role of formal analysis within it. One implication is that environmental policy, because it is necessarily formulated in the real world of hard political choices, makes predictable tradeoffs between the aggregate resource costs of regulation and its distributional consequences. Policies that achieve environmental objectives without generating serious losses for specific groups may necessarily sacrifice some of the allocative efficiency attributes of the pricing mechanisms often advocated by economists. In effect, under a wide variety of circumstances, the political process may rationally adopt a policy that increases regulation's real resource costs to achieve a politically feasible distribution of those costs.

However, this does not mean that economists have less of a role in policy formation or that we cannot design feasible pricing mechanisms that rely on decentralized decisionmaking to reduce aggregate regulatory costs. Indeed, the arguments in this paper for designing compensatory environmental policies both complicate and expand the role of formal analysis in real-world policy formation. But to achieve their full potential in policy formation, analysts must focus their creative energies not on abstract measures of aggregate social well-being, such as maximizing aggregate wealth or minimizing aggregate costs, but rather on the tradeoffs related to wealth distribution that are central to environmental policy choice.


RATIONALES FOR COMPENSATING REGULATION'S LOSERS

The question of even whether -- let alone how -- regulatory strategies should attempt to compensate regulatory losses is not uncontroversial. Some analysts seem to suggest that in the case of environ- mental controls compensation may be undesirable because it violates "the polluter pays" principle.[1] Others argue that, in practice, compensation programs often become unwieldy and fail to achieve their distributional goals.[2] Still other analysts conclude that while compensation of regulation's more serious distributional effects has merit, environmental policy is inherently ill-suited to achieveing distributional goals and should focus primarily on its allocative role.[3]

Despite these reservations, previous literature identifies at least three rationales for compensating the losses generated by regulation: the equity rationale, the Pareto rationale and the political ration- ale.[4]

The equity rationale reflects the argument that regulation, environ- mental or otherwise, should seek to advance (or at least not defeat) the broader distributional goals of society. Though this rationale seems to provide the basis for many previous distributional analyses of environmental regulation,[5] it is not relied upon here as a compelling justification for considering the design of compenstory environmental policies. As Baumol and Oates (1975) note, environ- mental policy is not a suitable mechanism for achieving a particular income distribution. Consequently, it is not surprising that there is little (if any) evidence that suggests environmental policymakers have attempted to advance the broader distributional goals of society through the choice of an environmental policy approach.

The Pareto rationale represents an essentially normative view of the acceptability of public policies. Taken to its logical extreme, this view holds that only policies that make the members of society unanimously better off are unambiguous improvements over the status quo. However, as the next section will suggest, it may be extremely difficult (if not impossible) to design policies that are strictly Pareto superior to the status quo. And the fact that virtually all public policies generate at least some opposition suggests that this extreme form of the Pareto rationale, like the equity rationale, has not been embraced by the policymaking process.

Nevertheless, the logic underlying this rationale may still provide the basis for compensatory policy design. Some regulatory policy designs relative to others may impose substantial losses for some specific groups. In the context of environmental policy, Buchanan and Tullock note that such policies may be viewed within the policymaking process as "punitive taxation" and that the "imposed destruction of property values may suggest the justice of compensation."[6] Thus, even when a policy cannot meet the strictest (and more clear-cut) requirements of the Pareto rationale, the policymaker may desire to implement policies that spread the losses (or benefits) of regulation more broadly in society rather than concentrating them on specific groups.

The political rationale stems from positive predictions about the behavior of the political process. This rationale reflects a simple fact of life: public policies are the outcome of a political process within which a number of affected groups have both the desire and ability to protect their interests by affecting the design of regulatory policies. And as Majone has forcefully argued, "it seems rather pointless to advocate policies that essentially deny the political character of environmental problems."[7] But what does the "political character of environmental problems" imply about the design of feasible regulatory strategies, especially as regards their distributional characteristics? The answer, of course, depends upon how we view the political process.

In this paper, the political process is viewed in a general equilibrium context. As such, the underlying positive model of political competition is Peltzmanian in nature.[8] Briefly stated, we assume that prior to regulation there exists an equilibrium property right structure and corresponding equilibrium distribution of wealth. When an externality problem disturbs this equilibrium in one way or another, the political process moves to protect the environment by altering the rules governing economic activity, eventually moving to a new political equilibrium.

Ultimately, the political process, once disturbed, must render two decisions related to environmental policy. First, it must decide,

either directly or indirectly, the level of environmental quality to
provide; second, it must select a policy design or property right
structure (e.g., direct regulation, residual tax, TDPs, etc.) to
achieve the environmental objective.  Both of these decisions will
reflect the nature of the forces that disturbed the initial equilibrium.  The first decision may reflect, as Weingast (1980) argues, the
increased political effectiveness of environmental groups, or it may
reflect only the increased damages resulting from pollution.  However,
the decision among alternative property right structures is the
primary concern here.  This decision will reflect primarily how
different policy decisions distribute the costs of regulation among
groups in the private sector, such as the regulated firm owners,
consumers and workers who ultimately may bear the regulatory losses.

The implications of a general equilibrium model of the political
process for the choice among alternative property right structures are
perhaps best described by what we shall call "political conserva-
tism."  Absent a shift in the relative political effectiveness of
these affected groups, the forces of political competition will
generate policy designs that protect what Owen and Braeutigam (1978)
call their "rights in the status quo."  In short, an equilibrium model
of the political process predicts that politically feasible public
policies must pay heed to the status quo distribution of wealth.

This view of the political process implies that feasible environmental
policy designs will attempt to avoid major redistributions of wealth
and the losses they portend for firm owners, consumers, workers and so
on.  Thus, compensation in some form is a political necessity within a
system in which the forces of political competition require that a
policy protect affected groups' "rights in the status quo."  In this
sense, the political rationale, although reflecting only the positive
predictions of a model of political behavior, has the same implications for policy design as does the normative Pareto rationale.  In
the absence of exogenous shifts in political power, we should expect
the adoption of policies that, through some form of compensation,
spread the costs of regulation more broadly, rather than allowing them
to fall disproportionately on a few isolated groups.[9]


## SOME DISTRIBUTIVE CHALLENGES TO THE DESIGN OF MARKET MECHANISMS

Whether based solely on the desire to make social change more
consistent with the Pareto ideal or in response to political realities, the designing of regulatory mechanisms that attempt to compensate potential losses is easier said than done.[10]  To illustrate,
this section discusses the consequences of alternative ways to
implement TDPs in the particular case of the control of chlorofluorocarbon (CFC) emissions.

Since the 1930s, CFCs have been used pervasively in the U.S., partly
because their chemical properties made them appear environmentally
safe relative to potential chemical substitutes.  In the early 1970s,
however, CFCs became suspected of depleting the earth's protective
ozone layer, thereby increasing the earth's exposure to potentially

harmful ultraviolet radiation. Though the scientific evidence
continues to generate some controversy, the use of CFCs as an aerosol
propellant was banned by the U.S. Environmental Protection Agency
(USEPA), and regulations are under consideration for the CFCs used in
nonaerosol applications, including a variety of refrigeration devices,
cushioning and insulating foams, and industrial solvents.

This section considers the consequences of three TDP policies designed
to eliminate growth in aggregate CFC use and emissions in nonaerosol
applications.[11] These policies are an auction, grandfathering and a
policy we will label the "final product formula." In each case, the
regulation sets a quota on aggregate CFC use equal to its 1980 level,
permits are issued to authorize use under the quota, and these permits
are freely transferable within a permit market (or "after-market").
The only difference among the policies is the method used to allocate
permits initially. Under the auction, permits are initially sold to
the highest bidders. Under grandfathering, firms that use CFCs are
given (at a zero price) a fixed number of permits based on each firm's
historic (1980) share of CFC use.[12] Under the final product
formula, a firm's initial allocation of permits is based on its
current share of final product output. Although these forms of
implementing TDPs differ in only this single respect, they have
dramatically different implications for the firm owners, consumers and
workers in the regulated industries and for the economy as a whole.


THE AUCTION: THE PROBLEM OF TRANSFER PAYMENTS

The economic effects of a CFC permit auction -- which is probably the
easiest form of TDPs to administer -- are illustrated in Table 1.
This table estimates trader surplus losses from two sources for 11
industry groups directly affected by regulation.

The first column of the table summarizes an auction's resource costs.
This policy sets into motion an allocative movement of resources that
raises CFC prices and final product prices, encourages the investment
of resources in improving the environment and discourages the use of
resources to make products with CFC. Resource costs represent the
sacrifice in other goods and services required to improve the
environment as a result of these allocative effects. These costs
summarize actions taken by consumers who switch to products that are
less CFC-dependent, and by firms which implement abatement technologies to reduce CFC use. Relative to direct controls, an auction
achieves a substantial savings in aggregate resource costs.[13]

For the regulated industries, however, the most important feature of
an auction by far is the generation of enormous government revenues,
or "transfer payments," shown in the second column of Table 1.
Transfer payments represent a unique flow of wealth under an auction
policy. This movement of wealth originates in the pockets of
consumers, flows through (and, in the short run, is enlarged by) firm
owners, and eventually winds up in the general treasury and benefits
general taxpayers. For the regulated industries, transfer payments
represent an added burden of regulation. Moreover, in the case of

CFCs -- and probably many other environmental problems -- column 3 indicates that these payments account for the vast majority (about 87 percent) of the trader surplus losses suffered by the regulated industries under the auction alternative.

Paradoxically, an auction defines allocative outcomes that have the potential for achieving a Pareto superior policy, but its treatment of transfer payments virtually assures that this potential is not realized. While the policy minimizes the impact of regulation for the economy as a whole, it maximizes regulatory losses for the CFC-using industries. Because of this significant redistribution of wealth, the policy certainly does not Pareto-dominate the status quo; it imposes substantial losses on some groups -- unless we are willing to make rather heroic assumptions regarding the environmental and/or tax benefits enjoyed by individuals in the regulated industries. Moreover, the policy is not a likely outcome of a conservative political process.

TABLE 1
Estimated Trader Surplus Losses by Industry Group
Under a CFC Permit Auction: 1981 to 1990[a]

| Industry | Cumulative Resource Costs | Cumulative Transfer Payments | Transfer Payments As Percentage of Total Loss |
|---|---|---|---|
| | (millions of 1976 dollars) | | (%) |
| Flexible foam | 82.9 | 94.2 | 53 |
| Solvents | 93.7 | 259.5 | 73 |
| Rigid foam | | | |
|   Packaging | 29.1 | 31.1 | 52 |
|   Insulation | 11.5 | 735.9 | 98 |
|   Other | 20.9 | 101.8 | 83 |
| Mobile air conditioning | | | |
|   Manufacturing | 23.3 | 123.5 | 84 |
|   Servicing | 6.0 | 338.8 | 98 |
| Retail food refrigeration | 4.8 | 32.6 | 87 |
| Chillers | — | 112.1 | 100 |
| Home refrigeration | — | 40.4 | 100 |
| Miscellaneous | 33.6 | 161.1 | 83 |
| Total[b] | 304.9 | 2,031.1 | 87 |

SOURCE: Palmer and Quinn (1981), Tables 2.2 and 2.3.

[a]Sum of annual resource costs and transfer payments from 1981 through 1990, discounted to 1981 at 11 percent.

[b]Detail may not sum to total due to rounding.

GRANDFATHERING:   THE PROBLEM OF HETEROGENEOUS INDUSTRIES

The efficient allocative consequences of an auction are, of course, not unique: any policy that defines complete private property rights would have identical allocative effects. And it is not the efficiency attributes of the policy that cause its potential political problems, but rather the distributional consequences that necessarily flow from the sale of the initial permit allocation. Therefore, one obvious alternative is simply to give away the permits to grandfather firms according to some neutral formula like historic use. This policy of grandfathered private property rights retains the efficiency attributes of an auction and eliminates the flow of transfer payments away from the regulated industries as a group.

However, a relatively simple grandfathering mechanism would probably not result in the accurate compensation of CFC regulatory losses. Like many environmental regulations, CFC regulation would cut across industry boundaries and involve a large number of highly differentiated firms. As a result, a grandfathering policy may result in substantial wealth redistribution.

The situation for CFCs is illustrated in Table 2 for a single year (1985), assuming that permits are allocated on the basis of historic use in 1980. As the table indicates, the policy creates some big gainers and some big losers, though all industries fare better than under the auction. Of the 11 industry groups in Table 2, five would be net sellers of permits and actually gain (sometimes substantially) under regulation. The remaining six industries are net buyers and incur substantial regulatory losses. In fact, for these latter industries as a group, grandfathering retains a political liability of the auction: transfer payments still account for the majority of trader surplus losses due to regulation.

Ultimately, the wealth disparities generated by grandfathering reflect the ability of the initial permit allocation formula to match the economic complexity of the regulated industries. The firms affected by CFC regulation represent a wide variety of industries that have very different input demand characteristics for CFCs and are growing at radically different rates. Yet these differences are ignored by the relatively simple, historically based "rule of thumb" for the initial allocation of permits (and, therefore, wealth). Consequently, firms with relatively inelastic CFC input demand schedules in rapidly growing industries (such as rigid insulating foams) incur substantial transfer payments, while firms with relatively elastic input demands in more stable industries (such as flexible foams) reap large windfall gains from the sale of grandfathered permits.

These considerations suggest that devising an acceptable grandfathering formula poses a significant analytical challenge when regulated firms are highly differentiated, as in the CFC case. To the extent that this challenge is ignored or cannot be overcome, the transferability of property rights inherent under a market-oriented regime will tend to create big gainers and big losers. And this may make it difficult for a market-oriented policy to achieve a regulated

equilibrium near the initial distribution of wealth and satisfy a
conservative political process.[14]

However, the potential for wealth redistribution among the regulated
firms is not the only distributional problem posed by grandfathered
private property rights.  Suppose, for example, that a formula can be
devised that encourages the efficient exchange of permits, but at the
same time reduces, to the extent possible, the flow of transfer
payments among the regulated industries.  Can we then assume that the
resulting pricing mechanism will be attractive to the political
process?  The answer is no.  And the reason is that we have so far
ignored the implications of the policy for some important groups, such
as consumers.

TABLE 2
Redistributive Effects of Grandfathered Private Property Rights
(millions of 1976 dollars)

| Industry | Resource Costs[a] | Transfer Payments[b] | Net Costs[c] |
|---|---|---|---|
| Flexible foam | 10.4 | −22.8 | −12.4 |
| Solvents | 12.3 | −12.7 | −0.4 |
| Rigid foam | | | |
|    Packaging | 2.7 | −3.0 | −0.3 |
|    Insulation | 0.5 | +32.4 | +32.9 |
|    Other | 1.9 | +1.7 | +3.6 |
| Mobile air conditioning | | | |
|    Manufacturing | 2.6 | −4.9 | −2.3 |
|    Servicing | 0.6 | +6.3 | +6.9 |
| Retail food refrigeration | 0.9 | −5.0 | −4.1 |
| Chillers | −− | +0.8 | +0.8 |
| Home refrigeration | −− | +3.3 | +3.3 |
| Miscellaneous | 3.0 | +3.9 | +6.9 |
|    Total[b] | 34.7 | 0.0 | 34.7 |

SOURCE: Palmer and Quinn (1981), Tables 2.2 and 4.2.

NOTE: Detail may not sum to totals due to rounding.

[a]Annual costs for 1985 only, measured in constant 1976 dollars.
Industry-specific estimates vary in other years.

[b]Positive (negative) sign indicates industry is a net buyer (seller)
of emission rights.

[c]Sum of resource costs and transfer payments.  Positive (negative)
estimate indicates a net loss (gain) from control.

THE FINAL PRODUCT FORMULA:   THE PROBLEM OF COMPENSATING CONSUMER LOSSES

For consumers, the only difference between an auction and grandfathering as defined above is whether the wealth that flows from their
pockets is ultimately received by taxpayers or firm owners.   These
policies have identical allocative implications, and both result in
the same higher product prices, which transfer wealth away from
consumers.   Thus, grandfathering does not alleviate the losses of
consumers -- the wealth that is allocated under this kind of "direct
compensation" approach is completely "captured" by firm owners who are
the recipients of zero-priced permits.[15]

When a regulatory policy attempts to protect the consumer's "rights in
the status quo," high transactions costs strongly suggest that
compensation will not be direct.   Giving a fixed number of permits (or
any other form of lump-sum compensation to thousands -- even millions
-- of affected consumers is impractical on administrative grounds:   it
simply costs too much.   Rather, compensation to consumers is more
likely in the form of policies that reduce the impact of regulation on
product prices in the first place.   But because the product price
increases under the previous policies are a necessary consquence of
complete private property rights, this means that policies designed to
compensate potential consumer losses must create incomplete property
rights.

This observation poses a significant challenge to the policy analyst.
It implies that the analyst's job is to innovate policy designs that
may necessarily sacrifice some of the allocative efficiency properties
of an auction or grandfathering in an attempt to satisfy a conservative political system and to approach the Pareto ideal.

One such policy is the final product formula.   Like a grandfathering
policy, the final product formula initially distributes transferable
permits to regulated firms at a zero price.   Unlike grandfathering,
the initial permit allocation is based on each firm's current share of
industry-wide final product output rather than on its share of
historic emissions levels.[16]   This means that the wealth that would
otherwise go to taxpayers under an auction or in lump sums to firm
owners under grandfathering is distributed in the form of a per-unit
subsidy to final outputs under the final product formula.

The result?   Firms compete for this wealth in a manner that "trickles
down" much of the compensatory benefits of the policy to consumers and
other groups (e.g., workers) who receive no compensation under
grandfathering.

The resulting level of product prices and output levels in a particular industry depends upon the strength of two opposing forces under
this policy.   Because of the final product subsidy, firms are induced
to lower consumer prices (relative to an auction) in an attempt to
sell more output and increase their permit allocations.   But this
pressure to increase output levels also generates pressure on the
demands for permits.   Consequently, if the same total number of
permits are available as under the previously considered policies, the

final product formula will necessarily require a higher permit price
to equilibrate the permit market.  The ultimate effects of the formula
depend upon the balance between the final product subsidy (which acts
to reduce product prices) and the higher permit price (which acts to
increase product prices).

In the case of CFCs, the final product formula would be highly
effective in mitigating the losses cosumers would suffer under either
of the alternative forms of TDPs considered here.  Palmer and Quinn
(1981) estimate that in 1985 the policy would eliminate about 76
percent of the increase in product prices that would occur under
complete private property rights.[17]  Further, while the regulated
firms do not gain the sometimes substantial windfalls that occur under
grandfathering, they too receive compensation for potential regulatory
losses under the final product formula.

In short, more than any other policy, the final product formula
achieves the CFC quota without serious harm to any of the participants
in CFC-related markets.  But this potential political attribute is
obviously not without cost.  This policy is administratively the most
complex and costly one considered in this paper.  Moreover, the policy
increases the resource costs of regulation in private markets relative
to complete private property rights.

The resource costs under the policy are compared to an auction in
Table 3.  When the formula is effective, consumers undertake less
product substitution to reduce pollution levels.  By itself, this
reduces resource costs, which in Table 3 are actually lower than under
an auction in two industries.  However, since the final product
formula achieves the same environmental objective, this difference
must be made up by firms that implement additional abatement procedures in response to higher permit prices.  Thus, relative to complete
private property rights, firms undertake "too much" pollution clean-up
and consumers undertake "too little."  This raises the value of the
resources consumed by these industries to reduce CFC use by $3.6
million in 1985.  In addition to this imbalance between firms and
consumers in CFC-reducing activities, the formula encourages the
CFC-related industries to expand their output beyond efficient
levels.  Thus, the economy produces too many CFC-related outputs and
not enough of other products.  As Table 3 indicates, this additional
product market efficiency loss is about $2.0 million in 1985 for
CFCs.  Overall, the final product formula increases the resource costs
of achieving the CFC quota by about 16 percent in 1985.

However, these added costs must be interpreted carefully.  The
policy's higher administrative costs are small compared to the wealth
losses prevented for the policy's beneficiaries.  And while resource
costs are higher than under an auction or grandfathering, they are
much lower than under direct controls.  Perhaps most importantly,
these added costs fundamentally reflect the assumption that high
transactions costs forbid any form of direct compensation for
consumers and other diffuse groups.  If we desire or are compelled by
the political process to compensate potential regulatory losses with
reasonable accuracy, a policy like the seemingly inefficient final

product formula may be the cheapest way to get the job done.  Simply stated, the policy does add to the total resource costs of regulation, but only because it achieves a distribution of those costs that is beyond the reach of the allocatively efficient policy prescriptions advocated by economists.

TABLE 3
Resource Costs under the Final Product Formula: 1985

(in millions of 1976 dollars)

| Industry | Resource Costs | | |
| --- | --- | --- | --- |
| | Permit Auction | Final Product Formula | Change[a] |
| Flexible foam | 10.4 | 13.1 | +2.7 |
| Solvents | 12.3 | 13.6 | +1.3 |
| Rigid foam | | | |
| Packaging | 2.7 | 0.7 | −2.0 |
| Insulation | 0.5 | 0.1 | −0.4 |
| Other | 1.9 | 2.3 | +0.4 |
| Mobile air conditioning | | | |
| Manufacturing | 2.6 | 3.1 | +0.5 |
| Servicing | 0.6 | 0.7 | +0.1 |
| Retail food refrigeration | 0.9 | 0.9 | —— |
| Chillers | —— | —— | —— |
| Home refrigeration | —— | —— | —— |
| Miscellaneous | 3.0 | 3.9 | +0.9 |
| Total CFC-related | 34.7 | 38.3 | +3.6 |
| Product market efficiency loss | —— | 2.0 | +2.0 |
| Total Resource Cost[b] | 34.7 | 40.3 | +5.6 |

SOURCE: Palmer and Quinn (1981), Table 5.1.

[a]Indicates increase (or decrease) of final product formula over the permit auction.

[b]Detail may not sum to totals due to rounding.

Though the final product formula may have some potentially desirable
features as a politically feasible policy, it is extremely important
to realize that we cannot advocate the implementation of this policy
for the regulation of CFCs or anything else. This policy does nothing
more than offer an alternative mechanism for making tradeoffs between
the aggregate costs and distributional consequences of regulation.
While analysis can highlight the attributes and faults of these
tradeoffs, it cannot decide on their ultimate desirability. In the
complex world of real policy choice, the decision among alternative
policies requires an evaluation of alternative wealth distributions
that is beyond the objective expertise of the analyst. Ultimately,
only the political process can render decisions on whether the
distributional consequences of the formula are desirable and whether
they justify the price that must be paid in terms of higher administrative and resource costs.[18]


CONCLUSION

In a world where transactions are not costless, regulated firms are
not identical, and the welfare of consumers and other diffuse groups
matters (not to mention a host of factors not considered here), public
decisionmakers must make tradeoffs in the choice among alternative
policy designs. Potential CFC regulations illustrate some alternative
tradeoffs between how much regulation costs the economy as a whole and
how it affects the distribution of wealth.

When such tradeoffs are manifested in actual policy decisions,
economic analysts often view them in unfavorable terms. To cite only
one example, one recent writer, after an insightful political analysis
of the Clean Air Act, could only lament political decisions that
result in "the shrinking pie syndrome"[19] -- a view that I suspect is
shared by many economists. However, neither the normative Pareto
rationale nor the positive political rationale offers support for such
lamentations. Certainly, improving the allocative efficiency of
environmental policies is one important goal for analysis. But this
paper strongly suggests that economic analysts should refrain from
themselves falling into the "increasing pie syndrome" and judging
policies solely (or even primarily) on the basis of their allocative
attributes.

But perhaps the most important implication of this paper is the
expanded and somewhat redirected role it defines for formal economic
analysis in policy formation. Within a model that accounts for both
the allocative and distributional dimensions of policy choice, the
relevant question is not how do we design policies that minimize
costs, but rather how do we design policies that make better tradeoffs
between aggregate costs and politically feasible distributions of
those costs. In this expanded framework, the role of the policy
analyst has already been defined by Buchanan and Tullock (1975): The
analyst's job is to become a "Good Wicksellian" -- that is, we should
use the formal tools of our trade to innovate policies that achieve
environmental objectives, reduce aggregate costs relative to prevailing policies and have the potential of achieving political consensus.

To be successful in this endeavor, however, we must expand our inquiry into policy design beyond the contribution of Buchanan and Tullock. We must be willing to consider the interests of a variety of groups besides the firms that generate pollution. And we must be willing to consider a wide variety of innovative regulatory mechanisms. In this paper, the key to the design of policies that survive the political market test is the innovation of ways to compensate reasonably accurately potential regulatory losses. The final product formula is one small step in this direction. Even if it can't do the job for CFCs or anything else, it does suggest that economic analysis has much to contribute to a largely unexplored realm of regulatory policy design.

FOOTNOTES

1    For example, Freeman and Haveman (1972, p. 325) and Kneese and Schultze (1975).

2    For example, see Goldfarb (1980).

3    See Baumol and Oates (1975, chap. 13) and Freeman (1972).

4    This classification was initially suggested by Frank Camm. For an insightful discussion of the desirability of compensation in deregulation, see Tullock (1978).

5    For example, Gianessi et al. (1979) and Baumol and Oates (1975, chap. 13).

6    Buchanan and Tullock (1975, p. 143).

7    Majone (1976, p. 611).

8    See Peltzman (1976). Quinn (1981) develops a general equilibrium model of the political process in the context of environmental policy.

9    For a similar argument, see Tullock (1978).

10   For example, see Goldfarb (1980) on the practical problems of compensating the potential losses of labor groups under deregulation.

11   In the absence of controls, CFC use is expected to grow rapidly. But there is no reason to believe that a zero-growth policy results in "optimal" emissions levels. The intent here is simply to compare the effects of three alternative policies that are equally effective in protecting the environment.

12   CFC regulation has direct implications for a variety of firms involved in the manufacture, distribution and use of these chemicals. In this paper, we focus on the "user industries," which use CFCs as a material input in the production of a final

output.  For a discussion of policies that allocate permits to other kinds of firms, see Palmer and Quinn (1981).

13  Palmer et al. (1980) estimates that in the case of CFC regulation, economic incentives would reduce resource costs by about 40 percent relative to direct controls.  A similar savings would apply here, although cost estimates for a direct control policy that conforms precisely to the zero-growth quota have not been calculated.

14  In contrast, the propensity to cause significant wealth redistributions is much less under direct controls.  And this appears to explain at least part of the political processes' past preferences for this policy.  See Quinn (1981).

15  While the wealth of consumers cannot be ignored when considering the Pareto rationale, you may question whether such a diffuse group can be considered politically effective.  However, for a variety of arguments that consumers must be considered in the political calculus, see Peltzman (1976), Owen and Braeutigam (1978), and Weingast (1980) among others.  Moreover, an implication of the political process as described in the previous section is that the regulated firms will gain wealth at the expense of consumers only if the political power of firms fortuitously increases relative to that of consumers.  So long as a pollution problem does not result in such a shift of relative political power, the consumer's preserved marginal political effectiveness will allow the protection of his interests through elected representatives.

16  One administrative complication under the final product formula reflects the inherent differences among regulated products.  For example, some products use only a few ounces of CFCs per unit of output, while others use thousands of pounds.  This requires a set of conversion factors to convert disparate outputs into a common unit of account.  In Palmer and Quinn (1981), these conversion factors are set equal to a firm's CFC use in 1980 as a fraction of its total 1980 final output level.  And a firm's share of the permit allocation is actually its share of total converted output.

17  Similarly, because the policy prevents reductions in final output levels, it benefits workers and other inputs whose employment levels are closely related to output levels.  The case of worker losses is not considered in detail here because of space constraints and because their interests are generally closely tied to those of consumers.

18  In addition, when the regulated industries are highly differentiated, the policy may be susceptible to the same wealth redistribution problem discussed in the context of grandfathering.  In fact, it can be shown that under some circumstances the final product formula can backfire, resulting in lower consumer prices in some industries only at the expense of higher consumer prices

in others. For a detailed discussion, see Palmer and Quinn (1981), especially the appendix.

19    Navarro (1980, p. 44).


REFERENCES

Baumol, W., and Oates, W. 1975. The Theory of Enviromental Policy. New York: Prentice Hall.

Buchanan, J. 1959. Positive economics, welfare economics and political economy. Journal of Law and Economics 2(October).

Buchanan, J., and Tullock, G. 1975. Polluters profit and political response: direct control versus taxes. American Economic Review 65(1).

Frech, H. 1979. The extended coase theorem in the long run: the nonequivalence of liability rules and property rights. Economic Inquiry 17(April).

Freeman, A. 1972. The distribution of environmental quality. IN: Environmental Quality Analysis: Theory and Method in the Social Sciences, A. Kneese and B. Bower, eds. Baltimore: The Johns Hopkins Press.

Freeman, A., and Haveman, R. 1972. Residual charges for pollution control: a policy evaluation. Science 177(July 28).

Gianessi, L.; Peskin, H., and Wolff, E. 1979. The distributional effects of uniform air pollution policy in the United States. Quarterly Journal of Economics 371(May).

Goldfarb, R. 1980. Compensating the victims of policy change. Regulation 4(5).

Kneese, A., and Schultze, C. 1975. Pollution, prices and public policy. Washington: The Brookings Institution.

Majone, G. 1976. Choice among policy instruments for pollution control. Policy Analysis 2(Fall).

Navarro, P. 1980. The politics of air pollution. The Public Interest 59(Spring).

Navarro, P. 1981. The 1977 Clean Air Act amendments: energy, environmental, economic and distributional impacts. Public Policy 29(2).

Owen, B., and Braeutigam, R. 1978. The Regulation Game: Strategic Use of the Administrative Process. Cambridge: Ballinger Publishing Co.

Palmer, A.; Mooz, W.; Quinn, T., and Wolf, K.  1980.  Economic
    Implications of Regulating Chlorofluorocarbon Emissions.    Santa
    Monica: The Rand Corp.

Palmer, A., and Quinn, T.  1981.  Allocating Chlorofluorocarbon
    Permits:    Who Gains, Who Loses, and What Is the Cost?    Santa
    Monica: The Rand Corp.

Peltzman, S.  1976.  Toward a more general theory of regulation.
    Journal of Law and Economics 19(May).

Quinn, T.  1981.  Pollution, property rights and public policy:
    A  more  general  theory  of  environmental  policy.    The  Rand
    Corporation (unpublished).

Tullock, G.  1978.  Achieving deregulation: a public choice
    perspective.  Regulation 2(6).

Weingast, B.  1980.  Congress, regulation and the decline of nuclear
    power.  Public Policy, 28(2).

# Nonoptimal Solutions Using Transferable Discharge Permits: The Implications of Acid Rain Deposition

**Scott Atkinson**

**Department of Economics**
**University of Wyoming**

## INTRODUCTION

Despite efforts spanning more than a decade to improve ambient air quality -- among them the increased use of tall smokestacks for plant emissions -- many urban areas appear unable to attain the 1982 federal ambient standards for ozone, sulfur oxide ($SO_2$), particulate matter, nitrogen oxide and carbon monoxide. In fact, many of these areas are projected to be in nonattainment for more than one of these pollutants.[1] An apparent result is that the extent of acid deposition (not currently governed by standards) has increased during the last decade in the Midwest and Northeast.[2] To reduce the costs of compliance with standards, the U.S. Environmental Protection Agency (USEPA) has proposed the trading of transferable discharge permits (TDPs) in local airsheds.[3] The trading of local TDPs for ambient degradation would minimize the costs of achieving ambient standards in competitive markets without administrative and political constraints on the trading of permits. (See Crocker [1966] for an early recognition of this point, and Montgomery [1972] for a detailed mathematical proof of this proposition. Also, see Tietenberg [1980] for a survey and synthesis of the literature in this area.) Each firm would equate the price of marketable permits to its marginal cost of control. The magnitude of permits issued would have to yield the allowed ambient degradation. However, because TDP strategies load the environment cost-effectively, TDP strategies for $SO_2$ control that are designed to meet only local standards will most likely lead to increased long-range sulfate ($SO_4$) deposition, popularly known as "acid rain." This paper examines the extent of this phenomenon and the cost implications of constraints on acid rain deposition.

Local TDP strategies are basically variants of either emissions discharge permit (EDP) or ambient discharge permit (ADP) control strategies. Under the EDP strategy, sources with the lowest marginal control costs will undertake the greatest control burden, independent of their degradation of local air quality. Under the ADP strategy, sources with the lowest marginal control costs per unit improvement of local air quality will undertake the greatest control. That is, cost-effectiveness of incremental local control in achieving ambient standards will determine control responsibility.

Both of the local ADP and EDP strategies have been modelled with mathematical programming techniques by Atkinson and Tietenberg (1982) in St. Louis, where particulate control was considered, and by Anderson et al. (1979) in Chicago, where nitrogen dioxide control was examined. Both studies indicate an order-of-magnitude reduction in local control costs under the ADP system, and a factor of five reduction under the EDP system as compared to the current system, which is based on State Implementation Plans (SIPs).

However, both of these TDP strategies result in greater loading of the environment with $SO_2$ emissions than the SIP strategy. First, the SIP system is not a cost-minimizing strategy and so requires more control to achieve the ambient standard than local TDP strategies. Secondly, the ADP strategy generally encourages sources with tall smokestacks (usually power plants) to undertake less control, since they degrade the local environment less than other sources. Thus, the potential for long-range residual transport is much greater under the local TDP strategies, whose economic incentives for adoption appear very strong.

The present study attempts to measure the extent to which the cost savings of the local ADP strategy is due to externalizing the costs of long-range $SO_4$ deposition for the Cleveland region of the Ohio River Basin. We examine this region because it is projected to be a nonattainment region for $SO_2$ and is presumed to contribute significantly to $SO_4$ deposition in the Northeast.[4] A quadratic mathematical program is used to model the ADP method of pollution control. The objective function is a quadratic cost function reflecting increasing marginal control costs. When only constraints representing local ambient standards are satisfied, a local or intra-regional ADP solution is obtained. By adding constraints on the long-range transport of $SO_4$, an inter-regional ADP solution is also obtained. Clearly, the inter-regional solution is more costly than the intra-regional ADP solution, since some externalities are internalized. Inter- and intra-regional strategies that allocate additional control in proportion to current SIP control requirements are also examined. The first assigns additional control until local ambient standards are met. The second assigns additional control to meet these standards plus constraints on long-range $SO_4$ transport.

The results indicate that the intra-regional ADP strategy is substantially more cost-effective than the intra-regional SIP strategy. However, this saving is due to cost-effective pollution control, which implies greater loading of the local environment with $SO_2$ and substantially reduced control of power plants with tall smokestacks. Both contribute heavily to long-range transport of $SO_4$. Once significant constraints on long-range transport are introduced into both strategies, the cost-savings of the inter-regional ADP strategy is substantially reduced relative to the inter-regional SIP strategy.


MODEL FORMULATION

This model compares the costs and control burdens of four strategies. The intra-regional strategy, which includes only local $SO_2$ ambient constraints, is modelled for both the ADP and SIP methods. The inter-regional strategy, which includes local $SO_2$ ambient constraints and long-range $SO_4$ transport constraints, is also modelled for both the ADP and SIP methods.

Although some additional switches to lower sulfur fuels may be possible (see Table 1), the greatest incremental improvements in ambient air quality through fuel switching have already been achieved. Further, as will be shown later, reduction of fuel sulfur content by 40-50 percent is required to meet the primary ambient standard, and a reduction of up to 90 percent is required to meet this standard plus constraints on acid rain deposition. Since it is unlikely that there will be an adequate supply of fuels clean enough to meet these constraints, we examine the mandatory retrofitting of all major point sources with flue gas desulfurization (FGD) equipment, commonly called "scrubbers." Based on Mitre (1981), we assume that the maximum scrubber efficiency is 90 percent.

The intra-regional SIP allocation strategy requires computing additional control requirements for each source in proportion to its percentage contribution to total regional uncontrolled emissions under the current SIP strategy. The additional emission control responsibility for each source is computed as:

$$AER_j^e = AER^e \; \frac{ue_j}{\sum_j ue_j}, \qquad j = 1, \ldots, n, \qquad (1)$$

where:
$AER^e$ = the required change in aggregate regional emissions,

and:
$ue_j$ = the uncontrolled emissions from the $j$th source under the current strategy in grams/second (g/s).

The value of $AER^e$ necessary to achieve the 24-hour maximum $SO_2$ standard is adjusted iteratively -- after an initial best guess -- by computing individual source $AER_j$, using (1) subject to the 90 percent efficiency constraint and running uncontrolled source emissions through a diffusion model to determine expected air quality at each receptor. Adjustments in $AER^e$ are then made in successive iterations until the required ambient standards are just met at the region's air quality receptor that has the highest pollutant reading. Since there is no guarantee that this receptor will remain the same in each iteration, the diffusion model results must be examined at each iteration.

The inter-regional SIP strategy requires, in addition, that the following constraint on long-range $SO_4$ transport be satisfied:

$$\sum_\ell a_\ell \sum_j PR_j \geq b, \qquad (2)$$

$$0 \leq PR_j \leq 90, \qquad j = 1, \ldots, n, \qquad (3)$$

where:

$a_\ell$ = the product of the long-range transport coefficient (in $\mu g/m^3/g/s$) mapping $SO_2$ emissions from Cuyahoga County into $\mu g/m^3$ of $SO_4$ in the $\ell$th neighboring region and $ue_j/100$, yielding $\mu g/m^3/100$,

$PR_j$ = the percentage of total emissions, $0 \leq PR_j \leq 90$, (in $g/s$) of $SO_2$ to be removed by the jth source,

and:

$b$ = the total required reduction in $SO_4$ concentrations ($\mu g/m^3$) in all regions due to Cuyahoga County $SO_2$ emissions.

We model the intra-regional ADP control method by assuming that the cost functions for the sources under study are convex, smooth and continuous, and that all firms minimize their control costs, given they must install scrubbers. We can write the cost-minimization problem for the intra-regional ADP method as a quadratic programming (QP) problem:

$$\text{minimize } z = \sum_j c_j PR_j + \sum_j d_j PR_j \qquad (4)$$

$$\text{subject to: } \sum_j a_{ij} PR_j \leq b_i, \qquad i = 1,\ldots,n, \qquad (5)$$

$$0 \leq PR_j \leq 90 \qquad j = 1,\ldots,n, \qquad (6)$$

where:

$c_j, d_j$ = coefficients representing the cost of greater $PR_j$ per day for the jth source ($j = 1,\ldots,n$),

$a_{ij}$ = the product of the transfer coefficient which relates emissions from the jth source to air quality at the ith receptor (measured in $\mu g/m^3/g/s$) and $ue_j/100$, yielding $\mu g/m^3/100$,

$b_i$ = the reduction in $SO_2$ concentration required to achieve the maximum 24-hour $SO_2$ standard at the ith receptor.

The product of $a_{ij}$ and $PR_j$ yields $\mu g/m^3$ air quality improvement at receptor i due to additional control by source j. If $u_i$ equals uncontrolled air quality at receptor i, and g is the air quality standard, $u_i - g = b_i$, $i = 1,\ldots,m$. This trading rule requires the purchase of ambient permits by each source for each receptor, plus monitoring by the control agency and possible adjustment of the total number of permits to guarantee that ambient standards are met.

Finally, the inter-regional ADP control method can be written as the QP problem in equations (4) - (6), plus the additional acid deposition constraint in equation (2).


DATA AND ALGORITHMS

This section describes the Cleveland area source inventory, the local $SO_2$ air quality diffusion model and the long-range $SO_4$ transport model, and the control cost algorithms, which are input to the quadratic programming algorithm employed in this study. The quadratic programming algorithm is SYMQUAD,[5] which is based on the work of Van de Panne and Whinston (1969).

## Source Inventory

The sources examined in this study comprise the 25 largest point source emitters of $SO_2$ in the Cleveland area as defined by Cuyahoga County.[6] Together, they account for 95 percent of total regional emissions from all major point sources and 60 percent of total ambient degradation. The remaining ambient degradation from excluded point sources and all area sources is treated as background. The facility name, $SO_2$ source, and the percentage of $SO_2$ in the fuel burned by each source are given in Table 1. Fourteen of the 25 sources generate electricity, one source is a steam-heat boiler, one a wastewater treatment plant, and the remainder are industrial sources. As shown in Table 2, utilities account for 94.85 percent of $SO_2$ emissions, and these sources also employ substantially taller stacks than the other sources. Thus, the potential for long-range acid deposition is great for these emitters.

## Local Diffusion Model and Long-Range Transport Model

Air quality diffusion modelling is performed using the RAM steady-state Gaussian dispersion model developed by the USEPA.[7] Principally, RAM determines one-hour to one-day urban air quality levels based on concentrations of pollutants released by point and area sources. The algorithm is applicable for locations with level or gently rolling terrain, where a single wind vector, mixing height and stability class are assumed representative of the entire area for each hour.

The following information is required for all point and area sources. Emission information for all point sources includes source coordinates, emission rate, physical stack height, stack diameter, stack-gas exit velocity and stack-gas temperature. Emission information required of area sources consists of location coordinates, source side-length, total area emission rate and effective area source height. The output of the RAM model consists of calculated ambient concentrations at each receptor for hourly averaging times. Computations are performed on an hour-by-hour basis as if the atmosphere had achieved a steady-state condition. Therefore, if pollutant concentrations build up gradually over time, as under light wind conditions, error may result. The total concentration for a given hour at a particular receptor is the sum of the estimated contributions from each source.

Source-receptor pollutant transfer coefficients are computed from the RAM-calculated contributions of each source to the ambient concentrations at each receptor by dividing each concentration in $\mu g/m^3$ by the emission rate of the contributing source in g/s. The RAM model was run to simulate a typical 24-hour interval. The maximum 24-hour $SO_2$ standard is 365 $\mu g/m^3$. Thus, the output of the diffusion model was examined to determine whether this standard was violated during any of the 24 hours. The hour and receptor associated with

each violation as well as the extent of each violation are given in
Table 3.  The required improvements in air quality at each of the
eight receptors in violation are employed as the right-hand side of
the ambient air quality constraints in the QP sollutions to the ADP
problem.


TABLE 1
Inventory of $SO_2$ Sources -- Cuyahoga County, Ohio

| Source | $SO_2$ Process | Percentage $SO_2$ | Fuel |
|---|---|---|---|
| 1 ALCOA | Industrial coal boiler | 3.57 | Coal |
| 2 ALCOA | Industrial coal boiler | 3.57 | Coal |
| 3 Cleveland Electric Illuminating Co. (CEIC) | Steam heat boilers | .7 | Coal |
| 4 CEIC – Avon Lake Plant | Electrical generation | .24 | Oil |
| 5 CEIC – Avon Lake Plant | Electrical generation | .24 | Oil |
| 6 CEIC – Avon Lake Plant | Electrical generation | .24 | Oil |
| 7 CEIC – Avon Lake Plant | Electrical generation | .24 | Oil |
| 8 CEIC – Avon Lake Plant | Electrical generation | 2.65 | Coal |
| 9 CEIC – Avon Lake Plant | Electrical generation | 2.65 | Coal |
| 10 CEIC – Avon Lake Plant | Electrical generation | 2.65 | Coal |
| 11 CEIC – Eastlake Plant | Electrical generation | 3.14 | Coal |
| 12 CEIC – Eastlake Plant | Electrical generation | 3.14 | Coal |
| 13 CEIC – Lakeshore Plant | Electrical generation | 1.62 | Oil |
| 14 CEIC – Lakeshore Plant | Electrical generation | 1.62 | Oil |
| 15 CEIC – Lakeshore Plant | Electrical generation | 1.62 | Oil |
| 16 CEIC – Lakeshore Plant | Electrical generation | 1.62 | Oil |
| 17 CEIC – Lakeshore Plant | Electrical generation | .74 | Coal |
| 18 Division Pumping Station | Water treatment plant | 2.24 | Coal |
| 19 Ford Engine Plant #2 | Coal boilers | 2.9 | Coal |
| 20 General Motors/Chevrolet | Coal boilers | 2.26 | Coal |
| 21 Lincoln Electric | Coal boilers | 2.9 | Coal |
| 22 Medical Center | Coal boilers | 1.88 | Coal |
| 23 Republic Steel | Boiler | Coke oven | Gas |
| 24 Republic Steel | Slab R.F. #1 | Coke oven | Gas |
| 25 Republic Steel | Slab R.F. #2 | Coke oven | Gas |

TABLE 2
Potential Long-Range Transport Under Existing Controls

| Source | Current Emission Rate (grams per second) | Stack Height (meters) |
|---|---|---|
| 1 ALCOA | 106.80 | 60.96 |
| 2 ALCOA | 72.20 | 45.72 |
| 3 CEIC – Steam | 79.60 | 95.71 |
| 4 CEIC – Avon | 148.9 | 84.40 |
| 5 CEIC – Avon | 148.9 | 84.40 |
| 6 CEIC – Avon | 148.9 | 84.40 |
| 7 CEIC – Avon | 148.9 | 84.40 |
| 8 CEIC – Avon | 1,578.9 | 152.40 |
| 9 CEIC – Avon | 1,668.0 | 119.50 |
| 10 CEIC – Avon | 4,501.3 | 182.90 |
| 11 CEIC – Eastlake | 5,067.4 | 163.00 |
| 12 CEIC – Eastlake | 4,986.0 | 182.80 |
| 13 CEIC – Lakeshore | 453.81 | 81.69 |
| 14 CEIC – Lakeshore | 453.81 | 81.69 |
| 15 CEIC – Lakeshore | 521.88 | 81.69 |
| 16 CEIC – Lakeshore | 521.88 | 81.69 |
| 17 CEIC – Lakeshore | 1,055.16 | 81.69 |
| 18 Division Pump Station | 40.80 | 69.49 |
| 19 Ford Engine | 329.51 | 41.76 |
| 20 General Motors | 35.44 | 27.43 |
| 21 Lincoln Electric | 44.60 | 18.59 |
| 22 Medical Center | 174.60 | 58.52 |
| 23 Republic Steel | 145.50 | 68.60 |
| 24 Republic Steel | 68.40 | 49.10 |
| 25 Republic Steel | 68.40 | 49.10 |
| | TOTAL: 22,569.60 | AVERAGE: 85.27 |

The long-range transport model utilized in this study employs separate matrices computed for utility sources (assumed stack height of 175 m) and industrial sources (assumed stack height of 75 m) for July meteorology, which corresponds to the month of the RAM diffusion model run.[8]  The matrix coefficients map millions of metric tons of $SO_2$

TABLE 3
Receptors Exceeding the Maximum 24-Hour Standard

| Receptor | Hour | Air Quality ($\mu g/m^3$) | Required Improvement to Achieve Standard ($\mu g/m^3$) |
|---|---|---|---|
| 1 | 20 | 600.12 | 235.12 |
| 2 | 16 | 366.85 | 1.85 |
| 6 | 23 | 366.44 | 1.44 |
| 9 | 16 | 443.90 | 78.9 |
| 14 | 23 | 439.54 | 74.54 |
| 19 | 2 | 546.51 | 181.51 |
| 22 | 24 | 662.45 | 297.45 |
| 26 | 23 | 375.25 | 10.25 |

emitted per day in one state into average concentrations in $\mu g/m^3$ of $SO_4$ in a receptor state. In constraint equation (2), employed by the inter-regional least-cost strategy, long-range transport coefficients are converted into units of $\mu g/m^3/g/s$. The total contribution of the 25 Cuyahoga County sources to other regions' $SO_4$ concentrations is computed as 13.33 $\mu g/m^3$ for all utility sources and .79 $\mu g/m^3$ for all industrial sources. In the following analysis of inter-regional strategies, the cost of reducing these contributions by 50 percent is computed. Biologists have specified that reductions of this amount are necessary to restore acidified lakes to normal conditions.[9] It should be recognized, however, that the exact link between emission and inter-regional air quality is still unsolved.

## Control Costs

The estimated costs of $SO_2$ control are based on data reported by Mitre Corporation (1981) for industrial and utility sources. Based on discussions with Ohio EPA officials, all industrial sources are assumed to be retrofitted with dual alkali FGD equipment, and all utility sources with limestone FGD equipment, both of which appear more likely to be adopted than spray dryer systems.

Very similar procedures are used to estimate source control costs as a function of percentage of $SO_2$ removal for q utility sources and k industrial sources where $q + k = n$. Estimation of utility cost-functions are based on data for 30 plants supplied by the Tennessee Valley Authority and reported in Mitre (1981). These data include the annualized control cost (annualized capital costs plus annual operating and maintenance costs) in mills per kilowatt hour (MKWH), the $SO_2$ percentage content of fuel burned ($SO_2$), the megawatt capacity of the plant (MW) and the percentage of $SO_2$ removal (PR). The assumed annualization factor for capital costs is .1494, based on

a 30-year plant life and 14.7 percent discount rate, equal to the
assumed regulated rate of utility financing. After converting MKWH to
total annual cost (TAC) using a load factor of 62.8 percent as
suggested in Mitre (1981), TAC was regressed on a quadratic function
of $SO_2$, MW and PR using ordinary least squares (OLS):

$$TAC = \alpha + \beta_s \cdot SO_2 + \beta_m \cdot MW + \beta_p \cdot PR$$
$$+ \beta_{ss} \cdot SO_2^2 + \beta_{mm} \cdot MS^2 + \beta_{pp} \cdot PR^2 \qquad (7)$$
$$+ \beta_{sm} \cdot SO_2 \cdot MW + \beta_{sp} \cdot SO_2 \cdot PR + \beta_{pm} \cdot PR \cdot MW + e.$$

This functional form was particularly justified since the marginal
cost of additional PR should differ across firms based on individual
MW and $SO_2$ levels and marginal cost should increase with PR, all
else constant.

By dropping the insignificant terms in equation (7) and re-estimating,
we get the following regression:

$$TAC = 430629 + 321.88 \cdot PR \cdot MW$$
$$(573482) \quad (17.47)$$
$$+ 464.74 \cdot PR^2 + 2881.06 \cdot SO_2 \cdot MW, \qquad (8)$$
$$(105.42) \qquad (260.80)$$

with an $\bar{R}^2$ = .98. Standard errors are given in parentheses. The
fixed cost ($FC_q$) component is computed for source $\underline{q}$ as:

$$FC_q = \alpha + \beta_{sm} \cdot SO_{2_q} \cdot MW_q = 430629 + 2881.06 \cdot SO_{2_q} \cdot MW_q, \qquad (9)$$

where the values of $SO_{2_q}$ and $MW_q$ are substituted.

The variable cost ($VC_q$) component is computed as a function of $PR_q$
for source $\underline{q}$ as:

$$VC_q = \beta_{pm} \cdot PR_q \cdot MW_q + \beta_{pp} \cdot PR^2 = 321.88 \cdot PR_q \cdot MW_q +$$
$$+ 464.74 \cdot PR_q^2, \qquad (10)$$

where the values of $MW_q$ are substituted. The $FC_q$ component is
reported in column two of Table 4 and the components of $VC_q$
corresponding to $PR_q$ and $PR_q^2$ are reported in columns three and
four, respectively, of this table.

A similar procedure was employed for the estimation of industrial cost
functions. Total annualized costs were computed on a plant utilization rate of 60 percent and a capital annualization factor of .1715,
assuming a 30-year plant life and a 17 percent discount rate. Data in
Mitre (1981) for 89 industrial plants was employed to estimate

TABLE 4

Estimated Coefficient Values for
Equation (6) for Significant Point Sources

| Parameter / Source $j$ | Fixed Cost Constant | Variable Cost $PR_j$ | $PR_j^2$ | Upper Limit of Emissions with 90% Control |
|---|---|---|---|---|
| 1  | 2613870 | 4532.72   |        | 96.12   |
| 2  | 1952340 | 4516.74   |        | 64.08   |
| 3  | 2106740 | 4666.80   |        | 71.64   |
| 4  | 456905  | 12231.50  | 464.74 | 134.01  |
| 5  | 456905  | 12231.50  | 464.74 | 134.01  |
| 6  | 457596  | 12553.40  | 464.74 | 134.01  |
| 7  | 457596  | 12553.40  | 464.74 | 134.01  |
| 8  | 1896510 | 61801.20  | 464.74 | 1421.01 |
| 9  | 2201910 | 74676.40  | 464.74 | 1501.20 |
| 10 | 5393260 | 209223.00 | 464.74 | 4051.17 |
| 11 | 6319920 | 209545.00 | 464.74 | 4560.66 |
| 12 | 6310870 | 209223.00 | 464.74 | 4487.40 |
| 13 | 720003  | 19956.60  | 464.74 | 408.42  |
| 14 | 720003  | 19956.60  | 464.74 | 408.42  |
| 15 | 780678  | 24141.10  | 464.74 | 469.69  |
| 16 | 780678  | 24141.10  | 464.74 | 469.69  |
| 17 | 974285  | 82079.70  | 464.74 | 949.64  |
| 18 | 1387310 | 4513.96   |        | 36.72   |
| 19 | 6751950 | 4666.85   |        | 296.55  |
| 20 | 1287730 | 4509.90   |        | 31.89   |
| 21 | 1458000 | 4509.42   |        | 40.14   |
| 22 | 3872940 | 4633.57   |        | 157.14  |
| 23 | 3087900 | 25687.50  |        | 130.95  |
| 24 | 1785080 | 14452.20  |        | 61.56   |
| 25 | 1785080 | 14452.20  |        | 61.56   |

equation (7) using OLS. After dropping insignificant variables and re-estimating this equation, the following regression was obtained:

$$TAC = 629276 + 4484.78 \cdot PR + .599402 \cdot PR \cdot MW \qquad (11)$$
$$(74491.3)(1216.51) \qquad (.082487)$$
$$+ 6950.57 \cdot SO_2 \cdot MW \qquad ,$$
$$(216.069)$$

with an $R^2 = .98$. Again, standard errors are given in parentheses. The fixed cost ($FC_k$) and variable cost ($VC_k$) components of equation (11) are computed as follows:

$$FC_k = \alpha + \beta_{sm} \cdot SO_{2_k} \cdot MW_k = 629276 + 6950.57 \cdot SO_{2_k} \cdot MW_k \qquad (12)$$

and:

$$VC_k = \beta_p \cdot PR_k + \beta_{pm} \cdot PR_k \cdot MW_k, \qquad (13)$$
$$= 4484.78 \cdot PR_k + .599402 \cdot PR_k \cdot MW_k,$$

where the values of $MW_k$ and $SO_{2_k}$ are substituted for the kth source. The $FC_k$ and $VC_k$ components are reported in columns two and three, respectively, of Table 4. For all n sources, these columns represent the $c_j$ and $d_j$, respectively, of equation (4).


RESULTS

The individual source control requirements and total fixed and variable annual costs for each of the four strategies of pollution control described in section two are presented in Table 5. The expectation was that the intraregional ADP strategy would be substantially cheaper than the intra-regional SIP strategy. Further, it was expected that inclusion of constraints on long-range $SO_4$ deposition in both systems would substantially reduce the cost advantage of the intra-regional ADP strategy. These expectations are in fact borne out by the simulation results.

First, at the intra-regional level, fixed costs are constant for all strategies at $56,016,059. However, the variable costs of the ADP strategy -- $26,952,379 -- are almost two and one-third times less than those of the SIP method -- $61,574-528 -- to satisfy the intra-regional 24-hour maximum $SO_2$ standard. This is due to the ADP strategy's allocation of control responsibility according to the lowest marginal cost per unit of local air quality improvement. The SIP method simply increases all sources' control responsibility by an equal percentage, regardless of each source's marginal cost per unit of air quality improvement.

However, this intra-regional cost savings is achieved through greater long-range transport of $SO_4$ under the ADP strategy. This is due to two factors. First, since the ADP strategy is cost-effective on an intra-regional basis, it leads to far greater intra-regional environmental loading with $SO_2$. The ADP strategy removes less than half of

TABLE 5
Control Responsibilities and Costs
Under Alternative Control Strategies

| SOURCE # | CONTROL REQUIREMENTS (g/s) | | | |
| --- | --- | --- | --- | --- |
| | SIP Method | | ADP Method | |
| | Intra-Regional | Inter-Regional | Intra-Regional | Inter-Regional |
| 1 | 48.06 | 53.40 | -- | 96.12 |
| 2 | 32.49 | 36.10 | -- | -- |
| 3 | 35.82 | 36.10 | -- | -- |
| 4 | 67.01 | 74.45 | -- | -- |
| 5 | 67.01 | 74.45 | -- | -- |
| 6 | 67.01 | 74.45 | -- | -- |
| 7 | 67.01 | 74.45 | -- | -- |
| 8 | 710.51 | 789.45 | 687.61 | 572.04 |
| 9 | 750.6 | 834.00 | 706.03 | 483.34 |
| 10 | 2025.58 | 2250.65 | 2451.90 | 2845.30 |
| 11 | 2280.33 | 2533.7 | 3.37 | 3152.98 |
| 12 | 2243.7 | 2493.0 | -- | 2887.89 |
| 13 | 204.21 | 226.91 | 169.80 | 169.39 |
| 14 | 204.21 | 226.90 | 169.80 | 169.39 |
| 15 | 234.85 | 260.94 | 215.54 | 215.95 |
| 16 | 234.85 | 260.94 | 215.54 | 215.95 |
| 17 | 474.82 | 527.58 | -- | -- |
| 18 | 18.36 | 20.4 | -- | -- |
| 19 | 148.28 | 164.76 | -- | 296.56 |
| 20 | 15.95 | 17.72 | -- | -- |
| 21 | 20.07 | 22.30 | 21.97 | 21.97 |
| 22 | 78.57 | 87.30 | -- | 157.14 |
| 23 | 65.48 | 72.75 | -- | -- |
| 24 | 30.78 | 34.20 | -- | -- |
| 25 | 30.78 | 34.20 | -- | -- |
| Total Removed (g/s) | 10,156 | 11,281 | 4,642 | 11,284 |

Total Annual Costs (Dollars per Year)

| | | | | |
| --- | --- | --- | --- | --- |
| Variable Costs: | 61,574,528 | 70,020,301 | 26,952,379 | 56,841,304 |
| Fixed Costs: | 56,016,059 | 56,016,059 | 56,016,059 | 56,016,059 |

the total $SO_2$ emissions controlled by the SIP method and achieves the same intra-regional $SO_2$ ambient standards. Ultimately, this implies greater long-range transport of $SO_4$ by the ADP strategy. Further, from Table 2 it can be seen that sources 10–12 are power-plants with the tallest stacks (from 163–183 m). Thus, these sources undertake far less control under the ADP strategy because they degrade local air quality relatively little. This also implies greater long-range transport of $SO_4$.

Once constraints on long-range transport are included, the intra-regional cost advantage of the ADP strategy is substantially reduced. Inter-regional solutions for both the SIP and ADP strategies require a 50 percent reduction of the contribution of the 25 Cuyahoga County sources to $SO_4$ concentrations in all regions. After imposing this constraint, intra-regional $SO_2$ emissions for both strategies are highly similar, and the $SO_2$ removal levels are almost two and one-half times larger under the inter-regional ADP and SIP solutions than under the intra-regional ADP solution. Further, the power plants with the tallest stacks (sources 10–12) are required to undertake substantially higher levels of control than under the ADP intra-regional strategy. In particular, the control responsibility for source 12 increases from zero to 2887.89 g/s. The variable costs of both inter-regional strategies have risen substantially relative to their intra-regional counterparts, since one-half of previous externalities are now internalized. However, the variable costs of the ADP strategy -- $56,841,304 -- have more than doubled, while those of the SIP strategy -- $70,020,301 -- have risen only 13.7 percent. Thus, the ADP strategy is now only 18.8 percent cheaper than the SIP strategy. It then remains to be determined whether the cost savings of the ADP system will be sufficient to offset any additional transaction and administration costs of the ADP system. Further, concerns about equity in changing from the SIP to the ADP strategy may prevent adoption of the ADP system, given its substantially reduced cost advantage under the inter-regional solution.

CONCLUSIONS

Considerable discussion has emerged recently regarding the appropriate strategy for achieving compliance with ambient standards. The use of TDP systems has been suggested by the USEPA as a far more cost-effective method of achieving this goal than the current SIP strategy. Using data from a set of 25 $SO_2$ sources in Cuyahoga County, this paper demonstrates that the intra-regional cost savings of the ADP strategy are substantial. However, this savings is largely due to the long-range transport of locally generated $SO_2$. The introduction of constraints on long-range $SO_4$ transport substantially reduces the cost-saving advantage of the ADP strategy relative to the SIP strategy. The question then becomes whether the remaining differential is substantial enough to cover any additional transaction and administrative costs of the ADP system and whether it outweighs concerns about equity losses.

FOOTNOTES

[1]    See the National Commission on Air Quality (1981), pp. 3.4-21 to
       3.4-34.

[2]    See the National Commission on Air Quality (1981), p. 3.9-19.

[3]    See the National Commission on Air Quality (1981), p. 4.1-41.

[4]    See the National Commission on Air Quality (981), p. 3.4-26.

[5]    See Cohen and Stein (1978).

[6]    The author wishes to thank Robert Hodanbosi, Chief, Division of
       Air Quality Modelling and Planning of the Ohio Environmental
       Protection Agency for supplying the source inventory and
       answering numerous questions about the compatibility of sources
       and scrubbers.

[7]    See Turner and Novak (1978).

[8]    See the U.S. Department of Energy (1981).

[9]    See Committee on the Atmosphere and Biosphere (1981), p. 181.

REFERENCES

Anderson, R.J., Jr., et al.  1979.  An Analysis of Alternative
     Policies for Attaining and Maintaining a Short Term $NO_2$
     Standard.  Report to the Council in Environmental Quality.
     Princeton, N.J.: Mathtech, Inc.

Atkinson, S.E., and Tietenberg, T.  1982.  The empirical properties of
     two classes of designs for transferable discharge permit
     markets.  Journal of Environmental Economics and Management
     9:101-121.

Cohen, C., and Stein, J.  1978.  Multi-Purpose Optimization System
     Users Guide, Version 4.  Evanston, Ill.: Northwestern University
     Vogelback Computing Center.

Committee on the Atmosphere and Biosphere, National Academy of
     Sciences.  1981.  Atmosphere-Biosphere Interactions:  Toward a
     Better Understanding of the Ecological Consequences of Fossil
     Fuel Combustion.  Washington: National Academy Press.

Crocker, T.D.  1966.  Structuring of atmospheric pollution control
     systems.  IN: The Economics of Air Pollution, H. Wolozin, ed.,
     pp. 61-86.  New York: W.W. Norton and Co.

Mitre Corporation.  1981.  Acid rain mitigation (ARM) study: Final
     utility and industrial boiler FGD costs derived-cost algorithms.

Montgomery, D.W.  1972.  Markets in licenses and efficient pollution
    control programs.  Journal of Economic Theory 5:395-418.

National Commission on Air Quality.  1981.  To Breathe Clean Air.
    A Report to Congress.

Tietenberg, T.H.  1980.  Transferable discharge permits and the
    control of stationary source air pollution: A survey and
    synthesis.  Land Economics 56:391-416.

Turner, B.D., and Novak, J.H.  1978.  User's Guide for RAM, Vol. 1:
    Algorithm Description and Use.  Research Triangle Park, N.C.:
    U.S. Environmental Protection Agency.

U.S. Department of Energy.  1981.  Matrix Methods to Analyze
    Long-Range Transport of Air Pollutants, DOE/EV-0127.

Van de Panne, C., and Whinston, A.  1969.  The symmetric formulation
    of the simplex method for quadratic programming.
    Econometrica 37:507-27.

# Planning for the Development of Economic Incentives under Institutional Constraints: The Role for Guided Incrementalism

**David Foster**

**U.S. Environmental Protection Agency**
**Washington, D.C.**

"Environmental pollution is a classic example of market failure."

I'm not speaking here about the "tragedy of the commons" or the inability of the market to handle public goods or even the failure to internalize externalities. I am speaking of the tragic failure of economists to adapt and implement sound market-oriented policies for the control of pollution. I think we have made some progress, but the progress has been agonizingly slow and even slower to be recognized. Alfred Marshall spoke of "putting a price on smoke" as early as 1890. By 1912, A.C. Pigou had developed the concept of externalities leading to the effluent tax approach geared only to marginal damages. Since that time, scores of other talented economists have expounded on a variety of attractive pricing policies. Why then has there been comparatively little progress in implementation?

My thesis is essentially that the economic concepts are sound, but our poor track record results from a failure to recognize and deal with the institutional constraints. How then do we overturn this "market failure," this failure to successfully employ market approaches in the control of environmental pollution? I believe that the solution lies in developing and guiding a well-planned series of incremental improvements toward the long-range goals of a comprehensive market system better adapted to the impact of the institutional constraints.

THE GENERIC EXAMPLE

Figures 1 and 2 illustrate both some of the constraints confronting the implementation of economic incentives and one means to adapt an incentive system to seemingly irreconcilable constraints.

The simple 2 x 2 diagram in Figure 1 has ordered the opportunities for additional pollution control according to two dimensions: marginal cost and "affordability." Marginal cost is approximated here by the cost per ton of the next increment of control. Affordability is measured by the ability to absorb (or pass on) additional pollution control costs and still remain in business. For purposes of this

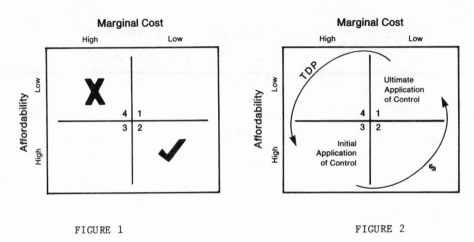

FIGURE 1                                    FIGURE 2

Constraints of Marginal Cost and Affordability on Pollution Control


example it is also assumed that all pollution reductions are fung-
ible.  That is, we are concerned with aggregate emission levels only
and will value a ton of emission reductions from one source as
environmentally equivalent to a ton of reductions from any other
source.  Hydrocarbon emissions leading to the formation of ozone and
emitted from the same major metropolitan area closely approximate this
condition.  Given free choice over pollution reduction opportunities
in all four quadrants and given the requirement to reduce aggregate
emission levels still further, everything else being equal, the local
air pollution control director will focus his attention on the lower
right-hand corner of quadrant 2 and avoid quadrant 4.

The  real  test  of  his  selection  criteria  arises  when  quadrant  2
opportunities have been consumed and yet further emissions reductions
are required to attain the ambient standard.  Does he seek to minimize
total pollution control expenditures by moving into quadrant 1 with
the concurrently high risks of shutting down certain businesses?   Or
does he seek to minimize, or at least postpone, business failure by
moving into quadrant 3 with the consequence of less cost-effective
pollution control?

Invariably, at both the local and national level there is a predictable pattern of decision-making that favors quadrant 3 over quadrant
1.   I suspect that this institutional pattern (along with source
variability and limited information) is one of the major causes of the
variation in marginal cost of control.   For example, electric
utilities, because of their monopoly position, have high affordability
and are the recipient of stringent pollution control requirements.
The copper smelting and steel industries have been the recipient of
far  more  lenient  requirements  and  have  frequently  been  granted
exemptions from even these, presumably because of their low affordability.

My intent here is not to denigrate environmental decision-making, but to identify this pattern as an important constraint and seek a means to minimize its impact. The pattern of bias favoring affordability over cost-effectiveness is so pervasive that any fee or marketable permit system that fails to take cognizance of it is immediately in jeopardy.

Figure 2 shows how a Transferable Discharge Permit (TDP) system could be adapted to this affordability bias.

The system in essence becomes a two-stage allocation process. The first stage recognizes the operant political constraints and allows for application of the control burden consistent with local concepts of equity, and the second stage minimizes the cost of the first stage by allowing sources to reallocate (transfer) emission reduction requirements among themselves.

The greatest virtue of a TDP system may be its ability to accept, survive and ultimately contravene an institutional constraint.


THE CONSTRAINTS

The constraints to the development of economic incentives are formidable. So strong, in fact, as to make the "great debates" over fees vs. marketable permits dwindle into comparatively minor quibbling over subtle nuances. By institutional constraints I mean all those factors that impede the application of otherwise viable theory. Institutional constraints are to the planner what friction is to the student of physics.

The Process
The first constraint -- and perhaps more like the forest than an individual tree -- is the presence of existing organizations and an ongoing process. Obviously, environmental control programs are already operating. With the possible exception of some newly identified toxic substances, we do not have the opportunity to start afresh. For better or worse, laws, regulations, control programs, procedures, institutions and other stakeholders are already in place, many with a vested interest in the way things are now run.

In his work on decision theory, Graham Allison classified decision-making models into three major categories: The Rational Model (decisions derive from objective evaluation of relevant benefits and costs of clearly identified courses of action); The Competitive Model (decisions derive from competition and compromise among relevant power groups, each seeking to further their own ends), and The Process Model (decisions derive from standard operating procedures and existing organizational relationships, which strongly tend to preserve the status quo and replicate earlier decisions). My own observations over the last 10 years confirm the common claim of all three forms of decision-making within the Environmental Movement, with the strongest -- albeit inadvertent -- emphasis on The Process Model. Historically at the USEPA, as in almost any other large bureaucratic organization, the best predictor of what will be done tomorrow has been what was done yesterday.

Methods of organization and operating procedures evolve, become standardized, and have a significant impact on the decisions that follow. A number of environmental historians have observed that the origins of the current system of air quality control regions, for example, has not so much to do with its inherent logic as with its having followed in the footsteps of earlier efforts to manage water quality on a river basins basis. Similarly, as the USEPA addresses any new pollution problem, it looks first to its repetoire of existing programs (usually to the exclusion of nontraditional alternatives) to determine which, if any, can be readily adapted to dealing with such a problem. Conversely, programs and policies not present -- at least in embryonic form -- during the early phases only rarely spring forth anew as those policies mature.

Where significant departures from traditional practice do occur, they usually appear only where all other options have first been exhausted and external pressures are of crisis proportions. The USEPA's issuance of the Offset Policy in December 1976 is a case in point. This major change and major new opportunity for economic incentives developed not because of newfound belief in economic theory, but because of a crisis in enforcing the Clean Air Act in the presence of widespread nonattainment. A literal interpretation of the 1970 Clean Air Act could have called for halting all major industrial growth in at least the nation's 100 largest cities because of the failure to attain the air quality levels specified in the National Ambient Air Quality Standards by the 1977 deadline. Forced to choose between ignoring the plain meaning of the Clean Air Act and resorting to such a politically, economically and administratively impossible task, USEPA chose instead to creatively reinterpret Section 110 of the act. Then-administrator Russell Train issued an "Interpretive Ruling" which held in part that the sanction against growth in nonattainment areas could be met by requiring sufficient offsetting emission reductions to assure that there would be no net growth in emissions in the non-attainment area. USEPA's "Offset Policy" therefore evolved not so much because of an interest in market mechanisms, but because the traditional avenues were unavailable.


The People
The heavy impact of the Process Model of decision-making would act as a major barrier to new methods of environmental control regardless of the individuals involved, but when this constraint is combined with the particular training and personalities of the early players in environmental decision-making, the impact of this constraint becomes even more formidable. This contraint derives from the historical origins and personal philosophy of USEPA personnel. USEPA's early origins were in public health service. A sister agency was the U.S. Food and Drug Administration. Early regulations of these organizations consisted of required work practices and prohibitions. The regulatory norm consisted of "thou shalts" and "thou shalt nots" rather than graduated incentives for better performance.

Historically, the Environmental Movement has been largely made up of lawyers, engineers and members of the health sciences. Economists have been conspicuously under-represented. Each program office, of course, has its economic branch or section, but these people are invariably assigned to calculate economic impacts of various emission standards rather than develop alternative control strategies. In USEPA's air office, for example, the Control Programs Development Division at last count had 15 engineers, nine environmental protection specialists, five secretaries, one attorney and one economist. That office is unusually low in the number of attorneys, but otherwise it is about normal. Top management at USEPA is typically 45 to 55 percent attorneys, 35 to 45 percent engineers and physical scientists, and less than 10 percent economists. These ratios remain essentially the same whether we are speaking of a Republican or Democratic administration, or one which is characterized by a strong or weak interest in the environment.

The training in these professions has led to a "command and control" orientation, not a market orientation. To the extent that people in these disciplines have studied market systems at all, one of the first things they seem to have learned is: "Environmental pollution is a classic example of market failure."

## The Laws

The existing laws are obviously a constraint, but frankly I believe we tend to overstate their importance, particularly when compared with the importance of the decison-making process and the backgrounds of the people involved. The laws themselves are a good deal more flexible than is generally assumed -- or than many of the regulations implementing them.

Numerous provisions of the Clean Air and Clean Water acts do form major constraints to the implementation of economic incentives. The major impediment is the requirement for technology-based emission standards. Whether these take the form of "best available tech-nology," "lowest achievable emission rates," or "new source perform-ance standards," they all have the consequence of reducing the opportunity for more cost-effective control programs. Prescriptive performance standards based on identified technology and generalized affordability (sometimes referred to as "squeeze til it hurts") not only create inefficiency through grossly unequal marginal costs of control, but also provide no incentive for innovation leading to eventual performance better than the prescribed standard.

Sometimes, however, an inconvenient law becomes a convenient excuse for not implementing change. Despite the conspicuous absence of explicit provisions for fees or marketable permits, various "proto" market systems employing such measures as "bubble," "offset" and "banking" have recently been implemented without legislative change -- under essentially the same laws that had previously been regarded as impenetrable barriers to change.

Furthermore, despite the frequent criticism of the law's inattention to economic incentives, I have yet to see a well-coordinated effort by

environmental economists to amend the Clean Air, Clean Water or
related acts with respect to this issue.  Clearly, if we are to
criticize lawyers or engineers for failing to make better use of
economic principles, then economists must also accept some blame for
failing to make better use of the policymaking process.  The real
problem, of course, is the failure to build any meaningful constituency.  Economists are see as "academics" in the end, and academics
don't count for much when it comes to votes -- unless they can
translate their ideas into approaches packaged for more popular appeal.


THE PROPOSED SOLUTION

If we are to accept the proposition that the constraints addressed
above are real and will remain so for the foreseeable future (and I
do), then the task is to adapt the development of a pricing policy or
an economic incentive system to the existing constraints rather than
lie in wait for a revolutionary change.  The proposed solution (and
the process now underway) has been to develop the concept of a
comprehensive economic incentive system and then to secure its
acceptance and institutionalization in small, bite-size increments.
Some have referred to this adaptive procedure as an "evolutionary"
process, as opposed to the "revolutionary" process of replacing
existing structures all at once.

I call this adaptive change process "guided incrementalism" and
believe it differs from social evolution as grafting differs from
biological evolution.  Evolution is an attractive but incomplete
metaphor for the adaptive change process.  True, the process moves in
slow, small (sometimes almost imperceptible) changes, but the changes
are neither random mutations nor may they risk the survival of the
whole organism as a consequence of some inappropriate change.
Grafting, in contrast, allows the innovative gardener to guide
development according to some comprehensive plan; joining small
branches of a new, more efficient variety one at a time without
threatening the livelihood of the root stock and yet still leading
over time to the creation of a system containing all the most
sought-after characteristics.


EARLY INCREMENTS OF CHANGE

Offsets
Chronologically, the first scion to be grafted onto the environmental
regulatory tree was the Offset Policy in December 1976.[1]  Biologically
it was a "sport."  The real impetus of change was more legal sleight
of hand to avoid political catastrophe than rational economic theory,
but the significance of this change was quickly recognized by
observant resource economists.  For the first time, a regulatory
agency would allow the emission burden imposed by one source to be
met, or "offset," through the voluntary contributions of another.
Though important, this was still a very narrowly constrained start.
It applied only to new sources in nonattainment areas, and before
those sources could seek relief by means of offsets, they had to first

employ technology sufficient to reach the lowest achievable emission rate (LAER). Furthermore, in the initial Offset Policy, any emission reduction to be used as an offset needed to be created simultaneously with the new source of emissions, and there was no provision of incentives to look for ways to reduce emissions now so that they might be sold or traded at some later time.

Notwithstanding these major restrictions, several offsets occurred during the first year. By March of 1981, Wes Vivian had documented over 1,500 offsets, and the offset concept had been adopted into the regulations of over 40 states. It is also significant to note that though the offset concept was first issued as an administrative change after almost nine months gestation, it was followed by a legislative change that ratified it into law. The small incremental change had become itself an institution.

### Banking

The next graft to take place was engendered out of the controversy surrounding the first. Revisions to the offset policy[2,3,4] formally recognized that simultaneous offsets in emissions rarely occur. Under the Banking Policy, emission reductions that precede emission expansions can be stored, or "banked," in a legally protected manner and used in future trades so long as the total allowable emission loading rates are not exceeded (e.g., if one plant reduces its emissions by 1,000 tons per year in 1982, then it may sell this emissions loading rate to another emittor in 1983 or whenever a buyer enters the market for emission permits).

If offsets were primarily a response to a political necessity, the call for Banking was clearly a sign that at least some economists recognized its significance. Bruce Yandle, now executive director of the Federal Trade Commission was one of the first to ask that the offset concept be expanded to allow Banking. The significance of the Banking concept has not simply been to allow for "storage" of emission reductions but to cause industry, environmental groups and regulatory agencies to think more clearly of emission reductions as a potential commodity of trade and for the first time to realize that failure to reduce emissions has an opportunity cost of its own. With the adoption of Banking provisions have come better measures for quantification, certification and record keeping, and with them the concept of an "emission reduction credit" -- all necessary if a market is to be achieved.

Although there are still only three or four formal emission-reduction Banking systems in the country, informally the concept has spread far wider, and every state experiencing growth is now debating how and under what circumstances to allow Banking.

### Bubbles

USEPA's Bubble Policy,[5] first issued in December 1979, followed the Offset Policy by nearly three years, but in some ways the concept was even older. Officials at Armco Steel claim that they, not the USEPA, invented the Bubble, while numerous state and local officials insist that the informal understanding had always been around in their areas that if an industry did better than was required on one source of emissions, they could expect to receive more favorable treatment in another where they were having more trouble. This early prototype "gentleman's agreement," though clearly not a market, did provide a fertile ground for grafting the more formal Bubble Policy.

If the Carter USEPA did not invent the Bubble, it did formalize, legitimize and publicize the program whereby it is not only okay but encouraged to get less pollution control where it is expensive in exchange for getting more where it is cheaper, provided the alternatives are environmentally equivalent. Where the Offset Policy allowed new industry to meet certain emission requirements through controls on other sources only <u>after</u> first employing all available technology on its own sources, the Bubble Policy for the first time approved the use of controls on other sources <u>in lieu of</u> controls originally required on the first source.

This program, like offsets and banking, did not displace any existing requirements but simply provided a supplementary alternative. States have always had the right to set their own limits on existing sources of pollution as long as they are consistent with an approved State Implementation Plan (SIP). The Bubble Policy calls attention to that flexibility and its financial advantages and provides increased confidence that emission trades will be kept consistent with the law.

Although the 1979 Bubble Policy was an important step forward, its restrictions were reminiscent of the old banking ditty (this time monetary banking, not emissions banking):

> "There is one rule of banking,
>     and woe to he who fails to heed it:
>  Never loan money
>     to anyone who needs it."

Thus the first incremental change that announced the Bubble did not approve trades for any source:

-- out of compliance, or
-- in a nonattainment area, or
-- seeking to trade with a different category, or
-- seeking to trade quickly, or, one could almost add, "to anyone who needs it."

Some critics felt that, to extract every last bit of rent out of the Bubble, the USEPA had removed its attractiveness.


RECENT INCREMENTS OF CHANGE

In response to criticisms and suggestions for change, most of which were raised at a USEPA-sponsored conference in September 1980, the agency has undertaken several changes to improve the Bubble and thereby facilitate a more efficient market for emissions trading. The Emissions Trading Policy Statement issued April 7, 1982, pulled the

various market-related elements into a more comprehensive framework
and approved the following changes:

### Approval Time
One of the major objections has always dealt with the time
required to get approval. Not only do the state and local
agencies have to approve emission trades, but the Clean Air Act
requires USEPA to review all substantive decisions with regard to
the setting of emission limits. The Generic Rule approach
responds to this problem by having states adopt generic criteria
for Bubble approval, and once these criteria are approved,
federal approval of an individual bubble is no longer needed.
Other administrative changes call for expedited processing of
noncontroversial Bubble proposals and simultaneous or parallel
processing of all other proposals along with the states. These
changes, together with the increasingly routine nature of many
proposals, should cut approval time by 50 percent or more.

### Nonattainment Areas
In recognition that the Bubble may actually be most useful in
nonattainment areas (presumably where control requirements are
most stringent), trading may now be approved for these areas
provided it in no way jeopardizes ultimate attainment.

### Noncompliance
The Bubble was once thought to be such a carrot that it should be
reserved only for those sources with good compliance histories.
It was later realized that not only would previously noncomplying
sources reap important benefits, but use of the Bubble could
frequently be the most effective means of bringing them into
compliance.


## CHANGES UNDER INVESTIGATION

Major improvements have been made since that first Offset Policy and
the first Bubble Policy. USEPA has approved or proposed to approve
two dozen bubbles, saving at least $50 million over the cost of
conventional air pollution controls, with 100 others averaging $2
million each in savings now under development. Several areas of
concern still remain, however, and additional opportunities for change
are now under investigation to further relax the barriers to a true
market system in air pollution control.


### NSPS Compliance Bubble
All USEPA policy statements and regulations dealing with emissions
trading still expressly exclude emissions subject to New Source
Performance Standards. Though the ASARCO decision expressly prohibits
the use of a bubble to avoid applicability of the NSPS requirements,
USEPA is now investigating the feasibility of allowing a "compliance
bubble" as a means of minimizing the cost of achieving the same
aggregate emission reduction required by compliance with the NSPS.
One electric utility has stated that use of this approach on just one

of their installations would enable them to reduce the cost of
compliance by $15 million per year while still achieving the same
emission reduction.

## Indirect Offsets

Even though multiplant or external trades are fully approvable and
even though available data indicate that these trades could result in
significantly greater savings than internal ones (because of the
typically greater variation in marginal cost), less than four percent
of total trades have been external. Though this pattern may change
over time, current indications are that it will be a very long time.
While this situation prevails, it can scarcely be claimed that
anything approaching a true market in emission reductions exists. Not
only are prospective users of emission reduction credits reluctant to
buy them outside their own firms, but more importantly few if any
sources are willing to sell. At least two major factors seem to
create this reluctance: first, environmental managers (who usually
make the decision) tend to be very risk-averse (particularly in
contrast with managers of profit centers); second, very few companies
can be sure that they themselves will not later need the emission
reduction credits. Faced with a high-risk premium and an uncertain
situation, most potential sellers are now hoarding.

One way to address this problem that is now under investigation
involves establishing a fee schedule based on the estimated cost of
offsets plus a margin of safety, and then giving new sources the
option of paying a fee or getting the offset, whichever they find more
convenient. Presumably, potential offset sellers would be more
willing to sell if they could be guaranteed the right to buy back in,
even at the higher price of the fee. All fee proceeds would be
specifically earmarked for the purchase of offsets.

Measures similar to this have already been introduced and passed the
relevant committees in both houses of Congress, and considerable
interest exists in both industry and environmental organizations,
particularly in areas faced with both high growth and serious
nonattainment. Other measures with similar intent include the use of
brokers, clearing houses and futures markets.


## CONCLUSIONS

Though neither the USEPA nor its fundamental authorizing legislation
ever officially espoused or adopted a comprehensive economic incentive
system such as emission fees or marketable permits for air pollution
control, and though resource economists continue to criticize the
agency for this apparent failure, USEPA is "evolving" in precisely
that direction through the adoption of many important incremental
changes. If one seeks to guide that change process, I believe the
following approaches are applicable:

    -- Identify major end-goals;

    -- Identify major constraints;

-- Identify major beneficiaries of proposed changes and build a
   constituency for change;

-- Concentrate on finding opportunities for change that have
   minimal impact on major stakeholders;

-- Introduce changes as small, self-sustaining supplements
   rather than as sweeping replacements;

-- Be prepared to capitalize on change induced from external
   forces; and

-- Be prepared to focus more on implementation issues and less
   on theory; and, lastly,

-- Be patient.

The resulting system will be neither a pure pricing policy nor a
traditional regulatory "command and control" approach, but a hybrid
blend responding to the technical, legal, institutional and political
constraints surrounding the administration of a pollution control
program.

DISCLAIMER

The opinions here expressed are those of the author and should not be
attributed to the USEPA or any other government entity.

REFERENCES

[1] Emissions Offset Interpretive Ruling, December 21, 1976, 41 FR
55524.

[2] Revisions to Offset Ruling, January 16, 1979, 44 FR 3274.

[3] Revisions to Offset Ruling, May 13, 1980, 45 FR 31304.

[4] Emissions Trading Policy Statement and Technical Issues Document,
April 7, 1982, 47 FR 15076.

[5] Bubble Policy, December 11, 1979, 44 FR 71779.

# Designing Markets in Transferable Property Rights: A Practitioner's Guide

**Robert W. Hahn**

**Dept. of Engineering and Public Policy**
**Carnegie-Mellon University**

## INTRODUCTION

Markets in transferable property rights have received a great deal of attention as an alternative for solving problems involving the allocation of a limited supply of resources. Working examples include markets for taxicab medallions, liquor licenses and land development rights.[1] Several potential applications are also under consideration. But if these applications are to become realities, serious thought needs to be devoted to the actual design of such markets. The basic problem underlying this research is the design of an institution that will work for different kinds of markets in transferable property rights. For concreteness, attention will be restricted to developing a system of transferable property rights to control pollution. The specific example against which the institution will be tested is the control of sulfur oxides emissions ($SO_x$) in the Los Angeles airshed.

This paper will set forth a framework for the design and testing of market mechanisms to control pollution. The next section reviews the classical arguments in favor of adopting a market approach. In the third section, literature relevant to the design of a market to control pollution is discussed. The fourth section develops a set of design criteria, and section five considers a market design that could meet these criteria. In the sixth section, preliminary experimental results are reviewed, and areas for future research are outlined in the last section.

## MARKETS VS. SOURCE-SPECIFIC STANDARDS

Past efforts to control pollution have relied heavily on the use of source-specific standards set by a central regulatory agency. Critics contend that this command-and-control approach to regulation is wasteful. Because of difficulties in obtaining accurate information or because of political pressures, regulators may select a set of standards that are not cost-effective. That is, other abatement strategies may exist that could reach a prescribed goal using fewer

resources.  The problem is to figure out a clever method for minimizing the costs associated with meeting a given level of environmental
quality.

A solution frequently advocated by economists is the creation of a
market in transferable property rights.  The principal reason that
economists have supported market approaches over standards is that
market approaches have the potential to be more cost-effective.  To
demonstrate this potential, a whole cadre of economists have attempted
to estimate the static efficiency gains that would result in certain
instances when a centralized standards approach is replaced by a
competitive market.  The principal conclusion to be derived from these
endeavors is that the static efficiency gains may be quite large.[2]

Static efficiency gains measure the immediate cost savings that could
result from substituting a competitive market for an existing
standards regime.  Another important concern in comparing a market
approach with standards is how the two systems affect the behavior of
firms over time.  Arguments on the dynamic effects of the two
approaches tend to be more speculative.  Because it is difficult to
develop a quantitative definition of dynamic efficiency, economists
generally resort to a more primitive defense of markets when promoting
them on dynamic efficiency grounds.  Arguments supporting markets on
dynamic efficiency grounds usually claim that incentives for cost-
effective innovation will increase.  In addition, it is often claimed
that a change from a nontransferable to a transferable property rights
system will lower barriers to entry.  Whether these claims would hold
in an actual application of a market in transferable property rights
remains an open question.

This paper starts with the premise that the methodology for estimating
static gains is well-known and a methodology for estimating dynamic
efficiency gains is likely to remain elusive.[3]  Thus, it may be time
to consider tackling a different set of research problems.  More
specifically, it is my view that social scientists concerned with
examining market approaches for a class of externality problems should
consider redirecting their energies to the actual development of
policies that may be feasible.  A first step in this process is to
review the pertinent information on issues in market design.


RESULTS ON MARKET DESIGN

A basic theme in the economics literature is that markets can work
wonders, provided they are competitive.  But in some cases, con-
vergence to the competitive equilibrium cannot be assumed.  As Plott
(1981) has demonstrated, the rules of exchange (i.e., the institution), can have a significant effect on the performance of the market
and who wins and loses.

There is a growing amount of literature in the social sciences which
can be drawn upon to develop a market to control pollution.  This
literature is primarily concerned with examining the relationship
between institutions and outcomes.  The basic approach is to have

human subjects voluntarily participate in a controlled experiment with well-defined rules and payoffs. In the experiments reviewed here, subjects are given a redemption value schedule which corresponds to a supply-or-demand curve. For example, a subject might be told he can redeem his first unit purchased for $5, his second unit for $3 and his third unit for $1. He would then be asked to participate in a market, receiving a cash payment based on his strategy and the outcome of the market. Smith (1976) provides the theoretical basis for this approach. The basic assumption is that subjects will attempt to choose a strategy that maximizes profits when the reward is a cash payment based on individual performance.

One purpose of laboratory experiments is to capture the essence of the institution under study. Of necessity, these experiments tend to simplify reality. If designed carefully, they can provide a useful check on the workings of different institutions: if an institution does not meet its prescribed objectives in a simplified setting, it is unlikely to perform well in more complicated environments.

The experimental literature reveals important insights for designing a market to control pollution. The contributions fall into three areas: testing the theory of externalities, testing the theory of derived demand, and identifying institutions that may fail to converge to the competitive equilibrium.

Plott (1977) has tested the theory of externalities using both taxes and marketable permits. A key finding was that markets behave in accord with the competitive model. Applying a tax reduced the equilibrium price and quantity, while using a marketable permit approach had a similar effect. Moreover, the efficiency of both markets — as measured by total earnings divided by total possible earnings -- was relatively high.

The above study and another study by Plott and Uhl (1981) provide a test of the theory of derived demand. In the externalities study, the transferable rights experiment is conducted with a primary market and a secondary market for licenses. Agents desiring to own units in the primary market must also cover themselves in the license market. Plott and Uhl examine the effects that middlemen between buyers and sellers have on equilibrium. The middlemen may be viewed as entrepreneurs who operate in a market for inputs as well as a market for outputs. This theory is relevant to the case of marketable permits because pollution can be viewed as an input to the production process. The demand for any input is based on the demand for the product it produces, and in that sense it is a derived demand. Both studies found that the prices and quantities converged to the results predicted by the competitive model.

The preceding experiments lend support to the view that market mechanisms can be used to control externalities. Specifically, they demonstate two points: (1) that subjects will internalize external costs when given appropriate incentives, and (2) that derived demands -- like the demand for transferable property rights -- do not pose any special problems for achieving the competitive equilibrium. While these results are encouraging, it must be noted that they were verified in the context of a specific institution -- a double-oral auction similar to the one used on the New York Stock Exchange. Because several institutions may be considered in designing a market in transferable property rights, it will be useful to know the type of situations where different market designs are likely to perform poorly. This question is particularly relevant to several potential markets in transferable discharge permits due to problems with market thinness and market concentration. Four key results on market power are:

1.  Experiments involving one seller and five buyers do not achieve the monopoly equilibrium; however, in some cases the competitive equilibrium is achieved (Smith 1981).

2.  Groups that conspire often make less than competitive profits. Prices and quantities do not seem to converge to the monopoly, monopsony or the competitive equilibrium (Smith 1981).

3.  In some markets, buyers can post bids on a take-it-or-leave-it basis. Smith (1981) has examined this institution for one seller and five buyers. He found that this institution can serve to limit monopoly power, but at the expense of not achieving the competitive equilibrium.

4.  Plott (1981) examined the posted pricing institution and found that, in general, it can induce higher prices.

The above findings on market power reveal two essential points. First, there are situations -- in this case with one buyer and five sellers -- where the market does not reach the competitive equilibrium. Second, the choice of institutions may be crucial in determining the type of equilibrium that is reached.


DERIVING DESIGN SPECIFICATIONS

The goals of the institution will be drawn from an examination of existing policy aimed at regulating the flow of pollutants. One of the critical problems in current trading approaches sanctioned by the U.S. Environmental Protection Agency (USEPA) is that relatively little trading is taking place. One reason may be that the property right is not well defined. A second reason may be that there is a great deal of uncertainty about a "reasonable" price for the commodity. Consequently, information on prices is not readily available to participants in the market and potential entrants. This raises the transactions costs associated with trading between parties. Indeed, this may be one of the reasons that, to date, more trades have occurred within individual firms than between firms.[4]

If a market is to effectively promote trading, it is important to establish a price signal at the outset. However, establishing a price signal is in itself not sufficient to warrant establishing a market. It is also necessary that the price be close to the competitive equilibrium so that the potential gains from efficiency can be reaped.

In establishing a market, issues of practicality also need to be addressed. One critical issue is the problem of potential wealth transfers. It is important, for reasons of both political feasibility and fairness, that the institution under consideration be able to address the questions of equity that are likely to arise.

To summarize, the three basic objectives to consider in the initial design of an institution are:

1.   Establish a price signal.

2.   Approximate the least-cost solution over time.

3.   Allow for equity considerations.

Of course, other issues -- such as the speed at which the price signal converges to an equilibrium and the robustness of the institution -- also need to be considered before informed policy recommendations can be developed. The three goals listed above must be viewed in the context of the particular application considered below. One feature that complicates the application is that one firm will own a large share of the permits in equilibrium. For example, if permits are grandfathered -- that is, distributed in accord with existing emissions -- the large majority of permits in the market would be sold to this firm.

Table 1 illustrates the point by identifying which firms are likely to be net buyers of permits and which firms are likely to be net sellers in a shift from the current standards approach to a competitive market approach for controlling $SO_x$ emissions in the Los Angeles airshed. The market is initiated by grandfathering permits. Firms then trade permits until the competitive equilibrium is achieved.

How permits are actually grandfathered depends crucially on the distribution and availability of natural gas. This is because $SO_x$ emissions in Los Angeles result largely from the combustion of petroleum products. When natural gas, which contains negligible amounts of sulfur, is substituted for these petroleum products, the overall level of $SO_x$ emissions is reduced and the distribution of emissions across source categories is affected.

Because of uncertainties associated with predicting the availability of natural gas, two cases are considered in Table 1 -- one assumes low availability of natural gas, and one assumes high availability. The only difference between the situations of low and high natural gas supply is that the latter substituted natural gas for 100 million barrels of residual and distillate fuel oil. In both cases, natural gas was allocated in accordance with existing regulations rather than through a market. The results for the two cases exhibit similar trading patterns. The two major utilities account for the bulk of permit purchases. Moreover, note that one of these utilities could be expected to participate in approximately three-fourths of the transactions that take place. This raises the possibility that some strategic manipulation of the market might occur if the institution is not designed carefully.

TABLE 1

Comparing 1977 Standards with a Competitive Market
for $SO_x$ Permits in the Los Angeles Airshed

| Source Category | Net Change in Permits (tons/day)[a] | | Number of "Major" Firms[c] |
|---|---|---|---|
| | Natural Gas Availability | | |
| | Low[b] | High | |
| Utilities | 56.0 | 51.9 | 2 |
| Refiners[d] | −27.9 | −25.4 | 6 |
| Calciners | −14.7 | −13.2 | 2 |
| Steel | −9.5 | −9.5 | 1 |
| Oil Field Process | −3.9 | −3.9 | 1 |

SOURCE:   Hahn (1981a)

[a]A positive/negative number indicates that the source category will use more/less permits if a market were initiated.

[b]Overall energy use remains constant for the two cases considered here.  In the low natural gas case, an additional 100 million barrels of oil is consumed in place of natural gas.  Note that the numbers in each column -- low and high -- may not sum to zero due to roundoff error.

[c]A firm is defined as "major" if it accounts for more than one percent of total $SO_x$ emissions under the 1977 low natural gas standards case.

[d]Includes emissions from refinery fuel burning, refinery gas and fluid catalytic cracking units.


DESIGNING AN INSTITUTION

After reviewing the relevant literature and developing a set of objectives, we are now in a position to address the problem of designing a market in transferable property rights for the particular problem at hand:  the control of $SO_x$ emissions in the Los Angeles airshed.  Recall that the basic objectives are to design a market that will elicit a price signal, induce efficient abatement decisions and satisfy considerations of equity.  One approach to the problem might be to distribute the permits to firms in some prescribed manner (e.g., grandfathering) and let them trade the permits as they see fit. The basic problem with this approach is that there is no guarantee that a quick price signal will emerge, because firms might be hesitant to trade. A second problem with this approach is that grandfathering of permits could result in a situation where one firm would be the principal purchaser of permits and most remaining firms would be sellers of permits.

One possible approach for dealing with these problems is the "zero revenue auction" suggested by Hahn and Noll (1982). The mechanics of the auction are relatively straightforward. At the outset, each firm would receive an initial allocation of permits, presumably based on considerations of equity. All sources would be required to offer their entire allocation for sale. An auction would then be held, where each firm would report its demand curve for permits. The sum of the demand curves would be used to calculate the market-clearing price for a permit and the final allocation of permits to the firms. A firm would make a gross payment to the state equal to the market price times its final allocation and would receive gross revenues from the state equal to the market price times its initial allocation. For example, suppose the market price were $2 million per permit. If a firm had an initial allocation of two permits and a final allocation of three permits, it would make a net payment of $2 million. Alternatively, if it had an initial allocation of five permits and a final allocation of three permits, it would receive a net payment of $4 million.

The zero revenue auction has several attractive features. It is designed so that net revenue collection by the state is zero.[5] All the revenues from the auction are completely redistributed to the participants. Firms who reduce emissions relative to their initial allocation receive a payment from firms who increase their emissions relative to their initial allocation; thus there is a net monetary transfer from polluters to abaters. Equity concerns can be addressed through a suitable initial allocation of permits. The auction also guarantees that a price signal will emerge quickly. Moreover, having such auctions at prescribed intervals would decrease problems with market thinness, where there are too few buyers or sellers.

The idea of returning some or all of the proceeds of an auction to the participants in the auction has been tried in several settings. For example, Plott (1977) uses a lump-sum transfer in testing the tax mechanism in his externalities paper. What is new, to our knowledge, is the proposed mechanism for redistributing revenues. This is why some further experimentation is in order.

Whether such an auction will work in practice remains to be seen. However, there is some reason to be optimistic. For example, Miller and Plott (1980) examined a multiple-unit, first-price auction and found that the result converged to the competitive equilibrium and was demand-revealing. However, the Miller and Plott result did not use initial allocations. Further research will be necessary to determine if the use of initial allocations induces firms to manipulate the market.

The only substantive design issue that remains is how the auction will perform on efficiency grounds. One of the reasons for using this auction is that it places all firms on the same (demand) side of the market. The hope is that this design will decrease the likelihood that a large net buyer or seller of permits would be able to influence the price.

To test the properties of an auction that returns the proceeds to the buyers, a small group experiment was designed that captures its essential features. In this experiment. subjects are given a list of possible equilibrium prices and asked to write down the quantity demanded of a fictitious commodity at each price. The fictitious commodity can then be redeemed for cash according to a payoff schedule provided to the subject. By varying the payoff schedule, different market structures can be tested. This enables a researcher to test the conditions under which the experimental institution produces a competitive equilibrium.

The experimental institution differs from one that would be used in practice in only one major detail. In the real world, participants in the auction would write down their entire demand curve. In the experiment, participants are asked to submit quantity demands at a predetermined set of prices. The reason for this design change is that instructing subjects in how to express demand functions -- that is, how price and quantity vary together -- is considerably more difficult and time-consuming than the procedure followed in the experiment. Though there is no reason to expect that this change in the procedures would affect the outcome of the institution, it is conceivable that it might.

Thus far, three experiments have been conducted using this auction. Eight subjects participated in each experiment. Subjects were not permitted to participate in more than one experiment, which means that a total of 24 different subjects participated, most of whom were students at the California Institute of Technology. Each subject received the same redemption value schedule. The horizontal aggregation of these schedules is shown in Figure 1 with the vertical supply constraint. The competitive equilibrium price was 500.[6] A critical parameter that differed among subjects was the initial allocation. Table 2 shows the initial holdings used in each experiment. As can be seen from the table, the total initial holdings were 1,000, which just equalled the quantity for sale in each period. Subjects were asked to submit purchase commitments at prices ranging from 100 to 1,000. These commitments were then aggregated into a willingness-to-pay schedule, and subjects were informed of the equilibrium price and quantity. One thousand units were offered for sale in each of 10 trading periods. The only public information was the quantity for sale in each period.


EXPERIMENTAL RESULTS

The results of the auction can be usefully separated into three parts: efficiency characteristics, demands patterns and equilibrium

TABLE 2
Initial Holdings in an Experimental Auction

| Experiment | Buyer | | | | | | | |
|---|---|---|---|---|---|---|---|---|
| | 1 | 2 | 3 | 4 | 5 | 6 | 7 | 8 |
| 1 | 100 | 100 | 100 | 100 | 150 | 150 | 150 | 150 |
| 2 | 25 | 50 | 75 | 100 | 150 | 175 | 200 | 225 |
| 3 | 50 | 50 | 50 | 100 | 100 | 150 | 150 | 350 |

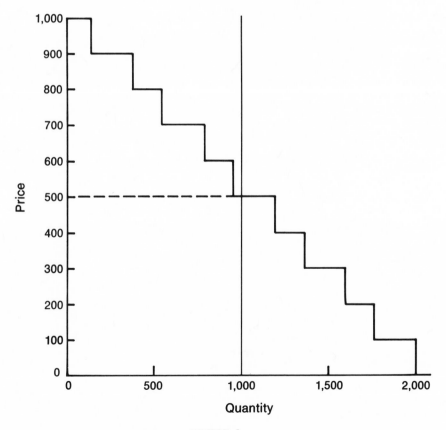

FIGURE 1
Horizontal Aggregation of Redemption Value Schedule
and Vertical Supply Constraint of Experimental Auction

price patterns.  An analysis of efficiency is presented below.  The
two remaining categories will be presented in a forthcoming paper.  The
basic measure of efficiency is the extent to which subjects have
exhausted mutually beneficial gains from trade.  The raw measure used
here is actual aggregate earnings divided by maximum possible
earnings.  Efficiency is defined to be one if actual earnings equal
total possible earnings.  It is defined to be zero for the case in
which earnings are just equal to the implicit value of the permits
associated with the initial allocations shown in Table 2.

Defining efficiency in this manner allows a straightforward comparison
of the "grandfathered" or initial allocation with the zero revenue
auction.  For example, a value of 0.5 would indicate that the auction
had exhausted half of the potential gains from trade.  A value of -0.5
would mean that the auction resulted in a loss (relative to the
grandfathering baseline) equal to half of the potential gains from
trade.  In the latter case, at least one subject would have preferred
his initial allocation instead of the allocation he received based on
the auction.

The results on the comparative efficiency of the zero revenue auction
are shown in Table 3.  The first 10 columns of data give the efficiency values for each period and each experiment.  The second-to-last
column averages the efficiency values for each experiment across all
periods.  The last column indicates how earnings associated with
grandfathering, G, compare with maximum possible earnings, M.  For a
given aggregate redemption value schedule, the fraction $G/M$ provides a
measure of the extent to which the initial grandfathered allocation
can be improved upon with trading.  A high value for $G/M$ would
indicate there is comparatively little room for improvement and vice
versa.  Note that this value cannot exceed one and will generally be
greater than zero if subjects attach any value to their initial
allocation.

Two interesting patterns emerge in analyzing the information contained
in Table 3.  The first is that the zero revenue auction tends to
dominate (in an efficiency sense) the institution of grandfathering
for cases in which there are significant gains from trade.  More
precisely, for values of $G/M$ less than .99 (i.e., experiments 2 and 3)
the efficiency values are positive in 19 of 20 periods.

Another approach to comparing these insitutions is to examine the
latter part of each experiment.  The objective is to control for
"learning" that may occur in the early stages.  The pattern that
emerges from this data set provides further support for the dominance
of the zero revenue auction.  Indeed, if one were to use the last
period as a measure of comparison, the auction fares better than
grandfathering in all three experiments.

The results provide preliminary support for the view that there are
several applications in which static efficiency gains could be reaped
from the introduction of an institution that returns the revenues of
the auction to the participants in a straightforward manner.  However,
the results also underscore the point that such institutions have

TABLE 3

Efficiency Results[a]

| Experiment | Period | | | | | | | | | | Average[b] | G/M[c] |
|---|---|---|---|---|---|---|---|---|---|---|---|---|
| | 1 | 2 | 3 | 4 | 5 | 6 | 7 | 8 | 9 | 10 | | |
| 1 | -3.00 | .75 | .75 | -2.75 | -4.56 | -4.00 | .19 | .75 | .75 | .69 | -1.04 | .99 |
| 2 | .96 | .96 | .90 | -0.14 | .73 | .96 | .99 | .35 | .98 | .99 | .77 | .91 |
| 3 | .75 | .83 | .99 | .84 | .90 | .69 | .97 | .97 | .98 | .98 | .89 | .85 |

[a]Figures rounded to nearest hundredth.

[b]Average efficiency over 10 periods.

[c]Grandfathered earnings/maximum possible earnings.

limits.   Further  research  will  be  needed  to  determine  the  robustness
of the institution studied here and its limitations.


## CONCLUDING REMARKS

A primary aim of this paper was to stimulate thought on the contribu--
tions  that  social  scientists  can  make  to  implementing  markets  in
transferable  property  rights.   Current  work  on  the  actual  design  of
market  mechanisms  is  in  its  infancy.   There  is  room  for  significant
theoretical and applied research.

At a theoretical level, very little is understood about the nature of
equilibria  that  could  arise  in  different  types  of  auctions.   For
example,  it  is  not  clear  that  the  theoretical  existence  of  an
equilibrium can be guaranteed in the zero revenue auction, even when
there  is  only  one  object  for  sale.   The  auction  literature  provides
little  guidance  in  the  case  where  bidders  are  not  identical  and
participants  in  the  auction  receive  a  rebate  based  on  their  initial
allocation  of  permits.   Moreover,  in  the  case  of  multi-object
auctions, even less is known.

While  theorists  attempt  to  rectify  this  imbalance,  it  is  imperative
that we forge ahead on other fronts.   There is a pressing need for the
development  and  testing  of  different  institutional  designs.   This  will
allow policymakers to choose from a wider array of alternatives in the
event  they  decide  to  implement  a  market  approach.   In  addition  to
designing  new  institutions,  it  also  makes  sense  to  monitor  the
progress of ongoing efforts in this area to gain an appreciation for
actual implementation problems and see how they vary with institutions.

It  is  clear  to  me  that  the  question  for  this  decade  will  not  be
whether markets in transferable property rights will be implemented,
but rather how many and in what form.   We now have the opportunity to
help frame a response to these questions.   To this end, I think it
behooves  us  to  take  a  serious  look  at  how  such  markets  could  be
designed.


## ACKNOWLEDGEMENTS

Roger Noll helped design the experiment discussed in this paper and
provided comments on an earlier draft.   Karen Close, Charles Cuny and
Jim  Merino  provided  valuable  research  assistance.   I  have  also
benefited from discussions with Donna Downing, Linda Cohen and Greg
McRae.   The usual disclaimer applies.

FOOTNOTES

1   Downing et al. (1981) provide a useful summary of actual and
    potential applications for marketable rights.

2   A survey of this literature can be found in Teitenberg (1980).
    Another perspective is provided in Chapter 2 of Hahn (1981b).
    With regard to the issue of estimating static cost savings, there
    are two reasons that such estimates may have been biased upwards
    -- one methodological, and one related to incentives. The basic
    problem with the methodology for estimating static efficiency
    gains is that it was usually assumed, either implicitly or
    explicitly, that the estimation of the demand for permits was
    accurate and certain. If uncertainty were admitted into the
    demand estimation procedure, it would be possible to construct
    cases where the static cost savings were positive, but not
    statistically significant (even if the estimate of demand were
    unbiased). The point is that no study that I am aware of uses an
    approach that would allow statistical error bounds to be placed
    on the estimate of static cost savings. While this could be done
    in principle, difficulties arise in practice due to limited data
    availability.

    A second reason that cost savings may have been biased upwards is
    that, at least initially, economists probably had strong
    incentives to obtain such results. Potentially large cost
    savings would be viewed as confirmation of the (induced?)
    preference that many of us share for markets over "centralized"
    forms of regulation like standards. Confirmation of this
    preference would probably be sufficient for publishing in a
    prestigious economics journal. Of course, with the passage of
    time, the finding of large static cost savings became less
    fashionable. This may be one of the reasons that applied
    economists are now beginning to think more seriously about the
    implementation issues that arise in moving from a standards
    approach to a market approach.

3   This is not to belittle the importance of estimating the
    efficiency gains associated with market approaches. For specific
    applications, this can be a useful exercise. Moreover, the
    methodology for estimating efficiency gains is only well
    understood for a small set of cases amenable to solution through
    basic techniques of mathematical programming. There is a class
    of nonlinear problems such as the formation of photochemical smog
    for which the best approach to optimizing is not straightforward.

4   Current issues faced in the trading of air pollution emission
    reduction credits are spelled out clearly in the recent GAO
    report (1982). One approach to dealing with the problem of
    insufficient trading has been suggested by Foster and Weiss
    (1981).

5   It would be a simple matter to allow the state to retain some of
    the revenues if this were viewed as desirable. For example, in

the context of the auction presented here, the state could hold part of the initial allocation.

6  Prices are dimensionless in the diagram.  Subjects were told how to convert price–quantity information into dollars in the instructions.  A copy of the instructions is available from the author on request.


REFERENCES

Downing, D.; Foushee, M., and Keeley, M.  1981.  Marketable rights:  A practical guide to the use of marketable rights as a regulatory alternative.  Menlo Park, Calif.:  SRI International.

Foster, J.D., and Weiss, M.D.  1981.  Indirect offsets:  A supplemental program to facilitate interfirm trades in emission reductions.  Paper presented at the 74th annual meeting of the Air Pollution Control Association, June 21–26, Philadelphia, Pa.

Hahn, R.W.  1981a.  An analysis of the effects of grandfathering permits.  Environmental Quality Laboratory working paper. Pasadena: California Institute of Technology.

Hahn, R.W.  1981b.  "An Assessment of the Viability of Marketable Permits."  Ph.D. dissertation, California Institute of Technology.

Hahn, R.W., and Noll, R.G.  1982.  Designing a market for tradable emissions permits.  IN: Reform of Environmental Regulation, W.A. Magat, ed.  Cambridge, Mass.:  Ballinger.

Miller, G.J., and Plott, C.R.  1980.  Revenue generating properties of sealed-bid auctions:  an experimental analysis of one-price and discriminative processes.  Social Science Working Paper No. 234. Pasadena:  California Institute of Technology.

Plott, C.R.  1977.  Externalities and corrective policies in experimental markets.  Social Science Working Paper No. 180 (revised Jan. 6, 1982).  Pasadena:  California Institute of Technology.

Plott, C.R.  1981.  Theories of industrial organization as explanations of experimental market behavior.  Social Science Working Paper No. 388.  Pasadena:  California Institute of Technology.

Plott, C.R., and Uhl, J.  1981.  Competitive equilibrium with middlemen:  An empirical study.  Southern Economic Journal 47:1063–71.

Smith, V.L.  1976.  Experimental economics:  induced value theory. American Economic Review 66:274–79.

Smith, V.L.  1981.  Microeconomic systems as an experimental science. Economic Discussion Paper 81-32, October.  University of Arizona.

Teitenberg, T..H. 1980. Transferable discharge permits and the control of stationary source air pollution: a survey and synthesis. Land Economics 56:391-416.

U.S. General Accounting Office. 1982. A market approach to air pollution control could reduce compliance costs without jeopardizing clean air goals. PAD-82-15, March 23.

Vivian, W., and Hall, W. 1981. An examination of U.S. market trading in air pollution offsets. Working paper, March. Institute of Public Policy Studies, University of Michigan.

# Coalition Formation and the Size of Regional Pollution Control Systems

James P. Heaney

Florida Water Resources Research Center
University of Florida

## INTRODUCTION

The economic efficiency of water resource projects can be improved by using optimization methods that take advantage of (1) economies of scale in production and distribution facilities, (2) the assimilative capacity of the receiving environment, (3) excess capacity in existing facilities, (4) multipurpose opportunities and (5) multigroup cooperation.

However, this optimal solution often specifies a relatively complex blend of management options, which may be quite difficult to implement unless an acceptable apportionment of project costs can be found. Indeed, the search for enhanced economic efficiency exacerbates the financial analysis.

For example, if the problem of regionalization of sewage treatment facilities among $n$ cities is being examined, the optimal solution may call for one large plant. To realize these savings, the $n$ communities must somehow apportion the cost of this regional facility among themselves in a "fair" manner. At the other extreme, the $n$ cities could forego the savings due to regionalization to have a simple solution to the financial analysis (i.e., each city constructs and pays for its own plant). Intermediate possibilities exist. The preferred answer may be to select a "good" solution to the economic analysis that is easy to implement from a financial point of view.

Concepts from cooperative $n$-person game theory are used to apportion costs among project participants in a fair manner. The result, called the minimum costs, remaining savings (MCRS) method, is a direct generalization of the widely used separable costs, remaining benefits (SCRB) method. These results are applied to an eight-city cost game to illustrate the MCRS method and the desirability of looking at intermediate solutions. An extension of the MCRS method is presented, which enables us to select fair cost alleviations to good solutions.

INSTITUTIONAL SETTING

The majority of papers in this compendium deal with the use of economic incentives in the form of transferable discharge permits (TDPs) (see Tietenberg 1980 for a summary of this literature). This paper does not address the issue of TDPs directly; rather, the discussion focuses on the process of coalition formation among interested participants. The analysis is presented in the context of cooperative n-person game theory in characteristic function form (see Heaney and Dickinson 1982 for a general introduction).

Earlier work on this problem by Sorenson (1972) and Heaney and Sheikh (1975) indicates the fundamental importance of defining ownership of pollution rights. In the game theory context, for any subcoalition, S, of the grand coalition, N, the characteristic function $c(S)$, is defined as the optimal solution for that coalition. If ownership of the assimilative capacity has been appropriated to each of the participants, then the value of the characteristic function can be determined directly. In this case, the game will be cooperative. If ownership is unspecified, a priori, then Sorenson (1972) suggests two definitions of the characteristic function for any S-member coalition:

$c_1(S)$ = value of coalition if S is given preference over N-S.

$c_2(S)$ = value of coalition to S if N-S is given preference.

For example, assume $\underline{k}$ units of assimilative capacity are available. Then in finding the optimal solution for coalition S, they may use up to $\underline{k}$ units (case 1), or whatever portion of $\underline{k}$ is left over after coalition N-S determines their optimal solution (case 2). These two definitions lead to competitive (case 1) or cooperative (case 2) games. The analysis to follow assumes either that:

1. The assimilative capacity has been appropriated among the participants, a priori, or

2. Definition $c_2(S)$ above is used.

These two scenarios lead to cooperative games.

Summary of MCRS Method

In the vernacular of cooperative n-person game theory, assume a characteristic function which assigns the real number, $c(S)$, to each nonempty subset, S, of players. Cost games are subadditive; that is:

$$c(S) + c(T) \geq c(S \cup T) \text{ for } S \cap T = \Phi , \; S, \, T \subset N \tag{1}$$

$\Phi$ is the empty set. S and T are any two subsets of N. If the economic optimization has been done correctly, then the subadditivity conditions should be satisfied automatically since, by definition, the least-cost solution is used for each coalition. Satisfaction of subadditivity is a prerequisite for voluntary cooperation. If it is not satisfied, then at least one coalition exists for which costs would be lower if the members did not form the coalition -- but this is impossible if the least-cost solution has been found for each coalition. At worst, no lower costs would result when the coalition formed, in which case the coalition is said to be inessential; that is:

$$c(S) + c(T) = c(S \cup T) \text{ for } S \cap T = \phi, S, T \subset N \qquad (2)$$

Game theorists enumerte three general axioms that a "fair" solution to a cost game should satisfy. First, the costs assigned to the $i^{th}$ group, $x(i)$, must be no more than their costs if they acted independently; that is:

$$x(i) \leq c(i) \qquad\qquad\qquad \forall i \in N. \qquad (3)$$

Second, the total cost, $c(N)$, must be apportioned among the $\underline{n}$ groups; that is:

$$\sum_{i \in N} x(i) = c(N) \qquad (4)$$

All solutions satisfying criteria (3) and (4) are called imputations. The third criterion extends the first criterion by insisting that the cost to each group be no more than the costs they would receive in any coalition S contained in N; for example:

$$\sum_{i \in N} x(i) \leq c(S) \quad \forall S \subset N \qquad (5)$$

All solutions satisfying criteria (3), (4) and (5) constitute the core of the game. For subadditive games, the set of imputations is nonempty, but the core may be empty. A cost game has a convex core if:

$$c(S) + c(T) \geq c(S \cup T) + c(S \cap T) \text{ for } S \ T \neq \phi S, T \subset N \qquad (6)$$

In general, the more attractive (lower costs) the game is, the greater the chance that the core is convex. Conversely, the less attractive the game is, the greater the chance that the core is empty. Table 1 shows how the core changes for a three-person normalized savings game as a function of the savings available to the two-person coalitions.

For games with a core, the upper and lower bounds on each $x(i)$ can be found by solving the following linear program:

maximize or minimize:     $x(i)$

subject to:          $x(i) \leq c(i)$        $\forall i \in N$

$$\sum_{i \in N} x(i) \leq c(s) \qquad \forall s \in N \qquad (7)$$

$$\sum_{i \in N} x(i) = c(N)$$

$x(i)$ unrestricted    $\forall i \in N.$

The 2n linear programs can be solved very easily since the constraint
set is identical. Additional solutions are obtained by bringing in a
new objective function and resolving the original problem.

| CHARACTERISTIC FUNCTION $v(1) = v(2) = v(3) = 0$ $v(123) = 1.0$ | | | | |
|---|---|---|---|---|
| $v(12)$ | $v(13)$ | $v(23)$ | $\Sigma\, v(ij)$ | GEOMETRY |
| .3 | .4 | .5 | 1.2 | HEXAGON |
| .35 | .47 | .58 | 1.4 | PENTAGON |
| .40 | .53 | .67 | 1.6 | TRAPEZOID |
| .45 | .60 | .75 | 1.8 | TRIANGLE |
| .50 | .67 | .83 | 2.0 | POINT |
| .55 | .73 | .92 | 2.2 | EMPTY |

TABLE 1
Core Geometries for 3:4:5
Normalized Three-Member Savings Game

If a game does not have a core, the solution to the linear program
will be infeasible. In this case, the values of the characteristic
functions for the S-member coalitions are relaxed until a core
appears. The linear programming formulation of this problem is:

minimize:   $\Theta$

$$
\begin{aligned}
\text{subject to:} \qquad & x(i) \leq c(i) & \forall i \epsilon\ N \\
& \sum_{i\ \epsilon\ s} x(i) - \Theta\ c(S) \leq c(S) & \forall\ S \subset N \qquad\qquad (8) \\
& \sum_{i\ \epsilon\ N} x(i) = c(N) \\
& x(i) \text{ unrestricted } \forall i\ \epsilon\ N.
\end{aligned}
$$

In summary, the procedure for the minimum-costs, remaining-savings
(MCRS) method is:

Step 1.   Find the minimum $[x(i)_{min}]$ and maximum $[x(i)_{max}]$ costs
          that satisfy the core conditions graphically or by solving
          linear programs 7 (core exists) or 8 (no core exists).

Step 2.   Prorate the nonseparable cost (NSC), using:

$$
\beta(i) = \frac{x(i)_{max} - x(i)_{min}}{\sum_{i\ \epsilon\ N} [x(i)_{max} - x(i)_{min}]} \qquad \forall i\ \epsilon\ N \qquad\qquad (9)
$$

$$
\text{and nsc} = c(N) - \sum_{i\epsilon\ N} x(i)_{min}
$$

Step 3.   Find the fair solution for each group, using:

$$
x(i) = x(i)_{min} + \beta(i)\ (nsc) \qquad\qquad (10)
$$

The MCRS method is preferable to the separable costs, remaining
benefits (SCRB) method because it uses bounds that are feasible; thus,
any convex combination of these bounds is feasible. The SCRB method
only analyzes coalitions of size 1, N - 1, and N. All other information is ignored. By contrast, the MCRS method includes all other
available information regarding intermediate coalitions. Note that it
is not required that all coalition values be available. A more
complete description of the development of this method is presented in
Straffin and Heaney (1981) and Heaney and Dickinson (1982).


TRANSACTIONS COSTS AND REGIONALIZATION

Economic optimization models usually ignore the transactions costs
associated with forming regional authorities. As the size of the
groups grows, transactions costs would be expected to increase at the
margin due to multiple political jurisdictions, growing administrative
costs, shifting environmental impacts, etc. Figure 1 shows the
general benefit-cost relationship as described by Young (1979). While

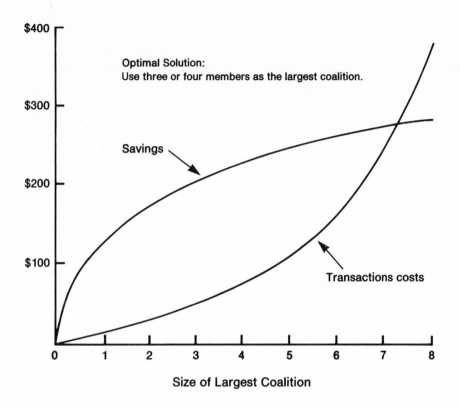

FIGURE 1
Savings-Transactions Costs for Hypothetical Regional Problem


I could not find hard data on transactions costs; they may well run
from 2 to 10 percent of total costs. Thus, it may be quite reasonable
to stop short of the optimum.

Lyon (1981) reports on attempts to simulate a market for phosphorus
control in 53 Wisconsin cities. The least-cost solution is 20 percent
less expensive than uniform treatment. Many difficulties arise in
setting up such a complex organizational structure with the hope of
such a relatively modest savings. It would be interesting to see the
results of selected intermediate "good" solutions with much simpler
market structure.

Very little work has been done in examining the possible efficacy of
using "good" but nonoptimal economic solutions. One reason for this
void is the availability of powerful optimization techniques, which
take us from the worst solution (no cooperation) to the best solution
in a few seconds of CPU time. The unfortunate side-effect of this

predilection with optimum-seeking methods is that very viable intermediate possibilities are ignored.

Similar problems arose in early attempts to apply optimization methods to engineering design problems. Enamored with our ability to rapidly analyze a myriad of alternatives, we attempted to remove existing engineering design constraints (e.g., the tank should be twice as long as it is wide) and institutional design constraints (e.g., interstate compacts don't work). The result of the unshackled optimization analysis is a bold, imaginative, creative but often totally naive engineering or institutional design.

Douglas Wilde, a pioneer in optimization theory, has recently demonstrated how the science of optimization methods can be interwoven into the art of engineering design (Wilde 1978). His ideas have relevance to social scientists interested in institutional design. Some quotes from Wilde (1978, p. 2) are appropriate:

> The way a design problem is formulated strongly affects its ease of solution. This may explain why elaborate computer studies all too often yield little or no improvement over a design made by a mathematically naive engineer familiar with the technology . . . Operating problems have generated an optimization theory of only limited worth to designers, who without knowing it face situations that are nonlinear, nonconvex, nonunimodel, noncontinuous, and consequently, at least to many an operations analyst, unsolvable.

With regard to wastewater treatment plants, a relatively wide variance in expected performance exists. Studies of the performance of 37 activated sludge plants (Niku et al. 1979) and 11 trickling filter plants (Niku et al. 1982) show that BOD removals are log-normally distributed with relatively high variance. Thus, the assumed constant loading rates may not be very realistic. Also, the cost data used in regional waste treatment models are usually based on simple power function approximations of available data. Site-specific circumstances can cause these estimates to err by 50 percent or more. Thus it may be counterproductive to fine-tune economic optimization well beyond the limits of the accuracy of the data.

The inaccuracies of the data on control costs, treatment plant performance and expected response in the receiving water have led water quality engineers to use approximate solution methods. In a recent book on water quality management, Krenkel and Novotny (1980) make the following comment about wasteload allocation models:

> While attempts at optimizing waste assimilative capacity are quite rational, their complexity and the many assumptions inherent in their use lead most regulatory agencies to use much simpler approaches.

Analogously, design of institutional arrangements for regional water quality management plans is a relatively crude process. Thus, primary concern should be placed on taking advantage of "significant" savings

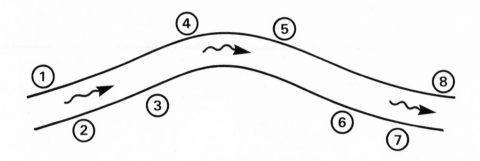

FIGURE 2
Hypothetical River with Eight Cities

from cooperation and avoiding the paranoia of feeling compromised if a regional solution other than the optimum is selected.

The next section presents this same perspective on problem-solving as related to the important problem of cost allocation. An eight-city example is used to illustrate how potential gains from cooperation vary as we move from simple solutions (e.g., build eight treatment plants), to the economic optimum (e.g., build one large regional plant).

EXAMPLE EIGHT-CITY COST GAME

An example eight-city cost game was created to illustrate various aspects of the cost allocation problem.

Assume eight cities are located along a river as shown in Figure 2.

Table 2 shows the characteristic function values for each of the eight cities (labeled row 1 through row 8) and all of the essential coalitions. By definition, all coalitions are subadditive. This game is a relatively attractive one in that the costs for the grand coalition, $c(12345678) = 29$, are 42 percent less than if the eight cities do not cooperate (i.e., $\Sigma c(i) = 50$). The upper and lower bounds of the core of the cost game are shown in Table 3. The largest coalition and its subgroups all have nonempty cores. This is to be expected, since the savings are relatively large.

The MCRS cost allocations for this game are shown in Table 4. Column 3 shows cost as a function of coalition size. Significantly, more than 50 percent of the savings can be realized by simply pairing off the cities. This is a seemingly attractive option, since the cost allocation procedure is so simple. Similarly, 76 percent of the savings can be realized using coalitions no larger than three cities.

TABLE 2
Cost Data for Hypothetical Example

| | Cities | | | | | | | | Cost |
|---|---|---|---|---|---|---|---|---|---|
| | 1 | 2 | 3 | 4 | 5 | 6 | 7 | 8 | Millions of Dollars |
| **E** | 1 | | | | | | | | 2 |
| **S** | | 1 | | | | | | | 4 |
| **S** | | | 1 | | | | | | 6 |
| **E** | | | | 1 | | | | | 8 |
| **N** | | | | | 1 | | | | 10 |
| **T** | | | | | | 1 | | | 4 |
| **I** | | | | | | | 1 | | 7 |
| **A** | | | | | | | | 1 | 9 |
| **L** | | | | | | | | | |
| | 1 | 1 | | | | | | | 5 |
| | 1 | | 1 | | | | | | 6 |
| | 1 | | | 1 | | | | | 9 |
| **C** | | 1 | 1 | | | | | | 6 |
| **O** | | 1 | | 1 | | | | | 10 |
| **A** | | 1 | | | 1 | | | | 12 |
| **L** | | | 1 | 1 | | | | | 10 |
| **I** | | | 1 | | 1 | | | | 13 |
| **T** | | | 1 | | | 1 | | | 8 |
| **I** | | | 1 | | | | 1 | | 12 |
| **O** | | | | 1 | 1 | | | | 14 |
| **N** | | | | 1 | | 1 | | | 10 |
| **S** | | | | 1 | | | 1 | | 14 |
| | | | | 1 | | | | 1 | 16 |
| | | | | | 1 | 1 | | | 11 |
| | | | | | 1 | | 1 | | 14 |
| **[S]** | | | | | 1 | | | 1 | 17 |
| | | | | | | 1 | 1 | | 9 |
| | | | | | | 1 | | 1 | 11 |
| | | | | | | | 1 | 1 | 12 |
| | 1 | 1 | 1 | | | | | | 7 |
| | 1 | 1 | | 1 | | | | | 12 |
| | 1 | | 1 | 1 | | | | | 11 |
| | | 1 | 1 | 1 | | | | | 11 |
| | | 1 | 1 | | 1 | | | | 14 |
| | | 1 | 1 | | | 1 | | | 9 |
| | | 1 | | 1 | 1 | | | | 17 |
| | | | 1 | 1 | 1 | | | | 17 |
| | | | 1 | 1 | | 1 | | | 12 |
| | | | 1 | 1 | | | 1 | | 16 |
| | | | 1 | | 1 | 1 | | | 16 |

TABLE 2 (cont'd.)

| | Cities | | | | | | | | Cost |
|---|---|---|---|---|---|---|---|---|---|
| | 1 | 2 | 3 | 4 | 5 | 6 | 7 | 8 | Millions of Dollars |
| E | | | | 1 | 1 | 1 | | | 15 |
| S | | | | 1 | 1 | | 1 | | 19 |
| S | | | | 1 | | 1 | 1 | | 15 |
| E | | | | | 1 | 1 | 1 | | 16 |
| N | | | | | 1 | 1 | | 1 | 18 |
| T | | | | | 1 | | 1 | 1 | 20 |
| I | | | | | | 1 | 1 | 1 | 14 |
| A | | | | | | | | | |
| L | 1 | 1 | 1 | 1 | | | | | 12 |
| | 1 | 1 | 1 | | 1 | | | | 15 |
| | 1 | 1 | | 1 | 1 | | | | 18 |
| | | 1 | 1 | 1 | 1 | | | | 18 |
| C | | 1 | 1 | 1 | | 1 | | | 13 |
| O | | 1 | 1 | | 1 | 1 | | | 15 |
| A | | 1 | | 1 | 1 | 1 | | | 17 |
| L | | | 1 | 1 | 1 | 1 | | | 18 |
| I | | | 1 | 1 | 1 | | 1 | | 22 |
| T | | | 1 | 1 | | 1 | 1 | | 17 |
| I | | | 1 | | 1 | 1 | 1 | | 20 |
| O | | | | 1 | 1 | 1 | 1 | | 19 |
| N | | | | 1 | 1 | 1 | | 1 | 22 |
| S | | | | 1 | 1 | | 1 | 1 | 24 |
| | | | | 1 | | 1 | 1 | 1 | 20 |
| | | | | | 1 | 1 | 1 | 1 | 21 |
| [S] | 1 | 1 | 1 | 1 | 1 | | | | 19 |
| | 1 | 1 | 1 | 1 | | 1 | | | 15 |
| | 1 | 1 | 1 | | 1 | 1 | | | 16 |
| | 1 | | 1 | 1 | 1 | 1 | | | 19 |
| | | 1 | 1 | 1 | 1 | 1 | | | 19 |
| | | 1 | | 1 | 1 | 1 | 1 | | 21 |
| | | 1 | 1 | 1 | 1 | | 1 | | 23 |
| | | | 1 | 1 | 1 | 1 | 1 | | 22 |
| | | | 1 | 1 | 1 | 1 | | 1 | 25 |
| | | | 1 | | 1 | 1 | 1 | 1 | 25 |
| | | | | 1 | 1 | 1 | 1 | 1 | 25 |
| | 1 | 1 | 1 | 1 | 1 | 1 | | | 20 |
| | 1 | 1 | 1 | 1 | 1 | | 1 | | 25 |
| | | 1 | 1 | 1 | 1 | 1 | 1 | | 23 |
| | | | 1 | 1 | 1 | 1 | 1 | 1 | 27 |

TABLE 2 (cont'd.)

| | Cities | | | | | | | Cost |
|---|---|---|---|---|---|---|---|---|
| 1 | 2 | 3 | 4 | 5 | 6 | 7 | 8 | Millions of Dollars |
| 1 | 1 | 1 | 1 | 1 | 1 | 1 | | 24 |
| | 1 | 1 | 1 | 1 | 1 | 1 | 1 | 28 |
| 1 | 1 | 1 | 1 | 1 | 1 | 1 | 1 | 29 |
| Σ S  16 | 28 | 39 | 44 | 43 | 37 | 28 | 16 | 251 |

TABLE 3
Lower and Upper Bounds on Costs for
Eight-City Cost Game for Various Coalition Sizes

| No. of Cities in Largest Coalition[a] | City Bounds: L = Lower, U = Upper | | | | | | | | | | | | | | | | TOTALS | |
|---|---|---|---|---|---|---|---|---|---|---|---|---|---|---|---|---|---|---|
| | 1 | | 2 | | 3 | | 4 | | 5 | | 6 | | 7 | | 8 | | | |
| | L | U | L | U | L | U | L | U | L | U | L | U | L | U | L | U | L | U |
| 1 | 2 | 2 | 4 | 4 | 6 | 6 | 8 | 8 | 10 | 10 | 4 | 4 | 7 | 7 | 9 | 9 | 50 | 50 |
| 2 | 1 | 2 | 3 | 4 | 2 | 6 | 4 | 8 | 7 | 10 | 1 | 4 | 3 | 7 | 5 | 9 | 26 | 50 |
| 3 | 1 | 2 | 1 | 4 | 2 | 5 | 4 | 8 | 5 | 10 | 1 | 4 | 3 | 7 | 5 | 9 | 22 | 49 |
| 4* | 1 | 2 | 0 | 4 | 0 | 5 | 5 | 8 | 7 | 10 | 1 | 4 | 3 | 7 | 5 | 9 | 22 | 49 |
| 5* | 1 | 2 | 1 | 4 | 2 | 5 | 4 | 8 | 5 | 10 | 1 | 4 | 3 | 6 | 6 | 9 | 23 | 48 |
| 6* | 1 | 2 | 3 | 4 | 2 | 6 | 2 | 8 | 3 | 10 | 0 | 4 | 2 | 7 | 5 | 9 | 18 | 50 |
| 7* | 2 | 2 | 1 | 4 | 0 | 5 | 1 | 8 | 3 | 10 | 0 | 4 | 0 | 7 | 5 | 9 | 12 | 49 |
| 8* | 1 | 2 | 0 | 4 | 0 | 5 | 1 | 8 | 3 | 10 | 0 | 4 | 0 | 7 | 5 | 9 | 10 | 49 |

*Lower and upper bound calculated using linear programming.

[a]Least costly partition of the coalitions is selected as best solution. For example, if the limit is three members, then the best partition is 123, 456, 78.

TABLE 4

Cost Allocations for Optimal
Solution and Intermediate Solutions

| Size of Largest Coalition | Coalition Structure for Least-Cost Solution | Least-Cost Solution | Minimum Costs, Remaining Savings (MCRS) Cost Allocation* | | | | | | | |
|---|---|---|---|---|---|---|---|---|---|---|
| | | | 1 | 2 | 3 | 4 | 5 | 6 | 7 | 8 |
| 1 | 1,2,3,4,5,6,7,8 | 50 | 2 | 4 | 6 | 8 | 10 | 4 | 7 | 9 |
| 2 | 12, 34, 56, 78 | 38 | 1.5 | 3.5 | 4 | 6 | 8.5 | 2.5 | 5 | 7 |
| 3 | 123, 456, 78 | 34 | 1.38 | 2.12 | 3.50 | 5.67 | 7.08 | 2.25 | 5 | 7 |
| 4 | 1234, 5678 | 33 | 1.46 | 1.85 | 2.31 | 6.38 | 8.07 | 2.07 | 4.43 | 6.43 |
| 5 | 123, 45678 | 32 | 1.38 | 2.12 | 3.50 | 5.33 | 6.67 | 2.00 | 4.00 | 7.00 |
| 6 | 12, 345678 | 32 | 1.5 | 3.5 | 3.88 | 3.75 | 6.28 | 1.88 | 4.33 | 6.88 |
| 7 | 1, 2345678 | 30 | 2 | 2.46 | 2.43 | 4.41 | 6.40 | 1.95 | 3.41 | 6.94 |
| 8 | 12345678 | 29 | 1.49 | 1.95 | 2.44 | 4.41 | 6.41 | 1.95 | 3.41 | 6.94 |

*See Table 3 for upper and lower bounds.

Thus, my initial feeling was that it may be best to simply accept the three-member solution as "good enough." Let's say that such an arrangement was proposed for cities 1 through 3. Comparing the assigned cost for the three- versus the eight-member coalitions, City 1 would prefer the three-member coalition, while City 2 has a slight preference for the eight-member solution. However, City 3 is the big loser if the three-member solution is selected. Further study of Table 4 reveals that the interior cities stand to lose the most if the eight-member coalition is not chosen. Thus, they might be expected to push for the eight-member solution not so much because the overall additional savings are that substantial, but rather to capture the larger percentage of the savings that they should receive because of their strategic location and contributions.

Table 5 shows the relative frequency that each city is a member of an essential coalition (i.e., one for which positive savings exist). For example, City 4 is a member of nearly 18 percent of the essential coalitions -- three times as many as cities 1 or 8 (see bottom of Table 2 for data).

In general, for polluters located along a river, the interior cities are more apt to be valuable. Consider the simple case where essential coalitions occur only when the cities are adjacent (e.g., coalition 23 is assumed to be essential; coalition 24 is not). For this assumed coalition structure, the results are striking (see Table 5). The interior members have much more potential influence. As in the eight-city case, middle City 4 is a member of nearly three times the number of essential coalitions as outer cities 1 or 8. Readers famililar with the related area of voting games may note the similar-ities of this calculation to determining the relative weights of a voting game (see Straffin 1980). In this case, the city is pivotal if it is a member of an essential coalition.

TABLE 5
Relative Frequency with which Cities
along a River Are in Essential Coalitions

| Size of Game | Relative Frequency (Adjacent Coalitions*) | | | | | | | | Total |
|---|---|---|---|---|---|---|---|---|---|
| | 1 | 2 | 3 | 4 | 5 | 6 | 7 | 8 | |
| 2 | .5 | .5 | | | | | | | 1.00 |
| 3 | .25 | .50 | .25 | | | | | | 1.00 |
| 4 | .17 | .33 | .33 | .17 | | | | | 1.00 |
| 5 | .12 | .24 | .28 | .24 | .12 | | | | 1.00 |
| 6 | .09 | .18 | .23 | .23 | .18 | .09 | | | 1.00 |
| 7 | .07 | .14 | .19 | .20 | .19 | .14 | .07 | | 1.00 |
| 8 | .06 | .12 | .15 | .17 | .17 | .15 | .12 | .06 | 1.00 |

*Only adjacent coalitions are essential.

In an actual regional case, the essential coalitions could be
tabulated in a similar manner. This calculation provides a simple
measure of the potential relative power of the cities. Of course the
actual economic power of the cities depends on their relative size and
associated treatment costs, their location relative to the limiting
water quality concentration, etc. These other factors are embodied in
the regional economic optimization model.

The results in Table 5 indicate the vital importance of identifying
essential intermediate coalitions and not just comparing the
go-it-alone solution to the overall regional optimum. Fortunately,
the MCRS incorporates the influence of the intermediate coalitions
directly using the core bounds.

### Cost Allocation for Nonoptimal Solutions

The suggested modification for stopping short of the optimal solution
is to apportion the costs among the subgroups according to the bounds
indicated by the grand coalition. Thus, the only change in the
calculations is that the bounds for the N-member coalition -- not the
S-member coalition -- are used.

For example, given that the eight-member coaliltion is optimal, the
cost allocation for the three-member coalition, 123, is:

Case 1: Three-member bounds -- three-person coalition optimal:

$$1 \leq x(1) \leq 2; \quad 1 \leq x(2) \leq 4; \quad 2 \leq x(3) \leq 5$$

$$\Sigma x(i) = 7$$

Case 2: Three-member bounds -- eight-member coalition optimal:

$$1 \leq x(1) \leq 2; \quad 0 \leq s(2) \leq 4; \quad 0 \leq x(3) \leq 5$$

$$\Sigma x(i) = 7$$

The MCRS cost allocations are:

|           | Case 1 | Case 2 |
|-----------|--------|--------|
| City 1    | 1.38   | 1.60   |
| City 2    | 2.12   | 2.40   |
| City 3    | 3.50   | 3.00   |
| TOTAL     | 7.00   | 7.00   |

This revised cost allocation recognizes City 3's value to other
coalitions. Given this straightforward modification, the cities can
use good, but not necessarily optimal, solutions without worrying that
the selected cost allocation does not reflect the relative bargaining
power of the cities if the grand coalition was formed.

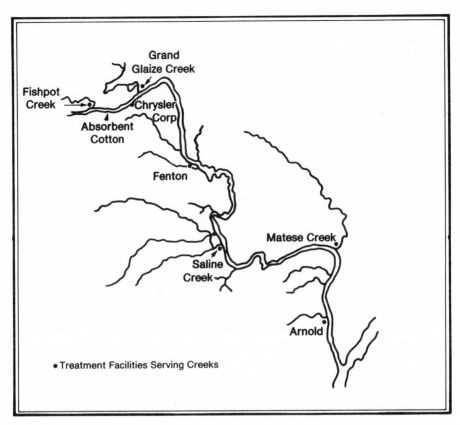

FIGURE 3
Major Dischargers to the Meramec River
(from Loehman et al. 1979)

EVALUATION OF THE MERAMEC EXAMPLE

Loehman et al. (1979) present a cost allocation procedure for eight
waste dischargers along the Meramec River in Missouri (see Figure 3).
An eight-member cost game was set up using optimal solutions for each
coalition as the characteristic function values.  Subsidized costs
were used.  Table 6 shows the 45 essential coalitions, the eight
individual costs, and the cost of the eight-member coalition.

In this example, the incentive to form larger coalitions is relatively
significant due in part to the assumed subsidies.  The least-cost
solution, as a function of the size of the largest coalition, is shown
in Table 7 and Figure 4.  Note in Figure 4 that total costs continue
to decrease at a relatively constant rate even up to an eight-member
coalition.  The overall savings of nearly 66 percent seem unrealisti-
cally high, but they will be accepted for the purpose of this
application.

TABLE 6
Cost Data for Meramec Example
(data from Loehman et al. 1979)

| | Cities | | | | | | | | Cost |
|---|---|---|---|---|---|---|---|---|---|
| | 1 | 2 | 3 | 4 | 5 | 6 | 7 | 8 | Thousands of Dollars |
| **ESSENTIAL** | 1 | | | | | | | | 631 |
| | | 1 | | | | | | | 789 |
| | | | 1 | | | | | | 1,447 |
| | | | | 1 | | | | | 540 |
| | | | | | 1 | | | | 413 |
| | | | | | | 1 | | | 365 |
| | | | | | | | 1 | | 605 |
| | | | | | | | | 1 | 226 |
| | | | 1 | 1 | | | | | 1,664 |
| | | | 1 | | 1 | | | | 1,181 |
| | | | | | | | 1 | 1 | 514 |
| **COALITIONS** | 1 | | 1 | | 1 | | | | 1,472 |
| | | 1 | 1 | | 1 | | | | 1,510 |
| | | | 1 | 1 | 1 | | | | 1,306 |
| | | | | | | 1 | 1 | 1 | 716 |
| | 1 | 1 | 1 | 1 | | | | | 2,468 |
| | 1 | 1 | 1 | | 1 | | | | 1,656 |
| | 1 | | 1 | 1 | 1 | | | | 1,585 |
| | 1 | | 1 | | 1 | 1 | | | 1,667 |
| | 1 | | 1 | | 1 | | 1 | | 1,800 |
| | | 1 | 1 | 1 | 1 | | | | 1,502 |
| | | | 1 | 1 | 1 | 1 | | | 1,466 |
| | | | 1 | | 1 | | 1 | 1 | 1,208 |
| | | | 1 | | 1 | 1 | 1 | 1 | 848 |
| **[S]** | 1 | 1 | 1 | 1 | 1 | | | | 1,766 |
| | 1 | 1 | 1 | | 1 | 1 | | | 1,875 |
| | 1 | 1 | 1 | | 1 | | 1 | | 1,995 |
| | 1 | | 1 | 1 | 1 | 1 | | | 1,809 |
| | 1 | | 1 | 1 | 1 | | 1 | | 2,001 |
| | 1 | | 1 | | 1 | 1 | 1 | | 2,051 |
| | 1 | | 1 | | 1 | | 1 | 1 | 1,448 |
| | | 1 | 1 | 1 | 1 | 1 | | | 1,603 |
| | | 1 | 1 | | 1 | | 1 | 1 | 1,344 |
| | | | 1 | 1 | 1 | 1 | 1 | | 1,878 |
| | | | 1 | 1 | 1 | | 1 | 1 | 1,309 |

TABLE 6 (cont'd.)

|   | Cities | | | | | | | | Cost |
|---|---|---|---|---|---|---|---|---|---|
|   | 1 | 2 | 3 | 4 | 5 | 6 | 7 | 8 | Thousands of Dollars |
|   |   |   | 1 |   | 1 | 1 | 1 | 1 | 1,308 |
|   |   |   |   | 1 | 1 | 1 | 1 | 1 | 1,014 |
| C | 1 | 1 | 1 | 1 | 1 |   | 1 |   | 2,160 |
| O | 1 | 1 | 1 |   | 1 |   | 1 | 1 | 1,565 |
| A | 1 |   | 1 | 1 | 1 | 1 | 1 |   | 2,187 |
| L | 1 |   | 1 | 1 | 1 |   | 1 | 1 | 1,469 |
| I | 1 |   | 1 |   | 1 | 1 | 1 | 1 | 1,507 |
| T | 1 |   |   | 1 | 1 | 1 | 1 | 1 | 1,235 |
| I |   | 1 | 1 | 1 | 1 | 1 | 1 |   | 2,091 |
| O |   | 1 | 1 | 1 | 1 |   | 1 | 1 | 1,473 |
| N |   | 1 | 1 |   | 1 | 1 | 1 | 1 | 1,475 |
| S |   |   | 1 | 1 | 1 | 1 | 1 | 1 | 1,462 |
|   | 1 | 1 | 1 | 1 | 1 | 1 | 1 |   | 1,616 |
|   | 1 | 1 | 1 | 1 | 1 |   | 1 | 1 | 1,650 |
|   | 1 | 1 | 1 |   | 1 | 1 | 1 | 1 | 1,629 |
| [S] | 1 | 1 |   | 1 | 1 | 1 | 1 | 1 | 1,379 |
|   | 1 |   | 1 | 1 | 1 | 1 | 1 | 1 | 1,587 |
|   |   | 1 | 1 | 1 | 1 | 1 | 1 | 1 | 1,545 |
|   | 1 | 1 | 1 | 1 | 1 | 1 | 1 | 1 | 1,712 |
| Σ S | 23 | 19 | 38 | 25 | 40 | 22 | 31 | 23 | 221 |

Loehman et al. (1979) compare three methods of cost allocation: general Shapley charge, minimize disruption and average cost. Their results are compared to the core bounds and the MCRS solution in Table 8. The results indicate that the generalized Shapley charge and the minimize disruption solution are unacceptable because some of the assigned costs fall outside of the core. The simple average cost method passes the core test. By its nature, the MCRS solution is in the core.

In this example, a relatively strong incentive exists to form the grand coalition, However, if it was desirable to select an intermediate solution, the core bounds could be used to prorate costs.

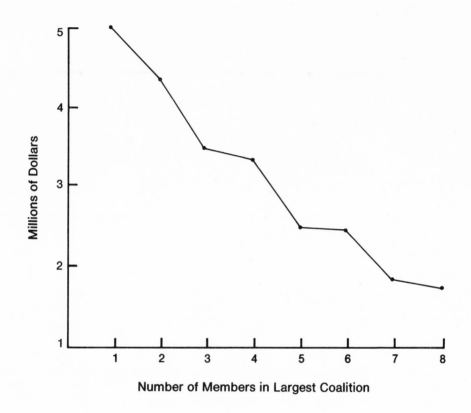

FIGURE 4
Optimal Solution as a Function of Coalition Size:
Meramec River Basin

Overall, a total savings of $3 million is realized due to coopera-
tion.   Table 9 shows how these savings are allocated if the MCRS
solution is used.   The percentage of membership in essential coalitions is also shown.   In this case, little correlation exists between
percentage of savings alloted by the MCRS solution and the extent of
participation in essential coalitions.


SUMMARY AND CONCLUSIONS

The water resources literature is replete with methods for increasing
economic efficiency by combining multiple purposes and/or groups in a
cooperative venture.   While the resultant savings are often impressive, the economic optimum may not be implemented because of difficulties in assigning the total cost among the participants in a fair
manner.   On the other hand, the simplest solution to implement

TABLE 7
Least-Cost Solution as a Function of Coalition Size:
Meramec River Basin
(data from Loehman et al. 1974)

| Size of Largest Coalition | Optimal Coalitions | Least-Cost Solution (Thousands of Dollars) | Percentage Savings |
|---|---|---|---|
| 1 | 1,2,3,4,5,6,7,8 | 5,016 | 0 |
| 2 | 1,2,34,5,6,78 | 4,376 | 12.8 |
| 3 | 1,2,345,678 | 3,442 | 31.4 |
| 4 | 1234,5678 | 3,316 | 33.9 |
| 5 | 12345,678 | 2,482 | 50.5 |
| 6 | 16,234578 | 2,469 | 50.8 |
| 7 | 1234567,8 | 1,842 | 63.3 |
| 8 | 12345678 | 1,712 | 65.9 |

from a cost allocation point of view is one in which all of the participants act independently. However, this can be quite ineffi-cient, so the analyst needs to search not only for the optimal solution to the economic efficiency problem but also for good solutions by which costs can be allocated in a relatively simple manner.

A hypothetical eight-city cost game was analyzed. Incremental savings as a function of the size of the largest coalition are seen to diminish. Accordingly, it might be better to stop at an intermediate, "good" solution. As the example clearly shows, however, this solution is unfair to the middle cities because it does not recognize fully the importance of their strategic location and contribution to a dis-proportionally large number of the intermediate essential coalitions. Thus, these interior cities could be expected to favor the grand coalition not so much because of the larger overall savings, but because of their larger share of the savings.

A very simple solution to the problem is recommended. In allocating costs, the core bounds for the overall optimal solution are chosen. This will result in a distribution of costs that recognizes the overall contribution of each participant.

The above ideas are used to solve an eight-discharger problem for the Meramec River Basin in Missouri. This application shows the impor-tance of using the core boundaries as a screening device.

TABLE 8

Core Bounds and Cost Allocations
for Eight-Member Group in Meramec River Basin, Missouri

(some data from Loehman et al. 1979)

| Number of Members | Costs in Thousands of Dollars | | | | | |
| --- | --- | --- | --- | --- | --- | --- |
| | Core Bounds | | Cost Allocations | | | |
| | Lower | Upper | General Shapley | Minimize Disruption | Average Cost | MCRS |
| 1 | 167 | 631 | 217 | 386 | 245 | 276 |
| 2 | 125 | 789 | 77* | 439 | 166 | 281 |
| 3 | 333 | 1,108 | 1,084 | 860 | 504 | 515 |
| 4 | 83 | 540 | 177 | 299 | 108 | 190 |
| 5 | 0 | 413 | -15* | -580* | 157 | 97 |
| 6 | 62 | 365 | 47* | 205 | 132 | 128 |
| 7 | 0 | 418 | 396 | -54* | 274 | 98 |
| 8 | 96 | 226 | -271* | 157 | 126 | 127 |
| TOTALS: | 866 | 4,490 | 1,712 | 1,712 | 1,712 | 1,712 |

*Assigned cost not in core.

TABLE 9

Allocation of Savings Based on MCRS Method
Versus Extent of Participation in Essential Coalitions

| Method | 1 | 2 | 3 | 4 | 5 | 6 | 7 | 8 | Total |
| --- | --- | --- | --- | --- | --- | --- | --- | --- | --- |
| MCRS | 10.7 | 15.4 | 28.2 | 10.6 | 9.6 | 7.2 | 15.3 | 3.0 | 100.0 |
| Coalition Count | 10.9 | 8.6 | 17.6 | 11.3 | 18.5 | 10.0 | 13.6 | 9.5 | 100.0 |

ACKNOWLEDGEMENTS

This paper is an extension of earlier research conducted for the U.S. Environmental Protection Agency Office at Cincinnati, Ohio. Financial support for this effort came from the Water Research Program of the Engineering and Industrial Experiment Station, University of Florida. Doug Dean and graduate students in the University of Florida Department of Environmental Engineering Sciences performed many of the computations. Their assistance and valuable suggestions are appreciated.

REFERENCES

Heaney, J.P., and Dickinson, R.E. 1982. Methods for apportioning the cost of a water resource project. Water Resources Research 18(3).

Heaney, J.P., and Sheikh, H. 1975. Game theoretic approach to equitable regional environmental quality management. Proceedings of NATO Conference on Mathematical Analysis of Decision Problems in Ecology, Istanbul, Turkey. Berlin: Springer-Verlag.

Krenkel, P.A., and Novotny, V. 1980. Water Quality Management. New York: Academic Press.

Loehman, E., et al. 1979. Cost allocation for a regional wastewater treatment system. Water Resources Research 15(2).

Lyon, R.M. 1981. Auctions and Alternative Procedures for Public Allocation with Application to the Distribution of Pollution Rights, NSF Award PRA 79-13131 Report 1. Urbana, Ill.: University of Illinois Department of Civil Engineering.

Niku, S.; Schroeder, E.D., and Haugh, R.S. 1982. Reliability and stability of trickling filter processes. Jour. Water Poll. Control Fed. 54(2).

Niku, S.; Schroeder, E.D., and Samaniego, F.J. 1979. Performance of activated sludge process and reliability-based design. Jour. Water Poll. Control Fed. 51(12).

Straffin, P.D. 1980. Topics in the Theory of Voting. Boston, Mass.: Birkhauser.

Straffin, P.D., and Heaney, J.P. 1981. Game theory and the Tennessee Valley Authority. International Journal of Game Theory 10(1).

Teitenberg, T..H. 1980. Transferable discharge permits and the control of stationary source air pollution: a survey and synthesis. Land Economics 56:391-416.

Tietenberg, T.H. 1982. Transferable discharge permits and the control of stationary source air pollution: A survey and synthesis. Land Economics 56(4).

Wilde, D.J.   1978.   Globally Optimal Design.   New York: John Wiley.

Young, O.R.   1979.   International resource regimes.   IN: Collective
    Decision Making-Applications from Public Choice Theory, C.S.
    Russell, ed.  Baltimore: The Johns Hopkins Press.

# Priority Pollution Rights:
# An Adaptation of Western Water Law
# to Pollution Control Problems

**Charles W. Howe**

**Department of Economics**
**University of Colorado**

**Dwight R. Lee**

**Center for Study of Public Choice**
**Virginia Polytechnic Institute and State University**

INTRODUCTION

Howe's Law: "Everyone has a scheme that will not work."

Time variability in the assimilative capabilities of the environment
and in demands for the waste disposal services of the environment have
long posed problems for pollution control systems. Streamflows vary
and atmospheric conditions change over both long and short periods,
requiring variations in permissible (nonworst-case) effluent discharges if ambient standards are not to be violated. Some tools for
environmental management just do not deal with this problem (e.g.,
pollution taxes) and must be supplemented by additional controls such
as maximum instantaneous effluent rates (Baumol and Oates 1975, pp.
162-68) or emergency powers to require effluent cutbacks and industry
curtailments. The main problem with these short-term measures is that
they are ordinarily applied uniformly across broad classes of
polluters (e.g., shutdowns of all heavy industries or prohibition of
all single-occupant automobiles). It is well known that policies of
uniform cutback across broad classes of activity are inefficient
because they fail to reflect differences in net benefit losses to the
various polluters (e.g., Johnson 1967; Teller 1970).

This article extends the work of Dales (1968), Tietenberg (1974),
Montgomery (1972) and others on transferable discharge permits by
proposing an adaptation of the long-standing system of "appropriations
doctrine" that is the basis of Western U.S. water law to the problem
of pollution control (i.e., the use of a "priority rights" system for
allocating available assimilative capacity). Appropriations doctrine
originated in the mountain mining camps of the West, where surface
water was relatively scarce (Hartman and Seastone 1969). Established
users frequently found their streamflows diminished by the arrival of
newcomers upstream. To avoid violent resolutions of such conflicts,
systems of priorities based on date of first use were established to
make clear who had call on available streamflows, how much they could
divert and what return flows were required of them. Each river came
to have a set of such priority rights, and these rights gradually were
incorporated into state law.

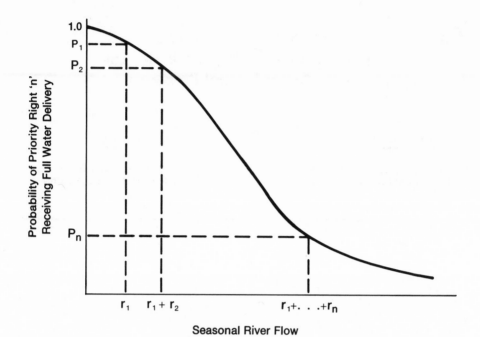

FIGURE 1
Probabilities of Water Availability
Associated with a Priority Rights System

In the case of surface water, the functioning of a priority system
depends on the probability distribution of streamflows: more senior
rights have a higher probability of getting their water than do more
junior rights. If the quantities of water associated with each right
are labeled $r_1$, $r_2$ ..., $r_n$ ... in descending order of priority,
the various probabilities of receiving water can be depicted as in
Figure 1. The degree of assurance of water availability increases
with the seniority of the right.

The economic efficiency argument favoring systems of priority rights
is that certain uses require the assurance of a highly reliable supply
of water before it becomes worthwhile to invest in the production
process. For example, a food processing plant or a citrus orchard
would not be profitable if the water supply failed frequently. Other
water-using activities, such as the growing of grains or mining
operations, may not be subject to as much damage from variations in
water supply. The former activities would presumably find it
advantageous to obtain quite senior rights, while the latter might
find more junior rights quite acceptable (and presumably cheaper to
buy).

The adaptation of appropriations doctrine as traditionally applied to
the ownership of surface water to a system of pollution rights

(priority pollution rights system [PPRS]) is accomplished in all important respects by substituting "available environmental assimilative capacity" for streamflow in the statements above. The economic efficiency of such a system will now be demonstrated in terms of the basic model of optimum pollution control.

## THE PERFORMANCE OF A SYSTEM OF PRIORITY POLLUTION RIGHTS

The basic model for deriving an optimum program of pollution abatement requires knowledge of the damages sustained by receptors and the abatement costs incurred by the polluters. The difficulty of obtaining damage information is a primary reason why systems of ambient air and water quality standards have been widely adopted. Under a system of standards, optimum control is reduced to minimizing the cost of meeting the standards. Assume that the least-cost solution in terms of aggregate effluent discharges for each zone of the system has been derived. In the notation of the basic model:

$$X_j^* = f_j (a_j, s_j) \qquad\qquad j = 1 \text{ to } m \qquad (1)$$

where the $a_j$ are vectors of the relevant physical environmental conditions in each zone, $j$, that determine the assimilative capacities of the environment, and $\bar{s}_j$ specifies the amount of this assimilative capacity that may be used without violating the zonal ambient water quality standard. That is, $X_j^*$ is the maximum amount of pollutant that can be discharged in that zone over a given amount of time.

At least three problems remain with the practicality of this solution:

1. The model is static and relates to the long-run abatement costs that would be faced by polluters in a steady-state situation, thereby failing to incorporate costs to polluters of short-term changes in the $X_j^*$ that would be required by changes in $a_j$.

2. The least-cost solution cannot be derived by inserting time averages of the $a_j$ into (1) above because of the non-linearity of the cost functions and environmental diffusion processes.

3. The solution still requires that the authority know the cost functions of the individual polluters.

What is needed is a system that is adaptable to short-term fluctuations in the assimilative capacity of the environment and that can cost-efficiently allocate short-term changes in allowable discharges among polluters, without the Pollution Control Authority (PCA) having to know the polluters' cost functions. This is the purpose of the PPRS.

To exhibit the basic properties of the PPRS, we first look at a simplified situation in which there is only one zone (i.e., m = 1, so $j$ subscripts can be dropped) for which the excess, or usable, assimilative capacity, S, has been established. Within this zone, the locations of the pollution sources are assumed to have no differential impact on the use of this available assimilative capacity.  Possible examples might include a small lake or reservoir in which quite thorough mixing of pollutants takes place, and the case of hydrocarbon emissions from vehicles in an urban airshed.  In this simplified case, the PPRS would operate according to the following sequence of steps:

1.  Pollution rights are issued without limit in the zone, each right having a priority number (1 being the highest) and entitling the holder to one unit of pollution per time period during any period for which that priority has been declared valid by the PCA;

2.  The vector of physical parameters, $\underline{a}$, that determine the assimilative capabilities of the environment are monitored at the beginning of each time period;

3.  The PCA determines the allowable aggregate level of pollution from all sources in the zone by using the relation:
$$g(X,a) \leq S$$
where g(.) is the physical diffusion process linking emissions, X, and use of the assimilative capacity.  S = total assimilative capacity -- the ambient water quality standard, $S^1$.

4.  The number X* is announced for that period and all rights numbered from 1 to X* may be exercised in that period;

5.  Over time, a set of prices will become established for the rights, the more senior rights presumably having higher prices because of the greater frequency with which they are declared valid;

6.  An efficient distribution of priorities is achieved as those parties to whom high priorities have greatest value acquire the higher priority rights.

To understand this process, we must consider the individual polluter's decision problem.  Since the assimilative capabilities determined by the physical parameters, $\underline{a}$, are random variables over time, the PCA's determination of X* over time establishes an observable frequency distribution of the values of X* and thereby a frequency distribution of the validity of each of the priorities.  Using this information and their private benefit-and-cost information, the individual polluters determine their own willingness to pay for the various priorities and presumably buy all rights with market prices below this level.


EXTENDING P.P.R.S. TO THE MULTIPLE-ZONE CASE (m $\geq$ 2)

Any system of pollution control is greatly complicated by the existence of multiple zones.  Zonal distinctions will ordinarily be necessary to take into account the different impacts of emissions at different locations on the various receptors or on the various zones for which standards have been established.  In the cost minimization case, the problem is that many sets of values of aggregate discharges in the zones, $X_1$ ... $X_m$, will be consistent with meeting ambient standards, $S_1'$... $S_m'$, and therefore using less than an equal to $S_1$ ... $S_m$.  An efficient determination of the optimum values, $X_1^*$ ... $X_m^*$ would still require a knowledge of the cost functions by the PCA.

We here propose a general, iterative procedure by which the PCA can obtain the required information for extending the PPRS (or other systems) to the multiple-zone case.  A summary of the sequence of steps in the operation of this iterative, multizone procedure follows:

1.  The zones are defined on grounds of physical homogeniety, greater accuracy being achieved by finer definition of zones;

2.  Standards are established for each zone;

3.  Pollution rights specific to each zone are issued without limit in that zone, each right having a priority number (1 being the highest priority) and entitling the holder to one unit of pollution in any period in which that priority is declared valid by the PCA;

4.  Assimilative capabilities represented by the $a_j$ are monitored in each zone at the beginning of each time period;

5.  The PCA parametrically solves a suboptimizing problem to be described later, producing a solution of the form (1) above;

6.  The number $X_j^*$ is announced for each zone, $\underline{j}$, at the beginning of each period, and all rights numbered from 1 up to $X_j^*$ may be exercised in that period;

7.  Over time, a set of prices becomes established for the rights in each zone, the more senior rights presumably having higher prices (the price sets will differ from zone to zone because of differences in other locational factors);

8.  Within each zone, those parties to whom reliable pollution rights have greatest value will come to own the more senior rights;

9.  As prices in each zone come to reveal the values to the polluters of the right to pollute, the PCA can use these prices in re-solving the optimizing problem referred to in step (5) above;

10.  Marginal location changes of polluters will take place as prices approach their equilibrium values;

11.  An intertemporally and locationally efficient solution is approached.

To understand this more complicated process, we must consider the PCA's decision problem referred to in steps 5 and 9 above. The PCA must announce in each period which seniorities will be valid in each one so that the standards will be met. Naturally, many sets of values $X_1, \ldots X_m$ will be capable of satisfying the standards, so a "solution" by the PCA requires the use of some criterion for selecting the $X_j$'s. Since the individual cost functions are not known, the minimum cost criterion cannot be used. Is there some other criterion that might be "reasonable"?

Since standards imply no benefits for achievement of super-standard ambient quality, it would be consistent with the use of standards for the PCA to seek to:

maximize        $\sum\limits_{j} X_j*$

$$(2)$$

subject to

$$g_j(X_j, a_j) \leq S \qquad \text{for } j = 1, \ldots, m$$

That is, the PCA starts out in step (5) of the preceding scenario by solving the problem of equation (2), maximizing the total allowable effluent load. This leads to a suboptimal solution that eventually induces the price sets $\Pi_{ij}$ ($\underline{i}$ referring to the priority and $\underline{j}$ to the zone). After prices have stabilized, the authority then has information on the values of pollution rights in the several zones.

How can this information be used? The observed prices in each zone are used to fit a pollution rights demand function for that zone by arranging the rights in descending order of seniority and price. This demand function, $P_j = P_j(X_j)$ exhibits the polluters' willingness to pay for rights of different priority. The areas under each zone's demand function can then be used in the second stage of the process, wherein the authority seeks to

maximize

$$\sum\limits_{j=1}^{m} \int\limits_{0}^{X_j} P_j(X_j)dX_j \qquad\qquad (3)$$

subject to

$$g_j(X_j, a_j) \leq S_j \qquad \text{for } j = 1, \ldots, m$$

Obviously, this step results in a revised set of allowable discharges, $X_j*$.

As the new rules are put into effect, price sets will again change because the probability distributions over the various seniorities in each zone will change. How many iterations might be required to converge on the optimal solution is not clear, but even stopping with one such step would come closer to an efficient solution than current procedures. Over time, the economic activities located in each zone will change, so prices will continue to change. The PCA should, therefore, redetermine the optimization problem (3) every few years.

COMPARISONS WITH OTHER CONTROL SYSTEMS
AND EXAMPLES OF POTENTIAL APPLICATIONS

Oates et al. (this volume) ably describe the advantages and disadvantages of the ambient-based permit system (APS), the emission-based permit system (EPS), and their own "pollution offsets" system. Each of these systems relies on the operation of competitive markets to approach the minimum-cost allocation of assimilative capacity among polluters. The role of the PCA differs with each system, being reduced to the provision of technical diffusion-process information (the transfer coefficients) and bookkeeping in the cases of APS and pollution offsets. None of the system deals by itself with the problem of short-term environmental variability.

The priority permit feature could be added to any of these systems. Naturally, there would have to be continuing activity by the PCA in monitoring changing environmental conditions and announcing the changing values of $X_j^*$, ..., $X_j^*$. Tietenberg (1974, p. 289) concluded that basing currently allowable rates of emission on current (say, daily) environmental conditions would involve excessive costs to the PCA and excessive uncertainty to polluters. But these are precisely the issues that a priority permit system is designed to handle: the efficient allocation of short-term changes in allowable discharges among polluters. Those for whom short-term adaptation is costly will buy the more senior rights.

Examples of possible application include control of point sources on a river system, point sources on lakes or seas (like the Baltic and North seas), stationary sources in an urban airshed, and urban automobile pollution. In all but the last case, the correspondence between elements of the preceding model and descriptions of the problem settings is obvious. For rivers, the diffusion processes $g_j(X_j, a_j)$ represent the Streeter-Phelps equations for BOD and dissolved oxygen, simple dilution processes for conservative wastes, and the transport equations for suspended solids. For urban airsheds, these functions will represent Gaussian plume models for important point sources and inversion models for acute episodes of airborne waste entrapment. In all cases, allowances must be made for the background ambient levels of pollution created by nonpoint sources, such as agricultural return flows and urban space heating.

The case of urban automobile air pollution warrants particular attention. In this case, the unit being controlled is the individual vehicle rather than a unit of pollutant (i.e., possession of a right of given seniority entitles the owner to use the vehicle on those days when that seniority is valid). Since the source moves from one zone to others, the simple one-zone model may be applicable. When serious inversions are in store, the value of $X^*$ declared for that day would be greatly reduced. Those who do not have access to public transportation or who highly value the convenience of private vehicles would presumably own the more senior rights.

While this system provides a convenient way of controlling the number of vehicles in daily use, vehicles are not homogeneous with respect

either to pollution per mile or miles driven. Thus different vehicles
might be required to hold different numbers of rights according to
their tested "smog rating." Another possibility would be simultaneous
use of a "smog tax" (see Freeman et al. 1973) that would depend on a
vehicle's tested "smog rating" and would be paid as an additional tax
when being refueled. This combined program would provide great
flexibility for the individual vehicle owner in choosing the person-
ally optimal mix of vehicle type, maintenance and reliability of
rights.

Institutional issues relating to the establishment and operation of the
PPRS are quite important and complex. The analogy to Western water
rights may again be helpful. Many Western U.S. rivers are interstate,
while the systems of water rights are established only within
individual states. The issue of interstate water allocation is
settled -- if at all -- by interstate compacts that tend to be fixed
for all time because of the complexity of their negotiation. At the
same time, some of the most important misallocations of water from the
economic efficiency viewpoint are interstate (e.g., between Colorado
and California on the Colorado River). This means that while
relatively efficient markets for water rights may exist within states,
there is no way to establish a market among states.

The same problem will exist with pollution rights as long as air and
water quality management are largely left to the states. The failure
of correspondence of political and pollution shed boundaries will
always pose problems and may require the establishment of special
interstate bodies such as the (now moribund) river basin commissions
or ad hoc commissions such as the Delaware River Basin Commission or
the Ohio River Sanitation Commission.

In summary, we feel that priority rights greatly increase the
adaptability of transferable permit systems to short-term fluctuations
in the assimilative capacity of the environment. They can be combined
with other systems such as APS, EPS or pollution offsets to obtin
compromise systems that may best fulfill the multiple criteria of
efficiency, equity, political feasibility and administrative feasibility. PPRS and the proposed iterative procedure for imputing values
to permits in the multizone case both appear worthy of further
consideration.

REFERENCES

Baumol, W.J., and Oates, W.E.  1975.  The theory of environmental
    policy.  Englewood Cliffs, N.J.:  Prentice-Hall, Inc.

Dales, J.H.  1968.  Land, water and ownership.
    Canadian Journal of Economics.

Dales, J.H.  1968.  Pollution, property and prices.
    Toronto:  University of Toronto Press.

Freeman, A.M. III; Haveman, R.H., and Kneese, A.V.  1973.  The
    economics of environmental quality, pp. 132–34.
    New York:  John Wiley and Sons, Inc.

Hartman, L.M., and Seastone, D.  1969.  Water transfers:  economic
    efficiency and alternative institutions.
    Baltimore:  Johns Hopkins Press.

Johnson, E.L.  1967.  A study in the economics of water quality
    management.  Water Resources Research 3(2).

Montgomery, W.D.  1972.  Markets in licenses and efficient pollution
    control programs.  Journal of Economic Theory 5:395–418.

Teller, A.  1970.  Air pollution abatement:  economic rationality and
    reality.  IN:  America's  Changing  Environment,  Revelle  and
    Landberg, eds.  Boston:  Beacon Press.

Tietenberg, T.H.  1974.  The design of property rights for air
    pollution control.  Public Policy 22(3):275–92.

Tietenberg, T.H.  1980.  Transferable discharge permits and the
    control  of  stationary-source  air  pollution:  a  survey  and
    synthesis.  Land Economics 56(4).

# A Tempest in a Teapot:
# The Analysis and Evaluation of Environmental Groups Trading in Markets for Pollution Permits

**Joe A. Oppenheimer and Clifford Russell**

**Resources for the Future**
**Washington, D.C.**

## INTRODUCTION

What if the Reagan administration took its rhetoric seriously and set up systems of marketable permits to pollute? Most discussions of such possibilities assume that the important actors in such markets would be polluters and government agencies (the latter's primary role being to determine the stock and quality of permits being traded). But imagine that environmental public interest groups (i.e., those organized to supply collective, or public, environmental goods to the society) join in market activity, becoming net buyers of these pollution rights. Such a possibility is not extremely farfetched. After all, even economists have considered it.

How would the actions of environmental groups in buying and "retiring" pollution rights change the equlibrium market outcome? Recent papers (Ryan 1981; Tietenberg 1980, 1981) express concern that the introduction of such market activities would throw the market equilibrium off from approximately Paretian outcomes. On the other hand, earlier and more casual treatments of this question usually did not find the prospect of environmentalist trading threatening; indeed, such a possibility was often held out as an advantage (Anderson et al. 1979; Tucker 1981).[1] For example, Tucker says that (p. 38) "...with the marketable-rights system, the possi- bility exists that the public, either through municipal bodies or environmental groups, can organize itself to <u>buy back</u> some of the rights to pollute and 'retire' them, thus eliminating more pollution from the atmosphere. This way, the public will be able to improve the air but will understand exactly how much it is costing. People can select it as a clear consumer choice..." Anderson says (pp. 3-20 to 3-21), "In this way, interested citizens would be able to influence the composition of the economy's output and its division between consumer goods and social amenities such as environmental quality."

We will here address some of these claims and concerns. We consider three levels on which it is useful to analyze the participation of environmentalists in pollution rights markets. First and most fundamentally, we consider the meaning of the comparison of the "optimal level of pollution rights" with a level of pollution that has been decided upon in the real world. More specifically, when pollution is but one item in the menu of public decisions, what consistitutes an optimal choice of ambient air quality standards? Can such a point be identified, let alone achieved? Such analysis rests, in part, on the social choice literature's questioning of the very notion of a social welfare function.

To understand the second level of this analysis, one needs to put aside some objections to the "meaning" of optimality. Thus, we adopt the more conventional perspective of welfare economics and apply it to the problem of standard setting. We try to specify when the actions of environmental groups in pollution rights markets would tend to improve, or undermine, economic efficiency. In short, we will comment on whether the resulting shifts in the equilibrium could be character- ized as an improvement or not.

We will then break away from public choice and economic theory altogether and discuss such practical matters as the likely cost of affecting environmental quality in a particular region through the purchase and retirement of discharge permits. This allows a compari- son of these costs with the resources likely to be available to environmentalists for that purpose.


COLLECTIVE CHOICE, ENVIRONMENTAL QUALITY
AND ENVIRONMENTAL GROUPS AS PURCHASERS OF RIGHTS

There are fundamental difficulties with the "efficiency" benchmark used by analysts like Ryan and Tietenberg. It is reasonable and useful to talk about the efficiency with which a politically given standard is met, but there is very little economists can say about the efficiency of the actual standard itself and hence of any departures from it. Only in the abstract world of the classroom and textbook do we have individuals' marginal benefit curves to add vertically and to match with a marginal cost curve. In reality, society lives with a necessarily imperfect aggregation process, which produces a more-or-less arbitrary answer to the question, "How much environmental quality should be provided?"

We emphasize that this is not due to a flaw in any particular system of government. After all, any political process imperfectly responds to what necessarily are surrogates for preferences. Such surrogates are needed for more than purely practical reasons. As Farquharson (1969) (and others) indicated several years ago, "voting one's preferences" is an ambiguous notion. Strategic elements stemming from the structure of an agenda make the relationship between voting and preferences ambiguous at best. Moreover, votes are aggregated to reach social decisions. When the social choice is based on an aggregation principle such as "whichever side gets the largest number of votes," the social choice is still further divorced from pref- erences.

Modern attempts to overcome these difficulties have stressed "tech- niques" or "procedures" which give individuals incentives to reveal their preferences. (See Tideman 1977 for an overview of such procedures.) But all of them are subject to severe limitations: for example, they only give an individual incentives to reveal his/her preference when individuals cannot form coalitions.

Working abstractly from the generally desirable characteristics of social decision procedures, we find that social outcomes cannot be assumed to involve a well-behaved function of individual preferences. This, of course, is but the practical manifestation of the Arrow (1963) theorem, or the general instatiblity theorem (Schwartz 1981).

To illustrate the general nonrelationship between social choice and individual preference in the simplest context, consider the connection between optimality and majority rule. When majority rule is used to reach a social choice about economic distribution, virtually <u>any</u> division can muster a majority; virtually any proposal is in a cycle of winning proposals.

To simplify matters, consider three individuals who are to use majority rule to divide a dollar. Imagine that the first proposal is 1/3, 1/3, 1/3. Now, any two of the individuals can better their payoffs by forming a coalition. So, for example, the first two might agree to split the dollar 50-50. This, then, leaves the third individual with nothing and gives him an incentive to propose a division that is asymmetric -- where he accepts less than half, but he gives more than half to one of the two coalition members to break up the coalition; for example, he might propose a 60-40 split.

Note that to this point we have only considered Pareto points. But this is clearly unnecessary. We could propose and reach Pareto inferior points. To see this, consider the fourth proposal in this sequence:

        Proposal 1:    1/3, 1/3, 1/3
        Proposal 2:    1/2, 1/2,   0
        Proposal 3:    .60, .00, .40
        Proposal 4:    .00, .40, .50

Obviously, such a Pareto inferior proposal is acceptable and can win a majority of the votes. To point out that, in turn, such a Pareto inferior point can be beaten (unanimously, even) is not interesting, since <u>all</u> proposals can be beaten, and it is true by definition of Pareto inferior points that alone they can lose unanimously) (see Sen 1970, Chap. 2). Thus, we can see that <u>if</u> the cycle is stopped by additional, arbitrary procedures, we have no assurance of a socially optimal group choice.

Only with extremely powerful -- and hence unrealistic -- assumptions can we formally relate social choices to individual preferences. So, for example, we could consider two models which develop such ties: that is, median voter analyses, as in Black (1958), or structurally induced equilibria, as in Romer and Rosenthal (1978), Shepsle (1979) and Shepsle and Weingast (1981). In the latter, the relationship is usually between the social choice and the preferences of representatives in a legislature -- not the preferences of the general members

of society.  Thus, the relationship is usually not specified in a
manner that identifies a social optimum.  In the former, the outcome
is not identified as Paretian, but rather only as stable.  Its roots
are procedural, not normative.

This, of course, has implications for our specification of a social
optimum.  Though such an optimum may exist in the "purely economic"
sense, there is no political path to get us there or even to identify
the optimum.  Or, said another way, political paths are often likely
to be indeterminate, leading to choices that are subject to cycles and
political instabilities, and where they stop is unknown.  On the other
hand, the political process may generate a quite stable set of choices
-- but then there is no reason to think that these choices will be
Pareto optimal.

In this light, a decision to allow environmentalists into a permit
market can be seen as a decision to open another route for the
expression of preferences over environmental quality and commodity
price combinations.  It will not be possible, in general, to say
whether the result of that expression is better or worse (i.e., more
or less efficient) than the original permit allocation.  Rather, one
will merely be able to say that the new political choice is a result
of the new political procedures.

WELFARE ECONOMICS AND ENVIRONMENTAL GROUPS AS PURCHASERS OF RIGHTS


If we relax slightly the strict public choice standards applied above
and allow ourselves to comment on the optimality of social (environmental quality) decisions, we can explore the relation between those
decisions with and without trading in discharge rights.  For example,
assume that a simple political system could be shown to deliver
supra-optimal levels of environmental protection.  If a modification
were to be considered, we could ask whether the modification (e.g.,
environmentalist trading in rights) would add to, or subtract from,
the supply of environmental protection.  The possibility of increases
in protection in such a situation would constitute a prima facie case
against the proposed procedural modification.  While only extremely
simplified models of social choice procedures yield simple, determin-
ate relationships between optimality and social choice, in this
section we illustrate the nature of the leverage one might get with
such models.

Our argument is built on a triad of assumptions regarding (1) the
relationships between (a) the regulations and the social optimum and
(b) political processes and the regulators; (2) the distribution of
costs and benefits among voters; and (3) the relationships between the
demands of environmental interest groups members' preferences and (a)
the preferences of the general population of the society and (b) the
groups' political agendas.

Assumption 1:  The Regulators and the Political Process
Consider the regulators.  If they were ideal economic actors and acted

strictly in the best interest of the society, we would expect that the marginal social benefit from tougher standards would just (barely) offset the marginal social cost. But a real agency such as the USEPA is all too imperfect, whatever the intentions of its leadership. Either such an agency is advocating too little regulation (i.e., too much pollution) or too much regulation (i.e., too little pollution) when judged against the efficiency standard.[2]

What detemines the direction of the "error" of the regulators? We assume the permitted level of pollution is a function of two things: the regulators' estimation of the set of social optima and their perceptions of sociopolitical forces impinging on their agency.

Political realities can take many different shapes. For example, direct payments could be made to regulators by industrial interest groups to tip the direction of regulation. But we assume here the simplest form of democracy: voters vote directly on the issues involved, and the outcome -- in the sense of impact on the regulatory decision -- is assumed to be a function of the placement of the median voter.[3]

## Assumption 2:  Distribution of Costs and Benefits
The costs of any program of improving environmental quality can be distributed in various ways. One way, which in a market society is quite natural, is to let costs be borne by changes in real income via market mechanisms. Of course, alternative ways of distributing the costs of environmental improvement are available. Taxes could be used to allocate the costs differently. Costs could be distributed equally to each individual by a head tax, for example. Our simple models of social choice will differ in their predictions when different assumptions are made about the distribution of costs and benefits.

## Assumption 3:  Environmental Groups' Actions and Membership Preferences
Various relationships may exist between the political actions taken by environmental groups and the preferences of their members. For example, the institutionalized group could be a "perfect" political representative of its members in the sense that it represents the median group member (voter) perfectly. Or, even better from an economic efficiency point of view, the group might in principle have a way of arriving at its welfare frontier (i.e., so that the sum of marginal benefits for the members of the group equal the total marginal cost for the group). More realistically, the groups, as microcosms of society, will face the same problems of preference revelation and registration as the nation at large.

Note that the environmental group is assumed to be interested in improving the quality of the environment. Retiring pollution rights is merely one strategy toward that end. To the extent that the group has the alternative of lobbying for a policy of issuing fewer marketable pollution rights to begin with, it may well prefer pursuing that alternative. Such a strategy could reduce pollution more cheaply for the members, for when the government restricts the original stock of rights, the cost is distributed over the entire population. But when the groups purchase the rights themselves the cost is borne

entirely by the members. On the other hand, once the rights are
defined and distributed, it may be that only the purchase option
remains to the group.

Finally, note that the response of the group, if it is a function of
its members' wishes, will also be a function of the quality of the
environment. To the extent that the regulatory agency is "lax," the
group will be pushier, and thus, other things being equal, it will be
willing to buy more, or spend more.


ANALYSIS


Varying the assumptions about the issues discussed above produces a
range of models and a range of implications for the normative status
of environmental group purchases of tradable discharge rights.

First, recall the requirements for efficiency in public goods
provision. The most important of these for our purposes is that at a
social optimum, the sum of the marginal benefits enjoyed by individuals is equal to the total marginal costs paid, or:

$$\sum_i MB_i = TMC \tag{1}$$

The average marginal cost to the citizen/taxpayer of any social
program is the total marginal cost of the program divided by the
number of taxpayers. The total marginal benefits can be also
expressed as $\underline{n}$ times the average per-capita marginal benefits, or from
(1) above:

$$[\sum MB_i/n(MB_i)] = TMC/n = (MC_i) \tag{2}$$

Now if the regulator's choice is in fact a function of the median
voter's position as well as of the social optimum, we can say more,[4]
for -- at least probabilistically -- each individual's preferences are
a function of the marginal benefits that he/she anticipates will be
associated with the program.[5] First, imagine ranking the voters by
magnitude of their individual marginal benefits. Now consider our
assumed political system, which is a direct translation of the median
preference into political action. The regulator, who aims (in our
benign world) for the social optimum, also responds to political
pressure and leans (never mind precisely how much) in the direction of
the median voter.

The predictive power of the approach stems from the simple numerical
property characterizing support for the winner of a majority-rule
contest. The winner in such a two-way contest (all the decisions will
be assumed to be made in a binary choice situation) must have more
supporters than opponents. If we were, therefore, to rank all
individuals by the degree to which they support a particular motion or
program, we could ask whether the median individual was, on net, a
supporter or not. If the median voter was not a supporter, then a
majority of the individuals (those with net evaluations below the

median valuation) would not be supporters of the program, and vice versa.

Combining the median voter analysis with the notions of optimality gives us considerable analytic leverage. We have shown that the average marginal cost and average marginal benefit must be equal at the social optimum. Thus, if we can establish the relationship between the median marginal benefit (or cost) derived from a program and the average marginal benefit (or cost), we will be able to ascertain whether there is support for increasing the program beyond the social optimum or holding the program to suboptimal levels.

## THE DISTRIBUTION OF COSTS AND BENEFITS

For the moment, assume that the benefits are equally distributed. This is obviously unrealistic for most real programs, but we can imagine a per-capita "bonus," given to everyone equally, which would be a suitable model for our purpose. Consider, then, the distribution of the costs of an environmental program. What happens if, at a social optimum, such a program is to be funded out of taxes? In particular, assume the tax is simply a neutral income tax (a fixed percentage of income at all income levels). Note that for the existing (as well as almost any imaginable) distribution of income, the mean income is above the median.[6] Under such circumstances, persons paying the median tax (and half of the people are paying this level of tax or less) are getting a program which at the margin is producing more benefits to them than the taxes they are paying for it. This follows from the requirement that the average marginal cost of the program must equal the average marginal benefit if society is at an optimum. Thus, the fact that the mean income is above the median means that there is an incentive for voters to favor a push beyond the optimum level of provision of the program. If this is true for neutral tax schemes, it is true a fortiori for progressive ones (where the average tax is paid by individuals with even higher income, and thus even further from the median.) It must also be true for many mildly regressive tax schedules as well.

We can think of tax systems that have the median and the mean at the same point; for example, one that taxes everyone the same amount -- a head tax. In that case, the median cost is equal to the mean cost and thus there will be no incentive to go beyond the optimum. Indeed, in our example there would be no point to the program, but in a real case of public good provision there might well remain a point.

It is also possible to devise tax systems in which the mean payment is less than the median. For example, the majority of individuals could pay a fixed fee, while others are given a "tax break." In this case, we would get suboptimal provision of the service or program that produced equally shared benefits, for the median voter is paying more than the average marginal cost, which, by construction, equals the average benefit. Thus, more than half the voters want to cut down the program.

A similar story can be told for benefits. If we assume that the costs are equally distributed across the population (for example, by a head tax), there are three cases differentiated by the relationship between the median and the mean marginal benefit. Again, there are real world analogues to each case.

First, consider the case where average marginal benefits are less than the median marginal benefits (e.g., because the frequency distribution of benefits is skewed with a long tail of small benefits). This creates pressure to increase the size of the program beyond the social optimum. At the social optimum, the average marginal cost equals average marginal benefit, and a majority of voters would want still more of the program delivered. The individuals with higher-than-average benefits constitute a majority, and for them the program looks good at the margin, with cost being equally distributed.[7] When the median and the mean marginal benefit coincide and costs are equally distributed, there is no political incentive to move from the optimum.

The final case is where the average benefits are greater than the median. Here the majority of the individuals would be for pulling back the program, and only a minority would be for its expansion, beyond the optimum.[8] We might characterize such programs as special interest efforts and can imagine such environmental examples as the provision of natural areas used principally by high-income recreationists or of playgrounds with facilities and in locations appealing only to particular ethnic or income groups, or the cleaning up of a single air pollution source affecting only one part of a metropolitan area.

To make the above discussion somewhat more formal and systematic, consider this model:

If costs are distributed in fixed proportion to income, we have:

$$MC_i = kY_i \tag{3}$$

Or, utilizing the same logic as above:

$$(n)(\overline{MB}) = TMB = TMC = (n)(\overline{MC}) = nk\overline{Y} \tag{4}$$

at any Pareto point.

Note that the voter is still deciding on the basis of the difference between his/her marginal benefit and cost (i.e., the net marginal impact on the individual). Assuming that the individual's marginal benefit is not a function of the individual's income, we can develop an argument similar to the one above, because the bureaucrats still are assumed to repond to the median voter.

Now if median income is below mean income and if the distribution of benefits is independent of the distribution of income, then the voter with median income is faced with the following: (1) the voter's income is below average; (2) therefore, his/her marginal cost associated with the program is below average; (3) the voter's marginal benefits are about average and thus, were the society at an optimum where average marginal benefits would equal average marginal costs, he/she would be in a privileged position: (4) the voter would want larger programs, or more environmental protection. This would imply that there would be political pressure, in this case, for the amount of regulation to be increased to above the socially optimal amount. Only if the average income were below the median would this not be the case.

If market forces operating via increased prices for manufactured goods are the primary means of "taxation," we would expect the incidence of cost to be similar to that of sales tax: distinctly regressive. A regressive tax schedule would imply that the pressures for strong regulation would decrease, and perhaps (depending on how regressive the policy) be reversed. For here the low-income voter would find himself/herself paying more. Whether this increased cost would offset the previously suggested "advantage" for the median cannot be "decided" without reference to further details of the distribution of costs.

But note: All indicators are that marginal benefits are a function of income. What could that relationship be? Assume it to be a simple linear one (almost certainly wrong; see Peskin 1978) but with a positive intercept (again, see Peskin 1978, who shows that $b$ is very likely to be greather than 0):

$$MB_i = b + 1Y_i \tag{5}$$

Then, if costs are strictly proportional to income again, as in (3), at the optimum it must be the case that:

$$b + 1\overline{Y} = k\overline{Y} \tag{6}$$

or $k$ must be greater than 1.

Now this implies that at a socially optimal level of regulation, the voter with the mean level of income is faced with offsetting marginal costs, but that those with lower incomes (i.e., the median voter) will find marginal benefits are greater than marginal costs and thus would support more regulations. In this case, then, we have an unambiguous signal for too much regulation. Note that if marginal benefits were progressive (they increased as a proportion of rising income) and marginal costs were regressive, we would again have an unambiguous tale to tell, this time that we would have too little regulation.

In summary, then, there are nine cases from the 3 x 3 typology that can be developed regarding the median/mean relationship for benefits and costs (see Table 1). Of the nine cases, only two are totally ambiguous as to the political result, given our simple median voter system: when the forces stemming from cost-benefit pressures work in opposite directions. In other words, when the mean benefits are in the same relation to the median benefits as are the costs, then there is ambiguity about the outcome of the political pressures. (These cases are labelled a in Table 1.) In the other seven cases, three are clearly unambiguous from the median voter point of view. <u>In these cases, either no pressures are generated (because average and median costs and benefits are equal), or both the pressures from the distributions of costs and benefits reinforce each other.</u>[9] In the

TABLE 1

Mean and Median Cost-and-Benefit Relations and
How They Generate Over- and Under-Regulation

|  |  | Marginal Costs | | |
|---|---|---|---|---|
|  |  | Median Greater than Mean | Median Equal to Mean | Median Less than Mean |
| Marginal Benefits | Median Greater than Mean | a | $b_o$ | $c_o$ |
|  | Median Equal to Mean | $b_u$ | o | $b_o$ |
|  | Median Less than Mean | $c_u$ | $b_u$ | a |

a   =   Ambiguous pressures
o   =   No pressures to move from optimum level of regulation
$b_o$  =   Balance is toward overregulation
$b_u$  =   Balance is toward underregulation
$c_o$  =   Clear pressure for overregulation
$c_u$  =   Clear pressure for underregulation

remaining four cases (labelled as b in Table 1), the median equals the
mean for either cost or benefit, but not both.  In these cases, the
median costs (or benefits) don't equal the mean costs (or benefits).
Presumably, this generates pressures for change along the lines
analyzed above.[10]

ENVIRONMENTAL GROUPS' ACTIONS AS A RESPONSE TO THEIR CONSTITUENCY

So far, we have merely considered the nature of the regulatory
equilibrium, specified some distributional and political parameters,
and wondered when these factors led to overregulation or under-
regulation.  Consider now the role of the interest groups that could
enter the market to purchase and retire rights so they cannot be
exercised.[11]  To relate this action to the models and result
developed above, we have to develop some functions for translating the
preferences of the members of the groups to the actions of the groups.

In what follows, note that the size of the group is important. When rights to pollute exist and are available at some market cost to the group, its size helps to determine its aggregate valuation of such rights and thus to constrain the group's leadership, their platforms and actions. For any particular group, the strategy of purchasing rights may be far too costly in relation to the size of the group.[12]

We would expect the average member of (one or more) environmental groups to value improving environmental quality more than the average nonmember. Or, in terms which do not require interpersonal utility comparisons, a member would on the average be willing to give up more so a particular environmental policy would be carried out than would the comparable nonmember. Monetizing the benefit figures permits us to talk about the mean marginal benefits to members and to nonmembers (or to the population as a whole). Define as a parameter the ratio of these monetized benefits:

$$h_j = (mb_i \text{ in the special group}) \, / \, (mb_i \text{ in society}) \tag{7}$$

The greater $h_j$, the greater is the level of dissatisfaction we can expect from members of the group with any given level of protection afforded by existing regulations (permit totals). For the individuals in the group, the ratio by which they hold these rights more dear ($h_j$) times the proportion of the population they represent ($S_j$) (i.e., group size) determines their relative effective aggregate valuation of the discharge permits. Note that for society as a whole, $h_j$ is one, and so is $S_j$. Thus, the product for any group may be considered (a surrogate for) the relative likelihood of the group making the purchase, though the scale is not zero-to-one and thus not a probability number. But we would conjecture that unless the product is greater than unity, there is little likelihood that the group would make the purchase.

To illustrate, consider a group with high relative monetized valuation of some environmental change (e.g., $h_j = 5$) and assume that the group would only buy rights if it is worthwhile for the membership. Then the product of $h_j$ and $S_j$ (which, recall, is less than .01; see fn. 11) would still be far less than one.

Thus, it would be highly unlikely that a small group would be willing to purchase the item for society: the smaller the group, the more extreme they would have to be to sustain the purchase. And if the society is near an optimum, we would expect that the average marginal benefit for a member of the society is equal to the average marginal cost. Indeed, at the social optimum, no subgroup of the population would find it worthwhile to make the purchase.[13]

Of course, the above analysis assumes that the leadership of the environmental group adopts actions in a democratic, representative fashion. Alternative scenarios are possible. Groups may adopt actions that represent only the interest of the leadership or the staff, using the resources collected from members to subsidize the leaders' interests.

PRACTICAL CONSIDERATIONS IN THINKING ABOUT ENVIRONMENTALISTS

Consider now the matter of the capability of environmentalists to buy
and retire permits.  In his discussion, Ryan (1982) refers to the
"considerable financial support" available to the Sierra Club.  A
little perspective is in order here.  Sierra Club spending for 1980
was almost $10 million, but less than $2.8 million of that was
available for action (i.e., studying and influencing public policy)
(Sierra Club 1981, p. 48).  The Environmental Defense Fund spent a
total of $2.3 million in 1981, of which $1.5 million went for programs
(Anderman 1982, p. 2).  Lobbying and public education (vs. research,
which the group would presumably want to continue even if all direct
action programs were changed to rights purchases) cost less than
$200,000.  Another, more politically activist group, the Natural
Resources Defense Council (NRDC), might be more indicative of what
could be spent on rights purchases.  In 1980, the NRDC had total
expenditures of $3.4 million, with lobbying and litigation costs
accounting for just over half of this.  Other program expenses
included scientific research and education (NRDC 1980, p. 30).  Even
the largest environmental groups have less money available for
politics than one would expect from their budget totals.  For example,
the National Wildlife Foundation, a relatively apolitical group, spent
$30 million in 1980.  After membership development expenses of about
$8 million, bread-and-butter programs run for federation members
(camps, magazines, etc.) account for about half of what's left,
leaving about $11 million for public education, research and politics.

Finally, for further perspective, consider The Nature Conservancy
(TNC), which specializes in buying and retiring (through transfer to
public agencies or continued management on its own) land of ecological
importance.  TNC was able to spend about $30 million during 1979 on
land acquisi- tion (TNC 1979, p. 28).  But $27 million of this was
used to buy land for resale to the U.S. government as part of a
program to cut down on profiteering in land speculation.  Only about
$4 million could be spent for land conservation involving permanent
purchase or purchase and subsequent gift to other organizations or
government agencies.  One might speculate that it would be easier to
raise money to retire land, which can be photographed and even
visited, than to retire permits to discharge $SO_2$, a colorless gas
with ill-understood effects on plants, humans and the rest of
nature.[14]

The contrast between these environmental group resources and the
prospective cost of permits could hardly be more stark.  Consider the
calculations of some researchers.  Hahn and Noll (1981), for example,
indicate that the annual cost of buying a close approach to the
attainment of ambient air quality standards for $SO_2$ in the South
Coast Air Basin of California would be close to $100 million.[15]

Similarly, water pollution rights would also be expensive.  O'Neil et
al. (1981) estimate the annual cost of buying improvements in the
dissolved oxygen level in Wisconsin's Fox River to be $4.9 million to
raise it from 2 ppm to 4 ppm, and $6.5 million more to improve it from
4 ppm to 6.2 ppm.[16]

These figures, of course, are merely suggestive. But what they suggest is that the costs of buying a significant improvement in environmental quality in even one major airshed or river would exhaust the resources of all the national environmental groups combined. Thus, far from being "considerable," these groups' resources are pitiful, considering that the groups try to cover the entire gamut of environmental concerns, and considering the resources of the firms against whom they would be bidding for permits.

We can conclude that any move to marketable permits is almost surely not going to lead groups to take collective action to purchase the rights. The notion that the introduction of environmental interest groups, as actors in these markets, will radically alter the outcome of the market equililbrium, is farfetched.[17]

How is it then that interest groups do supply the society with public goods? Usually this is achieved via lobbying, or efforts which give the groups "leverage" (Hardin 1982). Indeed, the pluralist political system might be seen as the method by which groups are given leverage via governmental action,[18] which brings us to a final point.

Environmentalists are unlikely to (and, as far as we have been able to tell, do not) favor marketable permits as an instrument of environmental policy. The reasons for this position range from ethical objections (e.g., see Kelman 1981) to a realization that they will be relatively disadvantaged by the change in regulatory agenda occasioned by a switch to marketable permits. Thus, while regulatory decisions and actions will continue to be made under a permit system, the matters decided will, we believe, tend to be of a more technical and less obviously important nature, so that environmental groups will have difficulty mobilizing support on any one of them and may find themselves on the wrong side of a tyranny-of-small-decisions problem.

CONCLUDING REMARKS

On the basis of the above considerations, we feel that the debate about the danger of environmentalists and a marketable permit system is largely an academic curiosum because:

1. A fully marketable permit is unlikely to be the instrument our society chooses to use in controlling air quality.

2. If such an instrument is chosen and environmentalists are allowed to buy and retire rights, no conclusions about the efficiency of the resulting air quality levels will be possible. We shall at most be able to conclude that expanding the set of mechanisms open for preference registration changes the observed public choice.

3. It is, moreover, unlikely that environmental groups will be able to mobilize enough money to significantly affect air quality (or industrial development) except perhaps in a very unusual situation. Certainly it would be surprising to find that

environmentalists could block development of any natural resource
deposit -- a special concern voiced in some contributions to the
debate.

FOOTNOTES

1    But see Rose-Ackerman (1973), who argues that if the quantity of
     permits is set at an optimal level, any group making further
     purchases to effect the quality of the environment would be
     engaging in "undesirable" activity.

2    A number of analysts have argued the various sides of this
     issue.  See Peskin (1978), for example, or Baumol and Oates
     (1979), who present material in support of the position that, in
     terms of cost-benefit analysis we probably have "over-
     regulated."  But other analysts and certainly environmentalists
     disagree (e.g., see Ophuls 1977).

3    This assumes some sort of independence of the issues in the eyes,
     or minds, of the voters, so that the median is an equilibrium.
     (See Black and Newing 1951.)

4    Here it must be noted that by making the model more realistic
     (i.e., by pointing out that the regulator is likely to filter the
     political inputs and respond to intense interests such as
     expressed by environmentalists and business interests), the
     conclusions of the logic would be modified.  For example, in a
     review Graff (1979, p. 283, fn.) writes that "bureaucrats ... are
     increasingly responding ... to the more general public outcry,
     often cynically manipulated by special interests anxious to avoid
     regulation, against big government."  Note that -- whatever the
     predicted choice would be under a model developed on these lines
     if the regulators also responded to the voters as we assume --
     the above analysis, or some suitable substitute, would be
     relevant.  The policy outcome would be the result of these two
     tendencies.

5    In this context, the term "marginal" takes on a somewhat new
     interpretation.  From the point of view of the voters on a
     particular motion, the unit of change is the content of the
     motion itself.  Thus, instead of a continuous function, they are
     faced with a step.  In addition, one marginal unit is not likely
     to have the same size and may not even be measured in the same
     dimensions as another.  But for the regulator, marginal benefits
     and costs relate to the stringency of the regulations and are the
     sum of the impacts of the possible marginal changes on the
     individuals.

6    This is the case in real-world income distributions.  It is easy
     to see why:  Income is "truncated" at the low end, and indeed
     there are very few persons with very low income.  But on the high
     end there is no fixed "top."  And the high-income individuals
     bring up the average.  In the U.S., the median family income in

1974 was $12,836, while mean family income for the same year was $14,502.

7    Under these circumstances, the minority that finds the program a burden often gets its way and reduces the program by combining with minorities on other issues and forming a logrolling coalition. See Oppenheimer (1975), or Frohlilch and Oppenheimer (1978), for a discussion of the properties of logrolls.

8    Note that this is also a situation that is amenable to logrolling (this time by the supporters, rather than the opponents, of program expansion.)

9    Note, however, that the possibility of multi-issue coalitions, or logrolling, raises further serious questions about actual outcomes even in these cases.

10   However, it should be noted that in reality the distribution of costs and benefits are a stochastic, or statistical, function of income, and therefore individuals may in fact have costs greater than the mean even when they have income lower than the mean and the tax system is progressive. We do not address such complications in this paper.

11   When substitute rights cannot be bought by polluters in other "airsheds" or ecosystems, such actions may be likened to purchase of industrial or commercial land by individuals who do not like urban sprawl. Those purchases would primarily effect the local neighborhoods, and groups usually would find similar results are obtainable more efficiently via pressures for zoning changes. Thus, such market actions may be quite unlikely. But in any case, we will pursue this question in the next section of this paper.

12   In the U.S., a <u>maximum</u> estimate of overall membership in environmental groups is two million individuals. Thus, for the U.S., the maximum value we would expect for $S_j$ would be about .01.

13   This conclusion is a straightforward derivation from the characteristics of the social optimum, as long as the environmental cleanup is positively valued by everyone. At the optimum, the total society's marginal benefit does not outweight the marginal costs. Thus there is no subgroup for whom the benefits outweigh the costs of making the purchase. We are not saying that such purchases could never be made. Obviously, for example, in the real world some groups find cleanup to be of negative value. Also, purchases could be made in spite of the interests of the members of the group, for example, by an exploitative leader of the group. Another way they could occur would be as a means to generate a negative externality, such as a restraint of trade to limit competition. Indeed, such manipulation of environmental regulations to decrease industrial competition seems to be one of the interesting stories Hassler and Ackerman (1981) have to tell.

[14]   Implicitly, it appears that Ryan and Teitenberg are assuming that
       these permits will in fact be cheap relative to other inputs to
       the offending production processes. Otherwise, we would expect
       them to be concerned about the possibility that the environmental
       groups would buy and retire land or water rights or some other
       key factor of production. It may be that at certain times and in
       certain places, bargains would be available in permits due to
       imperfect foresight, capital rationing or some other inconvenient
       attribute of reality. But to think that these bargains would
       fall to crafty environmentalists is to give the groups more
       credit in that area of skill than they would claim. On the other
       hand, coalitions of environmentalists and industrialists eager to
       restrain trade could occur (see fn. 13).

[15]   More specifically, they estimate the annual cost to achieve a
       level of pollution that would be in violation of California
       sulfate standards only 3-5% of the time at about $2,720/ton and
       that there would have to be a 34,405-ton annual decrease in
       emissions. Actually, to achieve the standards would cost
       approximately an extra $150 million. (All figures in 1977
       dollars and assume that there is a "low" natural gas supply. If
       natural gas is plentiful and can be utilized more fully in the
       generation of electric power, then the costs are considerably
       lower: $27.9 million and $69 million, respectively.) (See Hahn
       and Noll 1981, Tables 1 and 2.

[16]   Here the improvement costs were a function of the assumed
       temperature and flow regime in the river. These costs are for
       low flow and high temperature and are thus on the high end. The
       dollars are not identified with a particular year by the authors.

[17]   An aside: It could be that the above discussion focuses too much
       on the large, national public interest groups. Local special
       interest groups (such as anglers' associations) may be more
       likely to purchase discharge permits. This would especially be
       likely for smaller bodies of water where a few such purchases
       could make a substantial difference at a local site.

[18]   Note that this is in keeping with works on logrolling by Tullock
       (1968, chaps. 3-4), Oppenheimer (1975) and Bernholz (1973).

BIBLIOGRAPHY

Anderman, T. 1982. Memorandum to Finance, Executive and Development
     Committees. New York: Environmental Defense Fund.

Anderson, R.J., Jr.; Reid, R.O., and Seskin, E.P. 1979. An Analysis
     of Alternative Policies for Attaining and Maintaining a Short-
     term $NO^2$ Standard. Princeton: Mathtech, Inc.

Arrow, K. 1963. Social Choice and Individual Values, 2nd ed.
     New York: Wiley.

Baumol, W.J., and Oates, W.S.  1979.  Economics, Environmental Policy
    and the Quality of Life.  Englewood Cliffs, N.J.: Prentice Hall.

Bernholz, P.  1973.  Logrolling, Arrow's paradox and cyclic majorities.
    Public Choice, 16(Summer):87-102.

Black, Duncan.  1958.  The Theory of Committees and Elections.
    Cambridge, England: Cambridge University Press.

Black, D., and Newing, R.A.  1951.  Committee Decisions with
    Complementary Valuations.  London: Wm. Hodge.

Farquharson, R.  1969.  Theory of Voicing.  New Haven: Yale University
    Press.

Frohlich, N., and Oppenheimer, J.  1978.  Modern Political Economy.
    Englewood Cliffs, N.J.:  Prentice Hall.

Graff, Thomas J.  1979.  Stewart and Krier:  environmental law and
    public policy (a book review).  Harvard Law Review 93(1):282-89.

Hahn, R., and Noll, R.  1981.  Implementing tradable emissions permits.
    A paper prepared for Conference on Reforming Government Regula-
    tions, April 1981, Duke University.

Hardin, R.  1982.  Collective Action.  Baltimore: John Hopkins Press
    (for Resources for the Future).

Hassler, W.T., and Ackerman, B.A.  1981.  Clean Coal -- Dirty Air.
    New Haven, Conn.: Yale University Press.

Kelman, S.  1981.  What Price Incentives.  Boston:  Auburn House.

National Wildlife Foundation.  1980.  Annual Report.  Washington: NWF.

Natural Resources Defense Council.  Ten-Year Report 1970-80.
    Washington: NRDC.

Nature Conservancy.  1979.  Annual Report.  Alexandria, Va.: NC.

Olson, Mancur, Jr.  1965.  The Logic of Collective Action.
    Cambridge, Mass: Harvard University Press.

O'Neil, W.; David, M.; Moore, C., and Joeres, E.  1981.  Transferable
    discharge  permits  and  economic  efficiency.   Social  Systems
    Research Institute Workshop Series 8107, May 1981, Madison, Wis.

Ophuls, W.  1977.  Ecology and the Politics of Scarcity.
    San Francisco: W.H. Freeman.

Oppenheimer, J.A.  1975.  Some political implications of vote trading
    and  the  voting  paradox.   American  Political  Science  Review
    69(3):963-66.

Peskin, H.M.   1978.   Resources for the future.   IN: U.S. Environmental
    Policy, Paul R. Portney, ed.   Baltimore: John Hopkins Press (for
    Resources for the Future).

Romer, T., and Rosenthal, H.   1978.   Political resource allocation,
    controlled agendas and the status quo.   Public Choice 33(4):27-43.

Rose-Ackerman, S.   1973.   Effluent charges: A critique.
    Canadian Journal of Economics 6:512-28.

Ryan, D.R.   1981.   Transferable discharge permits and the control of
    stationary source air pollution: a survey and synthesis (comment).
    Land Economics 57(4):639-41.

Schwartz, T.   1981.   The universal instability theorem.
    Public Choice 37(3):487-501.

Sen, A.K.   1970.   Collective Choice and Social Welfare.
    San Francisco:   Holden Day.

Shepsle, K.   1979.   Institutional arrangements and equilibrium in
    multidimensional voting models.   Am. Journal of Pol. Sci.
    23:27-59.

Shepsle, K., and Weingast, B.   1981.   Structure-induced equilibrium
    and legislative choice.   Public Choice 37(2):503-20.

Sierra Club.   1981.   Sierra club financial report.   Sierra 66(2):46-49.

Tideman, T.N., ed.   1977.   Public Choice 29(Special supplement to the
    spring volume).

Tietenberg, T.H.   1980.   Transferable discharge permits and the
    control of stationary source air pollution: A survey and
    synthesis.   Land Economics 56(4):391-416.

Tietenberg, T.H.   1981.   Transferable discharge permits and the
    control of stationary source air pollution: A survey and
    synthesis: Reply.   Land Economics 57(4):641-44.

Tucker, W.   1981.   Marketing Pollution.   Harper's (May 1981):31-38.

Tullock, G.   1968.   Toward a Mathematics of Politics.
    Ann Arbor, Mich.: University of Michigan Press.

Ward, B.   1961.   Majority rule and allocation.
    Journal of Conflict Resolution 5(4):380-89.

# The Social Value of Tradable Permits:
# The Application of an Asset Utilization Model

**John J. Boland**

**Dept. of Geography & Environmental Engineering**
**The Johns Hopkins University**

The use of the environment as a waste sink, and the short-term and long-term consequences of this, has been a major focus of public policy development for several decades. In the U.S., the states and the federal government have revised priorities and reallocated responsibilities repeatedly since the late 1950s. Much attention has been given to this problem, and there has been no lack of study or experimentation with policies and institutions. Yet, even today, few would suggest that environmental policy is satisfactory, much less optimal.

Public policy with respect to waste discharge has at least three tasks: it must determine, directly or indirectly, (1) the total quantity of waste to be discharged at a given place and time, (2) the allocation of that discharge among the various agents that seek to dispose of their wastes, and (3) the costs to be borne by waste-discharging agents in complying with the public policy. The transferable discharge permit (TDP) has been proposed as a means of improving the performance of tasks 2 and 3: given any permissible discharge pattern (defined by task 1), TDPs improve the equity with which discharge rights are allocated while reducing the total cost of compliance (Eheart et al. 1981). Furthermore, TDPs provide, in some repsects, a more effective means of achieving the level of environmental quality that the target aggregate discharge is intended to represent (Brill et al. 1981).

As interest grows in developing practical policies based on the use of TDPs, some authors have addressed the need for efficient TDP market institutions (e.g., Eheart et al. 1981; Kshirsager and Eheart 1982; Montgomery 1972). Once the initial endowment of TDPs is complete, these markets are driven by differentials in the costs of complying with permit conditions. The benefits of compliance, which are the avoided costs of environmental degradation, are not known nor considered. In principle, avoided environmental costs should be instrumental in determining the initial endowment of permits and their distribution. In practice, however, substantial empirical diffi-culties may preclude quantitative estimates of abatement benefits. A major virtue of the TDP alternative, in fact, is that it promises some measure of efficiency in the absence of benefit measurements.

The purpose of this paper is to present an approach to the measurement of the social benefit of waste discharge abatement, an approach which may be useful in conjunction with TDP-based environmental policy. The approach is based on an asset-utilization model of the environment. The next section discusses reasons for choosing this type of model; the model itself is presented in the following section. A numerical example is provided to illustrate the application of this approach to a water quality problem.


SOCIAL VALUE MEASUREMENT

Any waste-discharging activity has the ability, through environmental linkages, to create costs that accrue to other users of the environment. Since there is no market in general for the services of the environment, and since these services range from privated goods (e.g., water supply) to pure public goods (e.g., visual amenity), there is little hope for a market solution to this problem. Similarly, there are few, if any, market measures of the costs imposed. Meanwhile, external environmental costs are generally believed responsible for substantial inefficiency in the allocation of goods and services throughout the economy. Waste discharges also have important equity consequences, as they may impose costs on participants in unrelated activities at different times and places.

In developing an optimal waste discharge policy, it would be desirable to know the magnitude of the external cost avoided for each increment of waste discharge abated. The avoided external costs are the benefits to other users of the environment, which are to be balanced against the private cost of abatement.

Mohring and Boyd (1971) suggest two distinct approaches to the identification and measurement of external (social) costs. The first of these, the direct interaction approach, requires attention to each environmental linkage and economic relationship that may tie a particular waste discharge to other users of the environment. This approach is exemplified by the use of externality models, or by conventional cost-benefit analysis. Many problems arise, however: the linkages and relationships are complex; an affected "party" may consist of many individuals; affected parties may overlap (the same individuals may be affected in more than one way by the same waste discharge); no data are available in many cases; relatively few effects are measurable in monetary terms, others are measurable only on a variety of dissimlar scales, and still others are not measurable at all (are entirely intangible).

The alternative approach, using an asset utilization model, addresses the same problems with the same data, but from a different perspective. The environment is viewed as an asset-like resource capable of sustaining many different service flows. The service flows are interactive, in that the use of one affects the availability or quality of others. Society's objective is taken as the maximization of some measure of satisfaction received from the environment as a whole. The social value associated with a change in the use of a resource service, then, is defined as the corresponding change in the optimal value of the objective function.

The asset utilization approach, while retaining many of the disadvantages of the direct interaction appraoch (e.g., complexity, lack of data, noncommensurability) offers comprehensiveness and logical consistency. As noted by Haveman and Kneese (1970), the asset utilization method seems "to go more directly to the heart of the problem of optimizing the use of common property resources and is also more readily adaptable to the analysis of many different users."

The major obstacles to the application of this method are associated with the nature of the services provided by the environment, services which are usually not readily described in monetary terms and may not be measurable in any terms. The specific technique presented here attempts to minimize these problems by transforming most variables into dimensionless relative rates of change. This reduces dependence on scales and measurements, and permits social values to be (at least) approximated in many cases.


AN ASSET UTILIZATION MODEL

The social value measurement technique described here is adapted from one originally developed and applied in the analysis of power plant siting decisions (Boland et al. 1974; Boland 1979). The original model is much more extensive in its treatment of resource services, economic activities, spatial locations and time periods.

In this paper, however, a simplified application is presented: the environmental resource is defined as a single river or stream (together with related shorelands), divided into two zones (spatial locations). A single year is considered, divided into two seasons: spring-early summer and later summer-fall. Finally, the stream is assumed to provide three types of resource service, which are utilized in three distinct types of human activity (see Figure 1).


ENVIRONMENTAL RESOURCE SERVICES

An environmental resource is a natural asset capable of supporting a number of resource service flows. The resource is defined by its services; its value is derived from the services. When the use of one resource service is increased (e.g., increased waste discharge), the impacts on all other service flows, concurrent and subsequent, must be evaluated. If these impacts result in a loss in value that exceeds the gain associated with the increased use, the environmental resource become less valuable as a result.

In the present example, three types of resource service are considered:

    1. Harvestable fish population;
    2. Visual amenity; and
    3. Waterborne waste assimilation.

Each service is offered at each of two locations (zones 1 and 2), and during each of two time periods, resulting in 12 distinct resource services.

In the case of harvestable fish and waterborne waste, it may be helpful to think of a single fish species, and a single type of waste (e.g., BOD). Additional resource services could be defined for other fish species or waste types, if necessary.

Each specific resource service (defined by type, place and time period) is assumed to be available in finite supply. The quantity of supply, or maximum availability, of a resource service may result from the physical nature of the service, from regulatory constraints, or from any other factor that is not subject to change by service users. For example, the supply of harvestable fish is simply the number of fish of harvestable size existing in a given zone of the river at a given time. The number that <u>will</u> be harvested, which is the level of <u>use</u> of the resource service, is determined by the number of fishermen and the effort they expend. The number that <u>can</u> be harvested, or <u>supply</u>, is the number of fish present.

The visual amenity resource service presents a different sort of problem. Since visual amenity is collectively rather than competitively consumed, the notion of maximum available supply has less significance. The major impact of conflicting resource service uses is to modify the character, rather than the quantity, of visual amenity. For purposes of consistency, it is assumed that a maximum quantity (fixed supply) exists, but in later application that supply is assumed to be always fully utilized. In this way, impacts of competing uses are limited to qualitative effects.

The supply of waste assimilation services, in this example, is assumed to be constrained by regulation. The maximum discharge of the selected contaminant at a particular place and time is specified by the relevant public body and is not subject to modification by waste dischargers. In the case of policies utilizing TDPs, the supply of waste assimilation service is the sum of the TDPs issued for that location and time period.

Resource services are inputs to human activities of various kinds. In this example, three types of activity are included:

1.  Recreational fishing;
2.  Passive recreation; and
3.  Manufacturing.

As in the case of resource services, each activity can occur in each of the zones and during each time period, giving a total of 12 distinct activities. Also, each activity is assumed internally homogeneous (all fishing activities are similar, all manufacturing activities are similar, etc.).

Passive recreation is included to represent the satisfaction individuals may derive directly from the qualities of the environment; it is not based on physical participation in environment-based activities

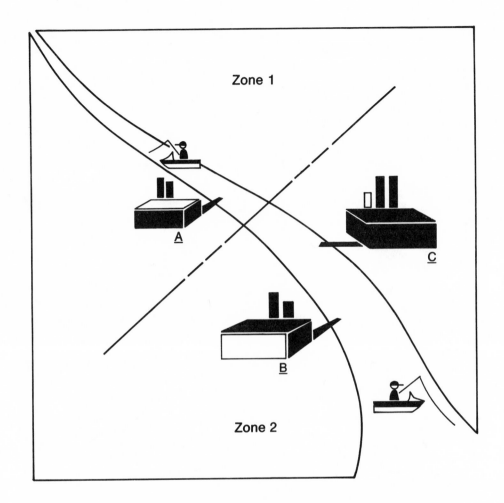

FIGURE 1
Environmental Resource:
Single Stream Example with Three Services

(fishing, boating, hunting, etc.). This type of passive activity can include, in principle, appreciation of aesthetic aspects of the environment (visual amenity), satisfaction derived from knowledge of environmental quality improvements, or a general desire for responsible environmental management.

THE MODEL

Generally speaking, the objective is to maximize the present value of all goods and services produced by activities that utilize services of the environment, net of the social opportunity cost of other inputs. This residual value is attributed to the use of the unpriced environmental services. In the present application, all activities occur within a single year, so the present value operator is omitted.

The objective function is stated as:

$$\text{Maximize: } \sum_{i=1}^{3} \sum_{s=1}^{2} \sum_{t=1}^{2} [Z_{i,s,t}(Q_{i,s,t}) - Y_{i,s,t}(X_{i,s,t})] \tag{1}$$

Where:   $Z_{i,s,t}$   = Social value of output of activity $\underline{i}$ in zone $\underline{s}$ during time period $\underline{t}$, expressed as a function of $Q_{i,s,t}$.

$Q_{i,s,t}$   = Physical measure of quantity of output of activity $\underline{i}$ in zone $\underline{s}$ during time period $\underline{t}$.

$Y_{i,s,t}$   = Social opportunity cost of other (non-environmental) inputs to activity $\underline{i}$ in zone $\underline{s}$ during time period $\underline{t}$ expressed as a function of $X_{i,s,t}$.

$X_{i,s,t}$   = Quantity of other inputs used by activity $\underline{i}$ in zone $\underline{s}$ during time period $\underline{t}$.

Maximizing the value of the objective function represents an improvement in social welfare from the standpoint of efficiency considerations alone. No equity objective is included in this model.

Three types of constraints are necessary to complete the model. First of all, the quantity of goods or services produced by each activity must be constrained by the production function for that activity. Second, the total use of each environmental resource service must be constrained by the available supply of that service, which in turn is a function of the use of related resource services. Finally, the total use of each resource service is defined as the sum of uses by individual activities.

The constraint sets follow, each defined over all $\underline{i}$, $\underline{s}$, $\underline{t}$, and $\underline{y}$:

$$Q_{i,s,t} = Q_{i,s,t}(R_{i,s,t,1}, R_{i,s,t,2}, R_{i,s,t,3}; X_{i,s,t}) \tag{2}$$

$$T_{s,t,y} \leq S_{s,t,y}(T_{p,j,g} \mid [p,j,g] \neq [s,t,y]; j \geq t) \tag{3}$$

$$T_{s,t,y} = R_{1,s,t,y} + R_{2,s,t,y} + R_{3,s,t,y} \tag{4}$$

Where:   $p = 1,2$;        $j = 1,2$;        $g = 1,2,3$

$R_{i,s,t,y}$   = Use of resource service $\underline{y}$ by activity $\underline{i}$ in zone $\underline{s}$ during time period $\underline{t}$.

$T_{s,t,y}$   = Total use of resource service $\underline{y}$ by all activities in zone $\underline{s}$ during time period $\underline{t}$.

$S_{s,t,y}$ = Maximum available supply of resource service $\underline{y}$ in zone $\underline{s}$ during time period $\underline{t}$, expressed as a function of the levels of use of other resource services (the argument list consists of all other resource services whose subscripts meet the conditions shown above).

Following suitable nonnegativity and nonzero assumptions, the method of Kuhn and Tucker is used to solve the constrained maximization problem. The first order conditions include the familiar results of welfare economics, which state that the value of the marginal physical product of each priced input is equal, at optimality, to its marginal social cost. In the case of environmental resource services, however, no prices or other exogenous opportunity costs apply. They are, therefore, imputed by the model.

The first order conditions applicable to resource services have the following form:

$$\frac{\partial Z_{i,s,t}}{\partial Q_{i,s,t}} \cdot \frac{\partial Q_{i,s,t}}{\partial R_{i,s,t,y}} = \mu_{s,t,y} -$$

$$\sum_{p=1}^{2} \sum_{j=t}^{2} \sum_{g=1}^{3} \left[ \frac{\partial S_{p,j,g}}{\partial T_{s,t,y}} \, \mu_{p,j,g} \right] \tag{5}$$

$$[p,j,g,] \neq [s,t,y]$$

Where: $\mu_{s,t,y}$ = Kuhn-Tucker variable associated with the supply of resource service $\underline{y}$ in zone $\underline{s}$ during time period $\underline{t}$.

Note that the Kuhn-Tucker variable is the shadow price for the associated resource service. Condition 5 states that the social value of the marginal physical product of each resource service (left-hand side) must equal a composite shadow price comprised of the shadow price of the resource service in question plus a weighted sum of all other resource service shadow prices (right-hand side).

Since the right side of Condition 5 is identical for all activities (over all $\underline{i}$), value represented by the left side must be equal for all activities. Without loss of generality, however, Condition 5 can be weighted (by resource service use) and summed over $\underline{i}$, yielding:

$$\frac{1}{T_{s,t,y}} \sum_{i=1}^{3} \left[ \frac{\partial Z_{i,s,t}}{\partial Q_{i,s,t}} \cdot \frac{\partial Q_{i,s,t,}}{\partial R_{i,s,t,y}} \, R_{i,s,t,y} \right] =$$

$$\mu_{s,t,y} - \sum_{p=1}^{2} \sum_{j=t}^{2} \sum_{g=1}^{3} \left[ \frac{\partial S_{p,j,g}}{\partial T_{s,t,y}} \, \mu_{p,j,g} \right] \tag{6}$$

$$[p,j,g] \neq [s,t,y]$$

This expression states that the weighted average social value of the marginal physical products of a resource service must be equal to the composite shadow price. Condition 6, therefore, represents the marginal conditions for optimal allocation of environmental resource services, assuming an otherwise well-functioning economy.


SOCIAL VALUE MEASUREMENT

While environmental resource services, as a class of economic good, do not lend themselves to the use of a price system for allocative purposes, the constructs and language of price theory are helpful in understanding fundamental relationships.

The left-hand side of Condition 6, for example, can be seen to represent the marginal benefit received by the average (or marginal) user of the resource service, while the right-hand side is the marginal social cost of that use. The relationship shown is of little practical significance, however, since it includes resource service use variables that may be difficult or impossible to measure, as well as unknown shadow prices.

Accordingly, the following variable transformations are made:

$$\mu_{s,t,y} = \frac{\pi_{s,t,y}}{T_{s,t,y}} \tag{7}$$

$$\frac{\partial Q_{i,s,t}}{\partial R_{i,s,t,y}} = n(Q_{i,s,t} \mid R_{i,s,t,y}) \frac{\partial Q_{i,s,t}}{R_{i,s,t,y}} \tag{8}$$

$$\frac{\partial S_{p,j,g}}{\partial T_{s,t,y}} = n(S_{p,j,g} \mid T_{s,t,y}) \frac{S_{p,j,g}}{T_{s,t,y}} \tag{9}$$

$$U_{p,j,g} = \frac{T_{p,j,g}}{S_{p,j,g}} \tag{10}$$

Where:  

$\pi_{s,t,y}$ = Product of shadow price of resource service $\underline{y}$ in zone $\underline{s}$ during time period $\underline{t}$ and corresponding total use of that resource service.

$n(Q_{i,s,t} \mid R_{i,s,t,y})$ = Elasticity of output of activity with respect to use of resource service.

$n(S_{p,j,g} \mid T_{s,t,y})$ = Elasticity of the supply of one resource service with respect to total use of another.

$U_{p,j,g}$ = Fraction of supply of a resource service used by all activities.

After substitution of (7), (8), (9) and (10) into (6), and some manipulation, the result can be stated in matrix notation as:

$$[V] = [E] * [II] \tag{11}$$

Where:   [V] = Vector of economic variables, which are:

$$v_{s,t,y} = \sum_{i=1}^{3} \left[ \frac{\partial Z_{is,t}}{\partial Q_{i,s,t}} \, \eta Q_{i,s,t}(Q_{i,s,t} | R_{i,s,t,y}) \right]$$

[E] = Matrix of environmental variables, which are:

$$e_{p,j,g;s,t,y} = \frac{\eta(S_{p,j,g} | T_{s,t,y})}{U_{p,j,g}}, \quad \text{or}$$

$$e_{s,t,y;s,t,y} = +1$$

[II] = Vector of shadow price-quantity products, which are:

$$\pi_{s,t,y}$$

The total external cost associated with a given pattern of resource service use, exclusive of any wholly inframarginal costs, can be given as:

$$TC = \sum_{s=1}^{2} \sum_{t=1}^{2} \sum_{y=1}^{3} (v_{s,t,y} - \pi_{s,t,y}) \tag{12}$$

Where:   TC = Total Pareto-relevant external cost.

This total cost can be decomposed in various ways to examine both the incidence and the source of external cost. One vector of costs, $[C_1]$, indicates costs imposed by users of individual resource services. Another vector $[C_2]$, reveals the costs imposed on users of individual resource services. These vectors are calculated as follows:

$$[C_1] = [1_r] * \left[ [E] - [I] \right] * [E]^{-1} * [V] \tag{13}$$

$$[C_2] = [V] - \left[ [E]^{-1} * [V] \right] \tag{14}$$

Where:   $[C_1]$   =   Column vector of costs imposed by resource service users.

$[C_2]$   =   Column vector of costs imposed on resource service users.

$[1_r]$   =   Unit row vector.

$[I]$   =   Identity matrix.

$[E]^{-1}$   =   Inverse of $[E]$.

The external social cost associated with the use of any particular
resource service, therefore, is equal to the corresponding element of
vector $[C_1]$. In the case of waste assimilation regulated by TDPs,
the corresponding element gives the social value of all TDPs issued
for a particular zone and time period.


AN ILLUSTRATION

Application of the measurement technique described here can be
illustrated for the resource configuration shown on Figure 1. As
noted earlier, three resource services are available in each of two
zones and two time periods. Also, three resource service-using
activities occur in each zone and time period. It is assumed that
TDPs have been issued to three manufacturing firms: Firm A is
permitted to discharge 500 pounds per day of BOD, Firm B is permitted
1,500 pounds per day and Firm C is permitted 1,000 pounds per day.

The data needed to estimate vector $[V]$ are obtained by analysis of the
resource-using activities and are shown as Table 1 together with the
resulting vector. Studies of the river and its ability to support
various uses lead to estimates of the variables needed to determine
matrix $[E]$, shown as Table 2. The resulting total cost vectors appear
on Table 3.

Referring to the cost vector $[C_1]$, it can be seen that the social
costs imposed by Firm A are $182,500 during time period 1 and $152,000
during time period 2. The combined social costs imposed by firms B
and C are $593,850 during time period 1 and $274,950 during time
period 2. It can also be seen from vector $[C_2]$ that Firms B and C
bear social costs as well as impose them. This is a result of
upstream (zone 1) discharges by Firm A, which reduce the maximum
permissible discharge in zone 2.

The combined costs imposed by firms B and C may be assigned proportionate to the permitted TDP quantities. For example, Firm B holds a
permit for 60 percent of the total zone discharge and may be assigned
60 percent of the social costs: $356,310 in time period 1 and
$164,970 in time period 2. The social costs may also be stated on a
per-unit-discharge basis: for example, $237.54 per pound of BOD per
day in zone 1, time period 1.


CONCLUSIONS

Social costs associated with specific uses of environmental resource
services can be identified by means of an asset utilization model of a
defined resource. The technique presented here does not require
direct measurement of any resource service. Instead, all values are
imputed from observable economic activities and from dimensionless
descriptors of environmental relationships.

The results can be used to value TDPs for the purpose of initial
distribution. They can also be used to determine the efficiency and

TABLE 1
Economic Variables

| Activity | Zone | Time | $\frac{\partial Z_{i,s,t}}{\partial Q_{i,s,t}}$ | $Q_{i,s,t}$ | $\eta(Q_{i,s,t} \mid R_{i,s,t,y})$ 1 | 2 | 3 |
|----------|------|------|------|------|------|------|------|
| Fishing | 1 | 1 | 20 | 4,000 | +0.5 | +0.1 | -0- |
|  |  | 2 | 30 | 5,000 | +0.5 | +0.1 | -0- |
|  | 2 | 1 | 25 | 2,000 | +0.6 | +0.1 | -0- |
|  |  | 2 | 30 | 4,000 | -0- | +0.6 | -0- |
| Passive | 1 | 1 | 15 | 3,000 | -0- | +0.6 | -0- |
| Recreation |  | 2 | 18 | 5,000 | -0- | +0.6 | -0- |
|  | 2 | 1 | 12 | 500 | -0- | +0.5 | -0- |
|  |  | 2 | 15 | 1,000 | -0- | +0.5 | -0- |
| Manufact- | 1 | 1 | 5 | 20,000 | -0- | -0- | +0.9 |
| uring |  | 2 | 5 | 20,000 | -0- | -0- | +0.9 |
|  | 2 | 1 | 5 | 100,000 | -0- | -0- | +0.9 |
|  |  | 2 | 5 | 80,000 | -0- | -0- | +0.9 |

| Resource Service | [V] Zone 1 Time 1 | Time 2 | Zone 2 Time 1 | Time 2 |
|------------------|--------|--------|--------|--------|
| Harvestable Fish | 40,000 | 75,000 | 30,000 | 72,000 |
| Visual Amenity | 35,000 | 69,000 | 8,000 | 19,500 |
| Waste Assimilation | 90,000 | 90,000 | 450,000 | 360,000 |

equity of proposed TDP market institutions. The proposed method is unique because (1) it provides a comprehensive framework within which all competing uses of a resource may be considered and (2) results are readily decomposed to the level of specific classes of waste discharges at specific locations and during defined time periods.

A previous application of the method (Boland 1979) included data collection for a large water resource, divided into eight locations, that was assumed to support 22 classes of resource service during each of seven time periods, providing inputs for 25 classes of economic

TABLE 2
Environmental Variables

$\eta(s_{p,j,g} \mid T_{s,t,y})$

**[η block]**

| Zone | Time | Service | | | | | | | | | | | $u_{p,j,g}$ |
|------|------|---------|---|---|---|---|---|---|---|---|---|---|---|---|
| 1 | 1 | 1 | -0.50 | | | | | | | -0.10 | | | 0.40 |
| 1 | 2 | 1 | -0.20 | 0.20 | | | | | | -0.08 | -0.10 | | 0.45 |
| 2 | 1 | 1 | -0.15 | | 0.50 | | | | 0.15 | -0.08 | | | 0.20 |
| 2 | 2 | 1 | | | | | | | -0.10 | -0.06 | -0.08 | -0.15 | 0.30 |
| 1 | 1 | 2 | | | | | | | | -0.20 | -0.35 | | 1.00 |
| 1 | 2 | 2 | | | | | | | -0.10 | -0.15 | -0.15 | | 1.00 |
| 2 | 1 | 2 | | | | | | | -0.10 | -0.10 | -0.10 | -0.15 | 1.00 |
| 2 | 2 | 2 | | | | | | | -0.05 | -0.05 | -0.05 | | 1.00 |
| 1 | 1 | 3 | | | | | | | | | | | 0.60 |
| 1 | 2 | 3 | | | | | | | | -0.35 | | | 0.60 |
| 2 | 1 | 3 | | | | | | | | | -0.70 | | 1.00 |
| 2 | 2 | 3 | | | | | | | | | | | 1.00 |

**[E]**

| Zone | Time | Service | | | | | | | | | | |
|------|------|---------|---|---|---|---|---|---|---|---|---|---|
| 1 | 1 | 1 | +1.00 | | | | | | | -0.25 | | |
| 1 | 2 | 1 | -1.11 | +1.00 | | | | | | -0.18 | -0.22 | -0.75 |
| 2 | 1 | 1 | -1.00 | +1.00 | +1.00 | | | | | -0.40 | -0.27 | -0.33 |
| 2 | 2 | 1 | -0.50 | -0.67 | -0.67 | +1.00 | | | | -0.20 | -0.35 | -0.10 |
| 1 | 1 | 2 | | | | +1.00 | +1.00 | | | -0.20 | -0.15 | -0.05 |
| 1 | 2 | 2 | | | | | +1.00 | +1.00 | | -0.15 | | -0.50 |
| 2 | 1 | 2 | | | | | | +1.00 | +1.00 | -0.10 | -0.15 | -0.15 |
| 2 | 2 | 2 | | | | | | | +1.00 | -0.05 | -0.10 | |
| 1 | 1 | 3 | | | | | | | | +1.00 | -0.05 | +1.00 |
| 1 | 2 | 3 | | | | | | | | | +1.00 | |
| 2 | 1 | 3 | | | | | | | | -0.35 | -0.70 | |
| 2 | 2 | 3 | | | | | | | | | | +1.00 |

TABLE 3

Social Cost Vectors

| Zone | Time | Service | $[C_1]$ | $[C_2]$ |
|------|------|---------|---------|---------|
| 1 | 1 | 1 | 163,194 | 22,500 |
|   | 2 |   | 120,296 | 105,444 |
| 2 | 1 |   | 816,042 | 459,625 |
|   | 2 |   | -0- | 1,381,588 |
| 1 | 1 | 2 | -0- | 18,000 |
|   | 2 |   | -0- | 58,500 |
| 2 | 1 |   | -0- | 57,150 |
|   | 2 |   | -0- | 105,525 |
| 1 | 1 | 3 | 182,500 | -0- |
|   | 2 |   | 152,000 | -0- |
| 2 | 1 |   | 493,850 | 31,500 |
|   | 2 |   | 274,950 | 63,000 |
| Total Social Cost: | | | 2,302,832 | 2,302,832 |

activity. Data on the characteristics of the economic activities (needed to produce vector [V]) were obtained from government and private statistical sources, from existing forecasts of economic activity, and/or were estimated based on existing data and forecasts. Environmental data (used to generate matrix [E]) were comprised of subjective estimates contributed, for the most part, by environmental scientists working in the related areas. In some cases, such as fisheries, quantitative models could be developed, which would provide estimates of supply elasticities and utilization ratios.

As a result, estimates of the external costs associated with a particular pattern of water discharge, or a specified change in an existing pattern of discharge, can reflect all available data on competing uses of the environment, as well as the best current judgment of environmental scientists on the nature of narrowly defined, specific interactions among the services of the environment.

While the social benefits of pollution abatement may continue to be but imperfectly known, the technique described here offers distinct advantages over previous proposals, including the direct relevance of its results to the analysis of TDP policies and institutions.

162                                          BUYING A BETTER ENVIRONMENT

REFERENCES

Boland, J.J.  1979.  Economic Considerations in Power Plant Siting in
    the Chesapeake Bay Region, 2 vols., PPRP-31.  Annapolis, Md.:
    Maryland Power Plant Siting Program, Dept. of Natural Resources.

Boland, J.J.; Geyer, J.C., and Hanke, S.H.  1974.  Economic
    Considerations in Power Plant Siting in the Chesapeake Bay
    Region, PPRP-2.  Annapolis, Md.:  Maryland Power Plant Siting
    Program, Dept. of Natural Resources.

Brill, E.D. Jr.; Eheart, J.W.; Kshirsager, S.R., and Lence, B.J.  1981.
    Water Quality Impacts of Biochemical Oxygen Demand under
    Trasferable Discharge Permit Programs, Report No. 2.  Champaign-
    Urbana, Ill.:  Dept. of Civil Engineering & Institute for
    Environmental Studies, University of Illinois.

Eheart, J.W.; Brill, E.D., Jr.; and Lyon, R.M.  1981.  Methods for
    Evaluation and Assessment of Transferable Discharge Permits for
    Control of Biochemical Oxygen Demand, Report No. 3.  Champaign-
    Urbana, Ill.:  Dept. of Civil Engineering & Institute for
    Environmental Studies, University of Illinois.

Haveman, R.H., and Kneese, A.V.  1970.  Incentives and common property
    resources:  with emphasis on the case of water pollution.  A
    paper prepared for the Study Group on Public Expenditures, April
    23, 1970.  The Brookings Institution (unpublished).

Kshirsagar, S.R., and Eheart, J.W.  1982.  Grouped markets of
    transferable discharge permits for water quality management,
    working paper no. 4.  Champaign-Urbana, Ill.:  Dept. of Civil
    Engineering, University of Illinois.

Mohring, H., and Boyd, J.H.  1971.  Analyzing "externalities":
    "direct interactions" vs. "asset utilization" frameworks.
    Economica 38:347-61.

Montgomery, W.D.  1972.  Markets in licenses and efficient pollution
    control programs.  J. Econ. Theory 5:395-418.

# Transferable Discharge Permits for Control of BOD: An Overview

**J. Wayland Eheart and E. Downey Brill, Jr.**

**Randolph M. Lyon**

**Department of Civil Engineering**
**University of Illinois**

**Department of Economics**
**University of Texas**

## INTRODUCTION

Transferable discharge permits (TDPs) have been examined over the past 15 years as a policy for managing pollution discharges (e.g., see Dales 1968; USEPA 1980; Atkinson and Tietenberg 1982; Tietenberg 1974, 1980; David et al. 1980; Noll 1982; Oates 1981). Under this policy, rights to discharge pollutants, once issued by the authority, may be transferred among users as property rights. The principal advantage of this policy, it is usually felt, is that the pollution control strategy that evolves at market equilibrium will be more cost-efficient than under alternative strategies, such as the uniform direct-regulation approach of many current federal programs (which often require dischargers to undertake similar efforts at waste abatement). Allowing permit exchanges among dischargers offers the potential for improving environmental quality while lowering overall costs, and provides an incentive for the development and adoption of innovative waste-reduction practices.

There are several other advantages of TDP policies over alternative schemes of both the incentive and regulatory type. One is that they can achieve this cost-efficiency without placing an additional financial burden on the dischargers. In contrast, another incentive program -- effluent charges -- shares the cost-efficiency advantage of the TDP policy, but typically requires charge payments on the part of dischargers (see Brill 1972; Buchanan and Tullock 1975; Brill et al. 1979). These payments are significant and may even exceed the waste treatment costs.

A second advantage is that the TDP approach allows an authority to control the aggregate level of waste discharge directly. Direct regulation programs and other incentive programs, such as effluent charges, do not.

A third advantage of the TDP program is its ability to accommodate newcomers, who may enter the system simply by purchasing permits. In contrast, direct regulation programs might require the redefinition of existing permits, and effluent charge programs would require a revision in the charge value.  Accomplishing the latter could prove difficult, due to changes in waste production levels and economic conditions (e.g., relative prices or inflation).  Furthermore, too many revisions could lead to cost inefficiencies.

There are, however, several complications in implementing the TDP approach in situations where the impact of a given pollutant discharge depends on its location.  For example, consider a permit to discharge P pounds per day of biochemical oxygen demanding (BOD) waste at location X on a given river.  If the permit is sold and the discharge site changes to location Y, then the impact on the dissolved oxygen (DO) level in the river at a critical water quality location Z could change considerably because of differences in the time of flow and other stream parameters.  Thus, an unrestricted permit transfer or set of transfers in a more complex setting could cause a violation of a water quality standard for DO.  This problem is shared by some regulatory-type programs and effluent charge programs.  For example, it is often necessary to add special provisions, such as those for "water-quality limited" streams as described in the federal Water Pollution Control Act (PL 92-500).

A second potential problem -- which applies to TDP programs in general but does not apply to other regulatory approaches -- is that the market for rights may not distribute the permits optimally.  Certain types of sales or auction mechanisms may fail to allocate the permits so that the water quality standards are achieved efficiently.

This paper summarizes the findings of a recent study (see Eheart et al. 1982) of issues associated with the application of TDPs to the management of BOD discharges.  The findings of the study, however, also apply to many types of waterborne pollutants besides BOD and to some extent to air pollutants, especially where there are location-dependent environmental impacts.

The principal objective of the study was to develop methods of analyzing TDP programs using data that could feasibly be collected by a water pollution control agency or authority (hereafter referred to as "the authority").  It was assumed that such an authority would exist and would evaluate any waste discharge management program with respect to the following objectives: (1) cost-efficiency, (2) equity, (3) ease of implementation, (4) water quality maintenance and (5) certainty of outcome.  It was further assumed that the authority would be able to gather the data necessary to calibrate and verify an acceptably accurate water quality model, and that it would have the right to allocate permits and conduct auctions to distribute them.  Though waste treatment cost data were used in market simulations in this research, the TDP programs considered do not require such data, and the authority was assumed not to have access to them.

The following section provides a qualitative discussion of the tasks and decisions facing the authority in designing a TDP program, and it describes several fundamental tradeoffs.  As an example, consider the situation described above where a permit transfer would cause a violation of the water quality standard.  This problem can be prevented by careful choices concerning the total number of permits to be issued and the rules that govern their exchange. There are different combinations of choices, however, and they differ with respect to cost efficiency, equity and administrative ease. As another example, discharge permits may initially be given away by the authority, or they may be sold through some procedure such as an auction. Because they would not have to pay for permits, dischargers may prefer the free initial distribution approach. Others, however, may prefer an auction approach, because revenue is provided to the authority and because it is theoretically possible to design an auction that will prevent market manipulation by individual dischargers.

The third section provides an overview of the quantitative results of four hypothetical case studies for which alternative designs of a TDP program were examined. Published waste-removal cost data and receiving-body modeling data were used. The four cases are the Willamette River in Oregon; the Delaware River estuary in Pennsylvania, Delaware, and New Jersey; and the Upper Hudson and Mohawk rivers in New York. Costs of various TDP designs were estimated by simulating the permits market for steady-state conditions using the waste removal cost data. Aggregate income transfers that would result from sales of permits by the authority were also estimated. In the Willamette case, the effects of income transfers on the individual dischargers were examined as well. These results and comparisons with other regulatory approaches are discussed.

The third section also presents quantitative examples, using the case studies, of several different ways to prevent or to reduce the likelihood of violations of a given water quality standard. The different approaches considered are: limiting the number of permits, limiting the aggregate discharge in subregions of the watercourse, preventing transfers across geographical boundaries, revaluing the permits automatically and uniformly when exchanged, and using combinations of these approaches. In the accompanying discussion, the worst possible violation of the given water quality standard that could occur under a set of rules is presented. It is shown that the results vary considerably from case to case. Furthermore, it may be possible to specify the number of permits and the rules governing exchanges in a manner that: (1) allows most of the cost efficiency gains that are possible from an initial round of exchanges, (2) treats the dischargers in a uniform fashion, (3) ensures that a specified level of water quality will be maintained and (4) allows automatic exchanges of permits without detailed administrative reviews.


DESIGNING A T.D.P. PROGRAM: A QUALITATIVE OVERVIEW

A TDP program may be viewed as a set of rules, chosen by the authority, which govern the dischargers. Important choices facing the authority are: (1) the water quality goals to be pursued, (2) the basis of definition of the permits, (3) the procedures for allocating and exchanging them, (4) their duration, (5) the number of permits to

issue, (6) the geographic and other restrictions on their exchange and
(7) implementation and administration. The following subsections
provide a discussion of these and related issues, with particular
emphasis on rules governing initial distribution and market options.

## Water Quality Goals

One of the most important decisions the authority must make in
designing any water quality management program for a particular water
body is the form and stringency of the water quality goal. This goal
is assumed here to be expressed as follows. A set of receiving body
conditions is chosen which represents a low extreme of assimilative
capacity. These conditions -- usually represented, for a stream, by a
streamflow and water temperature -- are referred to as the critical
conditions. All of the authority's decisions regarding numbers of
permits to issue, transfer restrictions, etc., are assumed here to be
undertaken on the basis of these conditions. A given water quality
standard is assumed to be expressed as a requirement that the
concentration of dissolved oxygen (DO) in the water not fall below a
certain level (e.g., 5 mg/L) at any point in the river under the
assumed critical conditions. Under most waste management programs
there will be points in the river that just barely meet the DO
standard. These locations of minimum DO are referred to as critical
points. Such a standard is typical of those traditionally used for
water quality control. The choice of critical conditions implies an
acceptable risk that a particular water quality standard will be
violated. The choices of the standard and the program to achieve it
are interrelated. The discussion here focuses on the analysis of
alternative water quality control programs for achieving a given
standard. Such an analysis may be needed for each of the contemplated
alternative standards considered in an actual planning effort.

Once the critical conditions have been chosen, a mathematical model is
assumed to be available for use by the authority to relate the water
quality (here represented by DO concentration) at all points in the
receiving body to the waste discharge rates of each discharger (a BOD
mass flow rate). The model is assumed to be of sufficient accuracy
that it may be used to determine, in advance, whether or not a given
waste management program will meet water quality goals. (Note,
however, that the agency is assumed not to have waste removal cost
data for the dischargers and would not be able to predict the exact
outcomes of alternative TDP policies.) It is assumed here that the
discharge allowed by a permit is not directly tied to the changing
assimilative capacity of the watercourse over time. Therefore, once
market equilibrium is attained and a particular set of waste treatment
efforts is established, it is assumed that these treatment efforts do
not change with time in response to changing conditions in the
receiving body. (O'Neil [1980] and Moore [1980] have explored the use
of permits that are indexed to ambient conditions.)

## Basis of Definition of Permits

Another policy decision is the basis of definition of the permits.
The authority must state just what a permit entitles its holder to
do. Two definition bases are considered here. The first, called a
BOD permit, entitles the holder to discharge a certain mass of BOD per

day. This type of permit would be used in the emissions permit
systems (EPS) cited elsewhere in this monograph. The second type of
permit entitles a discharger to deplete the dissolved oxygen at a
specific location (hereafter referred to as the defining point) in the
watercourse by a certain amount (in mg/L), as predicted by the water
quality model for the critical conditions chosen. It is termed a DODC
(dissolved oxygen deficit contribution) permit and is, in the
terminology of this monograph, a type of ambient (environmental
quality) permit system (APS). A DODC permit corresponds to a BOD
permit of a certain size when held by a given discharger, but, unlike
the BOD permit, is revalued when transferred to another location, so
that the DO deficit contribution at the defining point remains the
same under the critical conditions.

DODC permits are defined on the basis of dischargers' impacts on
dissolved oxygen at the defining point, but this point may not
coincide with the critical DO point. While the water quality standard
will not be violated under design conditions at the point used to
define the permits, violations might occur elsewhere. In some water
bodies, the critical point may remain fixed in space regardless of the
movement of permits (i.e., shifts in the pattern of discharges), and
for such cases the DODC program will achieve a high level of cost
efficiency in attaining the DO standard. In other cases, however, a
DODC program based on a single defining point may entail shifts of BOD
loading such that some point other than the defining point is
critical. In these cases, both cost efficiency and the certainty of
maintaining DO standards suffer. Higher cost-efficiency in such cases
could possibly be attained through multiple DODC markets, where each
discharger would be required to own a portfolio of permits to degrade
the water quality at a number of defining points on the watercourse.
This procedure would be administratively cumbersome, however, and only
single-point DODC markets are considered here.

In addition to being difficult to define for rivers with multiple or
nonstationary critical points, DODC permits present a potential equity
problem. Specifically, some dischargers -- those with substantial
impact at the defining point -- would have to purchase very expensive
permits to discharge a unit of BOD, while others could cheaply
discharge the same amount. (This nonuniformity results because of the
different impacts these dischargers have on the DO level at the
critical point, and it has a direct analog under effluent charge
programs. To achieve the particular pattern of discharges that
minimizes regional cost for a given DO standard, nonuniform effluent
charges are required. Dischargers would pay different charge rates
per pound of BOD discharged, depending on their locations on the river
[see Brill et al. 1979]).

Procedures for Initial Distribution and Exchanges

There are two major approaches to the initial distribution of permits:
they may be given away, or they may be sold by the government. In the
first approach, the authority must decide the basis of distribution
(i.e., who is qualified to receive permits and how many each should
receive); in the second, it must choose the type of procedure for
initial distribution (e.g., an auction) and the disposition of the

revenue thus generated. In either case, it must decide the procedures for exchanges of permits among the dischargers once they have been issued.

When the basis of free distribution reflects the status quo, the procedure is referred to as "grandfathering" (e.g., see Palmer and Quinn 1982). In considering such procedures for initially distributing permits, Eheart et al. (1980) discuss four possible bases of distribution (see also Lyon 1981, pp. 142–43). Among these is an approach whereby a direct regulation program is assumed to be the alternative to a TDP program. A set of permits that duplicates the pattern of discharges that would occur under the direct regulation program is issued, and trading of permits is allowed. This approach may appeal to regulators and environmentalists as well. It can be argued that as long as the environmental standard is met (and it may, in fact, be exceeded), the net social benefit will increase because the total cost of pollution control will generally be lower. In the discussions presented here, grandfathering is assumed to be based on uniform percentage removal of BOD by each discharger (the uniform treatment policy) corresponding to a uniform direct-regulation program.

The two approaches, distribution without charge or by sales, have quite different equity properties because the aggregate income transfer under a sales approach would typically constitute a considerable portion of the total financial burden on the dischargers for their wastewater management. (Financial burden is defined as the sum of waste reduction costs and net income transfers from the dischargers as a group.)

Aggregate transfer payments have been identified as potential barriers to implementation of effluent charge programs (Brill 1972; Buchanan and Tullock 1975; and Brill et al. 1979). One important potential advantage of the TDP program over effluent charge programs is that under TDPs there is a relatively straightforward approach to reducing dischargers' financial burdens by an initial free distribution of rights. Lump-sum refunds of tax payments to dischargers would be required to accomplish a similar reduction of financial burden under an effluent charge policy. (The financial burden can also be reduced somewhat through the use of charge schedules where the unit charge for BOD would decline as the waste removal level increases [see Brill et al. 1979].)

TDP programs with free initial distribution may be regarded as possessing favorable between-discharger equity properties in comparison to direct regulation programs like uniform treatment, especially if the latter constitutes the basis for the free initial distribution. The only departures with TDPs from the direct regulation strategy would be voluntary ones, which would presumably improve the financial lot of both buyer and seller. The authority would have, however, the nontrivial problem of determining an equitable or politically acceptable initial distribution of TDPs. Distribution based on uniform treatment may be preferred because of legal precedent, but no matter which basis is chosen, one type of discharger will usually be favored over another, which may lead to claims of inequitable treatment (see Palmer and Quinn [1982] for a discussion of this point). Of course, such claims may be made under direct regulation programs as well.

For initial distribution through government sales, two principal types of auctions are considered here. The first type is termed a single-price auction. Under this procedure, identical rights are sold by the government at a single market-clearing price (see Eheart et al. 1980; Lyon 1981, 1982). Dischargers submit bid schedules to the authority, and the authority determines the market-clearing price for the fixed number of rights to be sold. This price might be the lowest accepted bid, the highest rejected bid, or some value in between (e.g., see Lyon 1982). Smith (1976) terms this type of procedure a competitive auction, while Smith et al. (1982) term it a P(Q) procedure, to indicate that bidders submit demand curves to the seller.

The second type of auction is termed the incentive compatible auction. Incentive compatibility is defined as the property whereby the mechanism encourages truthful revelation of information by participants (Hurwicz 1972, 1973; Dasgupta et al. 1979). As long as bidder collusion may be ruled out, an individual discharger's dominant strategy under such an auction is to reveal (bid) his true value for the TDPs. This will result in an efficient allocation of aggregate discharge. (In contrast, procedures that are not incentive-compatible may not always be efficient because bids may reflect strategies rather than true values.) The incentive compatible auction is a part of the general class of preference revelation mechanisms investigated by Vickrey (1961), Clarke (1971), Groves (1973), and Green and Laffont (1977). Where homogeneous (i.e., identical) TDPs are being allocated, the mechanism operates as follows. Bidders submit binding bid schedules to the authority, which then allocates permits to the highest bidders, as under the single-price auction. Instead of paying a uniform price for permits, however, a discharger winning $\underline{k}$ permits would pay the $\underline{k}$ highest rejected bids of all dischargers except himself. So, for example, if a discharger wins two permits, he would pay the two highest rejected bids for permits submitted by other dischargers. This procedure has the property of encouraging bidders always to bid their true values for rights; it also may imply that bidders pay different prices for rights, instead of the uniform price paid under the single-price auction.

One problem associated with the free distribution of permits is that there is generally no way to guarantee that exchange procedures will not be manipulated through strategic bidding by either the buyers or sellers of permits. If these buyers or sellers act strategically, it is possible that not all attainable efficiency from the TDP policy will be realized, and it is very likely that the exchange procedure will be regarded as inequitable. In contrast, if TDPs are sold by the government, strategic behavior by individual dischargers can be avoided by using an incentive-compatible auction. Except for cases where there is collusion, it is each discharger's dominant strategy under this procedure to bid truthfully for permits. Unfortunately, this auction is only incentive-compatible as long as there are no refunds to dischargers (except for lump-sum transfers). This result

suggests a major tradeoff in designing a TDP program. To avoid
financial burdens on dischargers requires some sort of free initial
distribution or refund procedure, but such a procedure may be more
subject to strategic behavior than an incentive-compatible auction.

It should also be noted that the use of an incentive-compatible
auction implies that dischargers would pay nonuniform prices for
identical permits (though as the number of bidders and bids increases
the permit prices will tend to converge). If this unfamiliar feature
is viewed as inequitable, then a single-price auction may be preferred. The latter type of auction is not strictly incentive-
compatible, but might be expected to become so as the number of
participants increases, since no one bidder may expect to affect the
market price significantly. In fact, Smith et al. (1982) determined
experimentally, using student volunteers, that even a small number of
bidders (eight) was sufficient to achieve approximate incentive
compatibility. It is by no means certain, however, that their results
may be extended to TDP markets involving institutional bidders. To
illustrate, a simulation of a market following free initial distribution of phosphorus emission permits in the Lake Michigan basin
showed that despite the participation of 53 treatment plants in the
program, two plants under the same ownership would sell 75 percent of
the permits traded at the market-clearing price, and three plants
would sell 85 percent of the total (see Lyon 1981, 1982). Similarly,
in one simulated market for BOD discharge permits on the Willamette
River with 11 dischargers, one discharger would sell, and another
would buy, two-thirds of the rights exchanged. These results suggest
that even the participation of a fairly large number of dischargers in
a TDP market does not necessarily guarantee purely competitive (i.e.,
price-taking) behavior if certain participants have special size or
cost characteristics. Thus, in practice it may not be possible to
achieve relatively unmanipulated outcomes following a free initial
distribution of permits.

The potential efficiency of large markets leads to another important
tradeoff in the design of a TDP program. As the number of participants in the market increases, the operation of the market improves.
In order to achieve a sufficiently large market, however, it may be
necessary to expand the geographic area within which unrestricted
trading may take place. Such an expansion, though, may lead to permit
transfers that yield unfavorable water quality impacts. The likelihood of such impacts depends on the water body characteristics and the
prevailing local types of water use and economic activity; potential
impacts for some of the case studies are presented below.

There is yet a third type of auction mechanism that could be used to
determine an initial allocation of permits but that is not a sales
mechanism. This mechanism is termed a fair division procedure, and it
ultimately refunds all receipts from sales back to the bidders in a
manner which some investigators believe may have attractive equity
properties. Because no funds are received by the government, fair
division procedures are very similar in spirit to the grandfathering
approach and are not considered sales procedures here. This study
examined one such procedure -- Knaster's fair division procedure -- in

detail. The method has also been considered by Luce and Raiffa (1957), Tomasini (1976) and Samuelson (1980). Using a simplified game-theoretic model, bidders' expected profits were determined for a very broad class of fair division procedures, including Knaster's, by Lyon (1981, p. 72). As that paper points out, however, the substantial income transfers and incentives for strategic behavior under Knaster's procedure are likely to make it impractical for use in allocating TDPs.

Another major issue to be considered in designing a TDP program concerns the rules governing transfers of permits among dischargers. Exchanges of permits and funds would generally be necessary following free initial distribution to attain an efficient allocation of treatment effort. If permits are initially sold by the government, then allowing subsequent exchanges among dischargers would also generally increase efficiency.

The single-price procedure for redistribution is similar to the single-price auction for sales described above, except that the authority collects offers both to buy and to sell permits. All permits are exchanged at the single price at which the two sets of offers are equal. It may happen that, due to discontinuities in the bids, a single market-clearing price cannot be found. In such a case, a market-clearing rule -- in which the authority increases or decreases the supply of permits -- may be established.

## Permit Durations
Permits can be issued with finite durations or in perpetuity, though either type may be made contingent upon review and renewal by the authority. If permits are of short duration, the authority will presumably have more flexibility in altering the supply to adjust water quality. Long-term permits, on the other hand, would allow dischargers to plan capital investments with less uncertainty and might allow improved cost efficiency in waste management.

If TDPs are initially distributed free of charge, the authority should consider any potential equity issues associated with the new property right it is establishing and distributing. It should also consider the possible cost of repurchasing it in the future. A system of TDPs with staggered expiration dates, such as considered by David et al. (1980) is one approach that attempts to combine the benefits of long-term permits with the flexibility of frequent expiration dates. For example, staggered permits of 20 years' duration might be expected to provide a sufficiently long time-horizon for capital investment planning while allowing adjustment in the permit supply by as much as 5 percent per year.

## Numbers of Permits
The total number of permits to be issued initially, along with the type and severity of any restrictions on permit transfers, is a decision that is primarily based on water quality goals. There are several methods listed below for determining the aggregate permit supply. In general, these statements apply to both the BOD and DODC permit programs, though of course there would be some quantitative

differences between them with respect to cost, distributional
properties and the risk of violations of water quality standards.

1.  Adapted Uniform Treatment (AUT) -- If free permits are to be
    issued initially to reproduce some regulatory scheme (the scheme
    considered here is uniform treatment), the water quality model may
    be used to determine how many permits may be issued on that basis
    which achieve the water quality standard. Under such an approach,
    there is a risk that the standard will subsequently be violated
    after trading since the aggregate discharge -- under the initial
    uniform treatment spatial pattern -- would just barely achieve the
    standard. If violations of the standard could result from
    exchanges, then restrictions on exchanges would be needed (these
    are discussed in the next subsection). However, there is also the
    possibility that water quality will be improved, as in almost all
    of the case studies examined in the third section.

2.  Zero Reserve (ZR) -- Under a government sales approach, the
    authority may solicit bids prior to determining the number of
    permits to issue. By taking into account the location of the
    permit buyers, it could then sell the appropriate number which
    would just barely achieve the water quality standard. This
    approach was referred to as the zero-reserve policy by Eheart,
    (1980). Under this approach, there is no immediate risk of
    violating the standards (as there is under the AUT approach), but
    there is a risk that future changes in economic conditions will
    result in transfers of rights which will worsen water quality.
    Note that it is also possible to apply this approach to the type
    of grandfathering scheme which involves a centralized exchange
    procedure based on a single-price auction. Rather than distrib-
    uting permits prior to exchange, they could be sold in this
    manner, and auction revenue could then be refunded to the
    dischargers in proportion to the number of BOD permits that would
    have been awarded to them under the grandfathering scheme. The
    aggregate discharge (total BOD mass loading) under the ZR approach
    could be greater or less than that obtained using the AUT
    approach. It would be greater, for instance, in the examples
    described below in the third section, in which dischargers with
    high unit-DO impacts undertake a disproportionately large share of
    the treatment burden at market equilibrium. It could be less in a
    case where a large discharger purchased a relatively large number
    of permits and discharged waste at a location with a relatively
    large negative impact on water quality. (In general, large
    dischargers are not expected to buy disproportionately large
    number of permits because of economies of scale, but the situation
    is possible for several technical reasons.) In this case, the AUT
    approach would require market restrictions to prevent water
    quality violations.

3.  Higher-Reserve Policies (HR) -- As discussed by both Eheart (1980)
    and Brill et al. (1981), there are several possible bases for
    holding a certain number of permits in reserve to hedge against
    possible future violations of the standard. The choice of basis
    depends on how optimistic the authority wishes to be. Any such

approach would reduce the aggregate discharge level and increase the cost of the final solution in comparison to the above two policies. One approach is to base the number of permits to issue (i.e., the aggregate discharge level), on a worst-case basis so that no violation of the standard could occur under the assumed critical water quality conditions regardless of the geographical distribution of permits. Given an aggregate supply of permits, the worst possible DO level resulting from their redistribution can be calculated; conversely, the aggregate number of permits which would achieve the DO standard when distributed in the worst possible manner can also be calculated and can be used as a basis for the number of permits to issue.

There are alternatives to the worst-case analysis to determine the number of permits to issue. As described in the next section, stochastic simulation could be used to obtain a less pessimistic allocation. Eheart (1980) considered as one alternative the even more pessimistic assumption of zero river reaeration to accommodate possible changes in the chemical characteristics of the discharges as well as in their locations. The choice, of course, would depend on how conservative the authority wished to be in determining the aggregate discharge level.

Geographical and Other Restrictions on Transfers
To help ensure the continued maintenance of water quality, market restrictions may be added to prevent or discourage transfers of permits (discharges) that would cause violations. Since water quality problems depend in part on local physical features, the type of trading restrictions chosen by policymakers would be expected to vary from one water body to another. Several types of restrictions, discussed in more detail by Brill et al. (1981), are described briefly below, and policy tradeoffs among them are indicated.

1.  Ad Hoc Approvals -- One way to prevent violations of the DO standard under a BOD or DODC permit program is to require that any exchange be approved by the water pollution control authority. Proposed exchanges could be evaluated using a water quality model. One potential disadvantage of this approach is that perceived inequities could arise if similar dischargers are not treated similarly in the sense that they are not allowed to make similar market transactions. Another disadvantage is that transactions costs could be significant. Formal approval mechanisms could increase costs for the water quality agency, and dischargers could face the expense of countering public opposition whether it materializes or not. Also, significant time delays could occur.

The ad hoc approach could be formalized by automatically approving exchanges whenever the buyer or seller could demonstrate (using officially established impact coefficients) that no new violation of the water quality standard would occur. Inefficiencies could arise, however, because potential transfers would be evaluated independently. (For example, two possible transfers could be independently unacceptable, yet acceptable in combination.)

If the number of dischargers and the expected number of transfers are small, then an ad hoc approval mechanism may be desired. Other types of restrictions that would place general constraints on exchanges, but would not require the administrative burden of analysis and approval of each exchange, are outlined below. These restrictions could be applied in the context of a decentralized market or in the context of periodic trading sessions organized, for example, by the water quality agency.

2.  Limits on Aggregate Discharge in Sections of a River -- Under this type of restriction, the river would be subdivided into sections, and -- while trading both within and between sections would be allowed -- an upper limit would be placed on the aggregate BOD discharge in each section. Thus, once the limit is reached, a discharger in a given section could purchase a permit only from another discharger in that section.

3.  Zoned Markets -- Another way to restrict transfers is to define permits so that they can be exercised in only a certain region, or zone, in a waterway. The first consideration of zones for the Delaware River by other researchers was aimed at improving cost efficiency (Thomann 1972, p. 265) while maintaining certain equity properties, but such a trade restriction may also be effective in improving the worst possible DO levels. This mechanism allows equal opportunities for dischargers within a given zone to purchase BOD permits. Between-zone inequities could still be perceived, however, depending on the characteristics of the dischargers and of the physical river system under study.

4.  Uniform Revaluation Factors -- The DODC program would revalue permits based on the unique characteristics of both the buying and selling dischargers' locations; potential inequities that could occur under a DODC program would be avoided by applying the same revaluation factor (RF) to all first-time exchanges. For example, if RF = 0.75, a permit initially issued for a discharge of 1,000 kg/day of BOD would be devalued to 750 kg/day when sold. However, a program based on a uniform revaluation factor may be less cost efficient than a DODC program, since transfers that both improve and degrade the water quality may be equally inhibited.


Implementation and Administration

The ease of implementation and administration of a TDP program will vary according to the choices of policy options. All permit programs, even those of the regulatory type, that are based in any way on the amount of pollutant discharged by the regulatees require discharge monitoring for enforcement. The TDP programs considered here do not differ in this respect: all require monitoring of a BOD discharge whose allowable rate does not change with time. Additionally, any TDP program would require the operation of a registry of holdings and transfers to determine how much each agent is allowed to discharge. If an auction is utilized, the authority may wish to operate it, or it may be operated by private brokerage firms. The latter option is currently being used in an ad hoc fashion to transfer air pollution rights through the emission offset policy (see The Wall Street Journal, June 18, 1981). A TDP program would also require the development and operation of a water quality model, whose use would vary according to the options chosen.

In addition to these administrative tasks, some of the programs discussed above would require additional activities on the part of the authority. Grouping dischargers or separating the watercourse into free-trade zones would require delineating the zones or groups and would require the formulation of an assignment policy that strikes a favorable balance between the water quality and cost efficiency and distributional goals. In addition, any of the special trading restrictions discussed above would require decisions and continuous monitoring on the part of the authority. In particular, ad hoc review of permit transfers would require the maintenance of a panel or committee to conduct such reviews, and uniform revaluation would require the choice of a revaluation factor. In the final analysis, many of these decisions, while based substantially on technical considerations and analyses, would also be largely influenced by political factors.


QUANTITATIVE RESULTS AND TRADEOFFS IN DESIGNING
T.D.P. MARKETS FOR B.O.D. MANAGEMENT

This section presents the quantitative results of the study and draws upon these results to illustrate the tradeoffs that may be encountered in designing TDP markets for BOD management. It is assumed here that policymakers designing a program for controlling BOD would have multiple objectives, which would include: efficiency, equity, water quality maintenance, certainty of outcome and ease of implementation and administration. As the discussion indicates, fundamental compromises must generally be made among objectives in designing a TDP program. The discussion also suggests, however, that the TDP approach offers a number of important advantages over alternative environmental management strategies, such as uniform direct regulation and effluent charges.

Simulations of various TDP programs and alternative management programs under static conditions were carried out for the Delaware River in Pennsylvania, New Jersey, and Delaware; the Willamette River in Oregon, and the Mohawk and Upper Hudson rivers, both in New York. The TDP market simulations consisted primarily of equating the marginal BOD removal costs for all dischargers (in the BOD permit market case), or the marginal costs of DO improvement at the DODC defining point in the case of DODC permits. (For a more complete discussion of this method and a discussion of some additional complications related to cost curve concavity and discreteness, see Eheart et al. [1980].) These simulations, which set aside the potential problem of strategic bidding, were applied to programs with either government sales of permits or free initial distribution. Other analytical procedures used include least-cost analysis, worst-case analysis, stochastic simulation and water quality modeling.

In the first subsection, the alternative TDP programs are compared to uniform direct regulation, effluent charges and least-cost solutions with respect to treatment costs, payments for permits, and related considerations. In the second subsection, the degree to which various TDP programs ensure that a water quality standard would be achieved are evaluated. This evaluation is done through analyses of worst-case conditions and stochastic simulation techniques. In the third subsection, alternative approaches are then examined for restricting TDP markets to ensure achieving a water quality standard.

## Cost-Efficiency, Equity and Related Issues
The cost efficiency of a particular program is measured by the aggregate economic cost of achieving a given DO standard. Only the costs of real resources utilized are considered in calculating aggregate cost; payments for discharge permits are not included because they are transfer payments between parties. (These transfer payments do, however, represent a potentially important distributional issue, which is discussed later.)

To compare programs on the basis of cost efficiency and to evaluate the tradeoffs between this objective and other program goals, it is desirable that one important program goal be held constant. In the presentations of this subsection, the DO standard achieved under the assumed critical water quality conditions immediately after the program has been put into effect has been chosen as the basis of comparison. For TDP programs, it is the standard achieved at the initial market equilibrium. However, the degree to which this standard can be achieved may vary from one program to another; trading following this initial equilibrium in response to changes in economic conditions may result in a change in the level of environmental quality.

Table 1 presents selected results for the four case studies examined. Column 1 is the DO standard achieved for each policy. Column 2 presents the aggregate cost of waste treatment under the least-cost solution. This cost may be determined using mathematical programming (optimization) techniques such as the one described by Revelle et al. (1968). Column 3 presents the treatment cost under uniform treatment (UT) regulations, which require all dischargers to remove an equal percentage of their raw waste BOD (unless they initially treat at a higher level). Column 4 presents aggregate treatment cost under a TDP program based on BOD permits, where the appropriate number of permits are issued (after bidding) so that the DO standard would just be achieved (i.e., using the ZR method). Columns 5 through 7 are discussed below.

The results indicate that, as expected, aggregate treatment costs under the BOD permit program are less than the costs under the uniform treatment policy. These lower costs result because the TDP program allows increased flexibility in terms of dischargers' allocations of waste treatment effort. As under other programs providing economic incentives, dischargers with high marginal treatment costs would remove less BOD than under uniform treatment, while dischargers with low marginal treatment costs would remove more.

TABLE 1
Economic Characteristics of TDP Systems

| DO Standard | Least-Cost | UT Cost | BOD Permits Market | | | Clearing Price |
|---|---|---|---|---|---|---|
| | | | Cost (+) | Transfer (=) Payments | Total Financial Burden | |
| Column # 1 | 2 | 3 | 4 | 5 | 6 | 7 |
| mg/L | Millions of dollars per year | | | | | ($/kg) |

Willamette River

| | | | | | | |
|---|---|---|---|---|---|---|
| 4.8 | 2.86 | 3.20 | 2.86 | 0.64 | 3.50 | 0.02 |
| 7.5 | 3.84 | 4.60 | 3.84 | 1.32 | 5.16 | 0.11 |

Delaware River

| | | | | | | |
|---|---|---|---|---|---|---|
| 2.0 | N.A.* | 5.04 | 2.5 | 10.6 | 13.1 | 0.08 |
| 3.0 | 4.91 | 14.8 | 8.4 | 8.5 | 16.9 | 0.12 |
| 3.6 | 8.61 | 25.1 | 15.9 | 13.6 | 29.5 | 0.37 |

Mohawk River

| | | | | | | |
|---|---|---|---|---|---|---|
| 5.1 | 3.21 | 4.95 | 4.39 | 1.30 | 5.69 | 0.74 |
| 5.9 | 4.63 | 7.48 | 6.51 | 2.55 | 9.06 | 2.94 |

Upper Hudson River

| | | | | | | |
|---|---|---|---|---|---|---|
| 5.1 | N.A.* | 0.45 | 0.41 | 0.08 | 0.49 | 0.005 |
| 6.8 | 2.02 | 2.47 | 2.02 | 0.98 | 3.00 | 1.32 |

*Not Available

Figures 1-3 show similar economic data for three of the case studies for a large range of DO standards achieved. In general, the BOD permit program does not implement the least-cost solution, since it does not account for the effect of discharger location. However, as these figures illustrate, the cost of this program may be remarkably low. In the Willamette and Delaware cases, the dischargers whose impacts on the critical points per unit of BOD discharged are the greatest are also the dischargers who have the lowest treatment costs; thus, the simulated market solutions tend to be efficient. In the

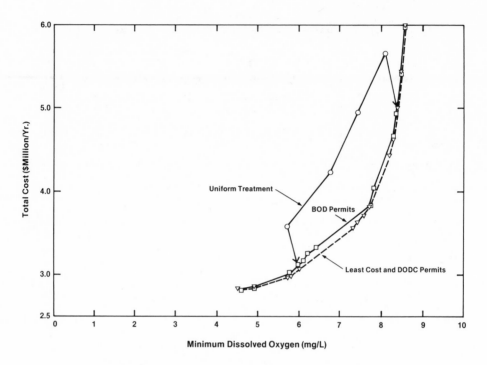

FIGURE 1
Cost Characteristics of TDP Programs for the Willamette River


Mohawk case, however, the dischargers with large impacts on the
critical points also tend to have high treatment costs. Here, the BOD
permit program is rather inefficient. In order to induce sufficiently
high treatment levels by the relatively high-cost dischargers with
large impacts on the critical point, the permit program must also
induce high treatment levels by the low-cost dischargers even though
they have a low impact on the critical point.

Figures 1 and 2 also show the simulated results, for the Willamette
and Delaware cases, of exchanges of BOD permits following free initial
distribution on a uniform treatment basis (the AUT approach discussed
earlier). The arrows connect points which represent the costs and DO
standard achieved before and after trading, with the total BOD load
held constant. The costs decrease substantially, but the DO standard
achieved increases in most cases and decreases only slightly in one
case. This improvement in efficiency may also be attributed to the
tendency of dischargers with low treatment costs to have high unit
impacts on the critical DO checkpoints. In the round of trading that
follows free initial distribution, permits tend to be sold by these
dischargers so that more discharge tends to occur in places where its
effect on the critical points is low.

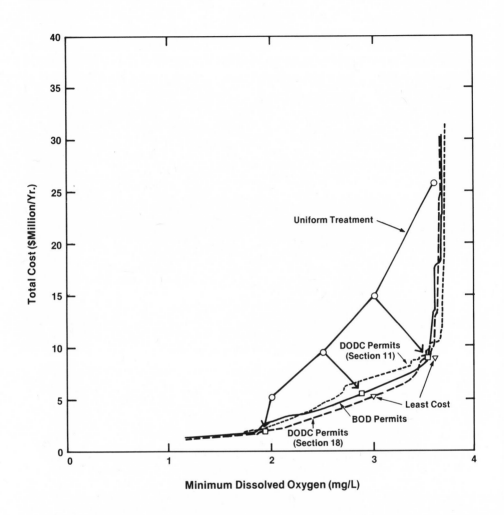

FIGURE 2
Cost Characteristics of TDP Programs for the Delaware River

Table 2 and Figures 1-3 present aggregate treatment costs for dischargers under DODC permit programs for three of the case studies. In each case, the number of permits was determined by the ZR method. The defining point chosen for the DODC permits either coincided with the critical point for most values of the standard, or constituted a "best compromise" choice over a large range of DO levels. The table also includes the treatment costs for the least-cost solutions. In the Willamette and Upper Hudson cases, the DODC program attains the highest possible cost efficiency since the minimum DO point stays at the mouth of the river under most BOD loading conditions. In the Mohawk case, DODC permits will implement the least-cost solution for

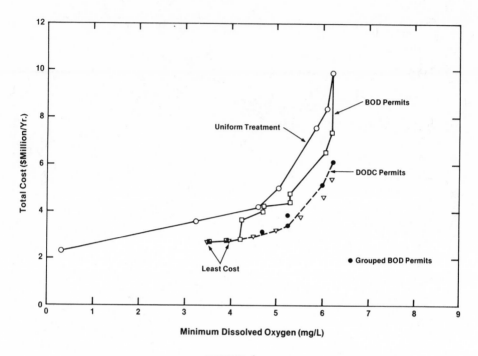

FIGURE 3
Cost Characteristics of TDP Programs for the Mohawk River

low DO levels, but for higher levels the critical point shifts and the
DODC program becomes less efficient (though it remains superior to the
BOD program).   In the Delaware case (Fig. 2), the critical point is
nonstationary, so regardless of which point is chosen to define the
DODC permits, there are violations of the DO standard at other
points.   In this case, DODC permits do not implement any of the
least-cost solutions.   River sections 11 and 18 of the Delaware
Estuary Comprehensive Study model were chosen as points for defining
the DODC permits, per Graves et al. (1970).   The least-cost solutions
were determined by the same investigators.

For certain types of rivers where neither the BOD or DODC permit
programs would be efficient, grouping or zoning of dischargers may
improve cost efficiency.   For high DO standards in the Mohawk case,
the large, efficient dischargers are either located downstream of the
critical point or have very little influence on it, and the upstream
dischargers exercise little influence on a local DO minimum point in a
downstream reach of the river.   By separating the river into two
distinct zones, each with its own BOD permit market, it was observed
that the cost efficiency of the BOD permit program might be improved
by allocating a relatively large number of permits to the downstream
zone  while  restricting  the  supply  of  permits  to  the  upstream

TABLE 2
Cost Comparisons of BOD Load and DODC Programs

| DO Standard | Least-Cost | BOD Program Cost | DODC Program Cost |
|---|---|---|---|
| mg/L | Millions of dollars per year | | |
| **Willamette River** | | | |
| 4.8 | 2.9 | 2.9 | 2.9 |
| 7.5 | 3.8 | 3.8 | 3.8 |
| **Delaware River** | | | |
| 2.0 | N.A.* | 2.5 | 2.5 |
| 3.0 | 4.9 | 8.4 | 8.8 |
| 3.6 | 8.6 | 15.9 | 20.0 |
| **Mohawk River** | | | |
| 5.1 | 3.2 | 4.4 | 3.2 |
| 5.9 | 4.6 | 6.5 | 4.6 |
| **Upper Hudson River** | | | |
| 6.8 | 2.0 | 2.0 | 2.0 |

*Not available

dischargers. (The supply of permits allocated to each zone was determined by a multizone adaptation of the ZR method.) The economic costs of the grouped program are shown in Figure 3; this program shows a definite improvement in cost efficiency in comparison to the single-zone BOD permit program (though it is, by and large, not superior to the DODC program). As a result of the different total permit allocations to the two groups, however, the market prices for BOD permits in the two groups differs substantially ($2.95 vs. $0.33 per kilogram for achieving a DO standard of 6.05 mg/L). This could result in the same sort of equity issue which might attend the use of DODC permits, as discussed above -- that is, some dischargers would be required to pay more than others to discharge a pound of BOD. These results are discussed more thoroughly by Kshirsagar and Eheart (1982).

In examining the distributional properties of TDP programs, both with respect to other programs and with respect to each other, there are two concerns. The first is the distribution of costs (or income) among dischargers, and the second is the distribution between dischargers as a group and the rest of society as a whole.

TDP programs in which permits are distributed by government sales have distributional properties similar to those of effluent charge programs. Table 1 demonstrates that the transfer payments required under governmental sales could be substantial. Column 5 gives the dischargers' aggregate payments for those permits if the permits were sold by the government via a single-price auction (with the permit supply determined by the ZR method). In the four cases the transfer payments for rights are seen to range from about 20 percent to 400 percent of the cost of treatment. (The permits payments in this case would equal the payments by dischargers under a program of uniform effluent charges for BOD discharge.) Column 6 presents the total financial burden given by the sum of the treatment cost (from Column 4) plus aggregate permit payments from a governmental single-price auction (from Column 5). As illustrated by all of the examples in Table 1, the dischargers as a group may pay more for treatment and permits under a TDP program than they do for treatment alone under uniform direct regulations. If permits are initially distributed free of charge, however, the aggregate payments for rights would be zero, while individual dischargers would have net payments or receipts, depending on whether they bought or sold rights after their initial allocation.

Figure 4 compares the distributional properties of BOD permit programs with those of other programs for the Willamette case study for a DO standard of 6.0 mg/L. The dischargers are arranged in order of decreasing influent load along the abscissa; that order corresponds roughly to decreasing efficiency of waste removal (due to economies of scale). The ordinate shows each discharger's individual net financial gain relative to a UT program. For both TDP programs, the permit supply is determined by the ZR method. Government sales of TDPs leave all dischargers worse off than under the least-cost program implemented by government fiat. Two dischargers are better off under government sales than uniform treatment.

Grandfathering of BOD permits on the basis of uniform treatment, of course, leaves all dischargers better off than under either government sales or the UT policy itself, but only three of the 11 dischargers would be better off under grandfathering than under the least-cost solution implemented by fiat. Thus, while it may be argued that TDP programs are more equitable than least-cost programs (since they do not place a disproportionately high burden on the more efficient dischargers), they may actually make only a minority of dischargers better off.

Column 7 of Table 1 presents the market-clearing price of the permits; these values would be the same either for a governmental auction or in an exchange following a free initial distribution (assuming no strategic behavior). Though the treatment cost data for the case studies are not all indexed to the same base year, inspection of the values still shows that the market-clearing price for permits -- even under the same water quality standard -- would vary considerably from one region to another. For example, the market price to achieve a DO standard of 3.6 mg/L on the Delaware is more than 10 times that necessary to achieve a standard of 4.8 mg/L on the Willamette.

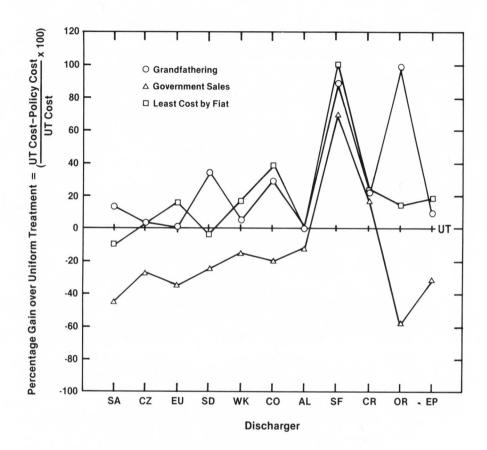

FIGURE 4
Distributional Characteristics of TDP Programs
for the Willamette River with a 6.0 mg/L DO Standard


Whether this type of disparity would be controversial depends in part
on the degree to which dischargers and others recognize the appropri-
ateness of regional approaches to environmental management.

Water Quality Assurance Under a TDP Program
This subsection illustrates briefly two methods of assessing the risk
of violating a given water quality standard under alternative TDP
programs. Details of these procedures are provided by Brill et al.
(1981).

Table 3 shows the worst possible DO level that could occur under the
assumed critical water quality conditions for a fixed aggregate BOD
discharge level for the Willamette and Delaware cases. Although the
initial discharge level was determined by the ZR method on the basis
of the bids (cost functions) of the existing (case study) dischargers

TABLE 3
Worst—Case Dissolved Oxygen Levels

|                   |                     | Worst—Case DO (mg/L) | |
| ----------------- | ------------------- | ----------- | ----------- |
|                   | DO Standard (mg/L)  | BOD Market  | DODC Market |
| Willamette River  | 4.8                 | 3.6         | 4.8         |
|                   | 6.0                 | 5.2         | 6.0         |
|                   | 7.5                 | 7.2         | 7.5         |
| Delaware River    | 2.0                 | 0.0         | 0.0         |
|                   | 3.0                 | 0.0         | 0.0         |
|                   | 3.6                 | 0.8         | 0.0         |

so that the standard would be achieved, future exchanges among these
dischargers and new ones could produce any geographical distribution
of permits.  In the Willamette case, a redistribution of discharges
under a BOD permit market designed to achieve a 4.8 mg/L standard
could violate the standard by as much as 1.2 mg/L (4.8-3.6).  Under a
DODC market for the Willamette, however, it is not possible to violate
the standard -- regardless of the location pattern of the discharges
-- because the critical water quality point remains fixed.

This finding implies that for cases like the Willamette River, the
authority could simply allow unrestricted transfers of DODC permits.
Nonetheless, there could be a tradeoff between the potential inequities of the DODC program in comparison to the BOD program and the
increased certainty of achieving the water quality standard and
attendant reduced administrative burden.  (Both the BOD and DODC
programs were shown to be very cost-efficient for the simulated static
market solutions for the Willamette.)

In the Delaware case, however, the worst possible location pattern
would deplete the dissolved oxygen completely (several times over)
under either type of market program.  In this case, the DODC program
would not function well because the location of the critical water
quality point changes by large distances from one solution to another.

Thus, the worst-case conditions vary greatly from one river basin to
another; the opportunity to use DODC permits to gain water quality
assurance that exists for the Willamette case is not present in the
Delaware case.  At the same time, the tradeoff that would exist
between equity and certainty of achieving the DO standard that would
arise in the Willamette case does not occur in the Delaware case.

The worst-case analysis is quite pessimistic.  An estimate of the
likelihood of DO violations can be obtained using stochastic

TABLE 4
Example Water Quality Results of
Stochastic Simulations of Biochemical Oxygen Demand Permits Programs

(All values in mg/L)

| Dissolved Oxygen (DO) Standard | DO for BOD Market | Worst-Case DO | Range of DO Values over 100 Simulation Runs | | |
|---|---|---|---|---|---|
| | | | Scenario 1 | Scenario 2 | Scenario 3 |
| 2.0 | 1.9 | 0.0 | 1.7–2.1 | 0.7–1.4 | 0.1–0.8 |
| 3.0 | 3.5 | 0.0 | 2.6–2.9 | 2.0–2.6 | 1.7–2.4 |

simulation. This approach was applied to the Delaware case for the BOD permit program. The aggregate BOD load (calculated to achieve a given standard by the ZR method) was divided into "packets" of 500 kg/day each, and each packet was randomly assigned to a location on the basis of a set of probabilities assumed for illustration purposes. The DO profile was then calculated for that location pattern for the permits (discharges). By repeating this process a probability distribution for the water quality impact in each section was estimated.

The probabilities chosen for each illustration were based on a scenario about economic development in the basin. Three scenarios are presented here. Scenario 1 implies that the future discharge pattern will tend to follow the current pattern, Scenario 2 implies that it will be very unpredictable, and Scenario 3 implies that future discharges will be concentrated in areas where there is little current discharge. The key results of these three scenarios are given in Table 4.

Scenario 1 most nearly duplicates the loading patterns of the simulated BOD market, and its range of minimum DO levels is also closest to the values corresponding to the BOD permit market. For the 3.0 mg/L standard, the minimum DO level along the DO profile for each of the 100 runs of the stochastic simulation falls below the DO value for the market solution and the standard. On the other hand, the minimum DO levels obtained for all simulation runs are considerably better than the worst-case DO levels for the same aggregate discharge. In the case of the 2.0 mg/L standard, some of the 100 simulation runs produced minimum DO values that exceed the standard and the DO value of the BOD permit program. Scenario 3, which implies growth in relatively undeveloped areas, approaches the worst case most closely. Scenario 2 produces minimum DO values that tend to fall between those of Scenarios 1 and 3. These results suggest that for the scenarios examined, it is quite possible that violations of the DO standard would occur, but it is quite unlikely that DO levels would approach worst-case values.

## Approaches to Preventing Violations of a Water Quality Standard

In the preceding subsection it was shown that in some cases unrestricted transfers of permits may over time allow violations of a water quality standard. As discussed above, there are several approaches that can be taken to maintain an adequate level of water quality in such cases. Two types of approaches are illustrated in this subsection. The first type limits the aggregate supply of permits, and the second type provides a set of rules a priori that restrict some subset of permit exchanges. As expected, there may be tradeoffs between water quality maintenance, cost efficiency and equity.

The first type of approach uses the higher-reserve (HR) method (based on the worst-case level of DO) for determining the number of permits to issue initially. Table 3 indicates for the Willamette example that the BOD permit program designed to achieve a 6.0 mg/L standard (where the number of permits is determined by the ZR method) has a worst-case DO level of 5.2 mg/L. Thus, the number of permits issued under that program (or slightly more) could be issued to ensure that a 4.8 mg/L standard will be achieved, regardless of future permit transfers. Table 1 indicates that the cost would increase from $2.9 million per year to no more than $3.1 million per year (cf. $3.6 million a year for uniform treatment). The Delaware case is quite different, however. Of the solutions in Table 3, the smallest aggregate BOD discharge level corresponds to the 3.6 mg/L standard (under the ZR method). That discharge level yields a very low worst-case DO of 0.8 mg/L and yet has a relatively high treatment cost. Thus, an attempt to maintain an even higher standard (such as 2 mg/L) by basing the aggregate discharge level on a worst-case analysis would be quite costly. In general, this HR approach might (as in the Willamette case) or might not (as in the Delaware case) be desirable.

The alternative approach establishes a set of rules that restrict permit exchanges. An example of this type of scheme limits the aggregate discharge in geographical sections and was evaluated for the Delaware data base. Limits were placed on the aggregate BOD discharge in each of 30 sections of the river. Under the assumed limitations, in sections where there was no existing discharger, none was allowed. In sections where there were dischargers, a limit on the aggregate discharge equal to some fraction of the existing (initial) BOD discharge was imposed. These restrictions might be viewed as equitable in the sense that the availability of permits is equivalent (in proportion to the initial aggregate discharge) in each section. For each level of the limit, both a worst-case minimum DO value under any possible set of future conditions and the economic cost for the simulated BOD permits market were determined. As before, the worst-case DO level was determined by allowing the BOD permits to be distributed in the worst possible set of locations from a water

TABLE 5
Tradeoff Between Cost and Worst-Case DO Level
with Limits on Aggregate Discharge in Each Section

| | | | | |
|---|---|---|---|---|
| DO Standard | (mg/L) | | 3.0 | 3.6 |
| Least-Cost | ($ million/yr.) | | 4.9 | 8.6 |
| Uniform Treatment Cost | ($ million/yr.) | | 14.8 | 25.1 |
| Worst-Case DO* | (mg/L) | | 0.0 | 0.8 |
| Case A | Worst-Case DO | (mg/L) | 1.7 | 2.8 |
| | Cost | ($ million/yr.) | 8.4 | 15.9 |
| Case B | Worst-Case DO | (mg/L) | 2.2 | 2.8 |
| | Cost | ($ million/yr.) | 10.0 | 16.5 |
| Case C | Worst-Case DO | (mg/L) | 2.7 | 2.9 |
| | Cost | ($ million/yr.) | 12.5 | 18.2 |

*BOD market with no section limits.

quality perspective, but subject to the sectional limits on aggregate discharge. The market was simulated subject to the sectional limits using cost data for the existing dischargers in the case study. Table 5 presents results for a BOD permit market with the initial supply determined by the ZR method to achieve the indicated DO standard. Cases A, B and C specify increasingly restrictive limits of 65 percent, 50 percent, and 25 percent of existing aggregate BOD discharge in each section of the river, respectively.

As the limits become more restrictive, the simulated cost for the existing dischargers increases, but the worst possible DO level improves. For example, under the 3.0 mg/L standard the cost increases from $8.4 million a year to $10.0 million a year and then to $12.5 million a year in cases A, B and C, respectively. Note that the least-cost and uniform treatment cost values are given for comparison, and that the cost in Case C approaches that of the uniform treatment solution. There is a tradeoff, however, since the worst-case DO level, 0.0 mg/L, improves considerably -- to 1.7, 2.2 and 2.7 mg/L in cases A, B and C, respectively. In general, market simulations indicate that some improvements in cost efficiency result from trading in comparison to the uniform treatment program even if restrictions are placed on the aggregate discharge in each section. Worst-case analyses indicate, however, that violations of the DO standard could still occur.

Zoned markets may also be used to restrict permit exchanges to minimize potential violations of a water quality standard. Table 6 illustrates the use of this restriction for the BOD permit market for the Delaware example. Two programs -- both of which attempt to

TABLE 6
Zoned BOD Permit Markets for Delaware River Example

| DO Standard | Basin-Wide BOD Market | | 3-Zoned BOD Market | | 4-Zoned BOD Market | |
|---|---|---|---|---|---|---|
| | Cost* | Worst-Case DO (mg/L) | Cost* | Worst-Case DO (mg/L) | Cost* | Worst-Case DO (mg/L) |
| Without Limits | | | | | | |
| 3.0 | 8.4 | 0.0 | 9.8 | 0.0 | 10.1 | 0.7 |
| 3.6 | 15.9 | 0.8 | 16.4 | 1.5 | 16.9 | 2.4 |
| With Limits | | | | | | |
| 3.0 | 8.4 | 1.7 | 9.8 | 2.1 | 10.1 | 2.7 |
| 3.6 | 15.9 | 2.8 | 16.4 | 2.9 | 16.9 | 3.3 |

*All cost figures in millions of dollars per year.

separate the river into zones that are relatively homogeneous with regard to water quality problems -- were examined. The aggregate supply of BOD permits was determined by applying the ZR method to the original (unzoned) BOD permits program to achieve the indicated standard. As more zones are defined the aggregate cost increases, but the worst possible DO level also improves. There still, however, could be significant violations of the standard for the examples shown.

Zones can also be used in conjunction with limits on aggregate discharge in each section. Example results are given in Table 6 for the Delaware River for zones combined with the least restrictive sectional limits discussed above (Case A in Table 5). In the case of a 3.6 mg/L DO standard, the use of four zones without sectional limits would ensure that the DO level would not fall below 2.4 mg/L under the assumed critical water quality conditions; when limits are also imposed, the DO level would not fall below 3.3 mg/L (within 10 percent of the standard).

In general, the imposition of sectional limits would be expected to increase the cost of a BOD permit program with a given zone configuration and aggregate BOD supply. For the Delaware data base, however, the Case A sectional limits correspond to the minimum required treatment level by individual dischargers. By itself this prevents transfers in the simulated solution which would exceed the Case A limitations. Thus, the substantial improvement in worst-case DO implied by the addition of sectional limitations would be attained at no extra cost as estimated by the simulated solution for the existing dischargers.

TABLE 7
BOD Permits Markets with Revaluation Factors
for Delaware River Example

| | Cost ($ million/yr.) | | | Worst-Case DO (mg/L) | | | |
| | BOD Market | | | | | | DO |
| | RF=1 | RF=0.75 | RF=0.35 | RF=1 | RF=0.75 | RF=0.35 | Standard |
|---|---|---|---|---|---|---|---|
| No Limits | 8.4 | 9.2 | 11.3 | 0.0 | 0.0 | 1.7 | 3.0 |
| Limits | NA | NA | NA | 1.7 | 2.0 | 2.6 | |
| No Limits | 15.9 | 17.1 | 18.8 | 0.8 | 1.8 | 2.8 | 3.6 |
| Limits | NA | NA | NA | 2.8 | 2.9 | 3.3 | |

Revaluation factors can also be used to reduce the potential violations of a water quality standard resulting from future permit
transfers. BOD permits markets with various uniform revaluation
factors (RF) were examined for the Willamette and Delaware examples
(for details, see Brill et al. 1981). As above, the permit supply was
determined by the ZR method to achieve the indicated standard. Subsequent permit trading was simulated by a special technique that could
accommodate revaluation; the imposition of a revaluation factor
decreases both the volume of exchanges and the aggregate BOD load.
Under revaluation, the worst-case DO level tends to improve, but the
cost of the simulated market solution tends to increase. As shown for
the Delaware example in Table 7, the worst-case DO values improve from
0.8 mg/L under the original BOD market to 2.8 mg/L if an RF value of
0.35 is applied. There is, however, a tradeoff with cost, which
increases from $15.9 million per year to $18.8 million per year. Even
with an RF value of 0.35, however, enough flexibility is allowed by
the market to produce a significant improvement in cost in comparison
to the uniform treatment cost ($25.1 million per year). In the
Willamette case study, it was shown that an RF value of 0.5 would
achieve a 6.5 or 7.0 mg/L standard, even under worst-case conditions.
Similarly, an RF value of 0.35 would ensure that a 4.8 mg/L standard
would be achieved.

Limits on aggregate discharge in each section in conjunction with the
use of an RF were also examined. In Table 7, it is shown for the

Delaware case that under a 3.6 mg/L standard the worst-case DO level improves to 3.3 mg/L if the least restrictive limits (Case A) are applied along with an RF value of 0.35. Revaluation factors may also be used in conjunction with zones, with or without limits on the aggregate discharges in sections. It was shown in the Delaware example that the application of the combination of all three types of market restrictions would ensure that the worst possible DO level would be within 0.1 mg/L of any of the water quality standards examined.

In general, it has been shown that in cases where water quality impacts resulting from market transfers could violate the given DO standard, market restrictions may be useful in reducing or possibly eliminating such violations. There are, however, potentially significant tradeoffs with cost and equity, and results vary from river to river. Details of the case studies are provided by Brill et al. (1981).


CONCLUSIONS

In the design of a program of transferable discharge permits for the control of BOD discharges, unavoidable tradeoffs exist among planning objectives. Furthermore, the system of rules that achieves the best compromise is likely to be unique to each application, and it would generally depend on the nature of the watercourse and the preferences of the policymakers, as well as on the number, types and locations of the dischargers. In the preceding sections, a framework for analyzing many of these issues is provided, and the application of this framework is illustrated. Several specific conclusions emerge from the results and are summarized as follows:

1.  The simulated market solutions for static conditions for the four case studies illustrate that BOD permit programs would consistently be much more cost efficient than a uniform treatment, direct regulation program. In several cases, the BOD permit programs would be nearly as efficient as the least-cost program.

2.  The Willamette case study illustrates that a DODC permit program may produce a least-cost solution and ensure that the water quality standard will be achieved regardless of future permit transfers. The Delaware case study shows that this program would not work well, however, in situations where it is not possible to select a stable defining point for DODC permits. In such situations, a much more complex program — involving either a portfolio of DODC permits or transfer restrictions — would be required.

3.  The case studies show that the aggregate payments for permits under a government sales mechanism could be very large. The total financial burden on the dischargers could exceed their costs under a uniform treatment, direct regulation program. On the other hand, under a free initial distribution program, these transfer payments would not be required. Furthermore, all dischargers

would be better off than under the UT program because there are
always mutual gains from voluntary exchanges. Free initial
distribution does involve another equity issue, however, since the
newly created property right would have considerable value.

4. Unrestricted transfers of BOD permits could cause violations of
   the water quality standard. The Delaware case study shows that
   such violations could completely deplete the dissolved oxygen in
   parts of the river if the permits were exchanged in the future so
   that the discharges were to occur in the worst possible locations. For the Willamette case, the worst possible violations
   would be approximately 1 mg/L.

5. A requirement of ad hoc approval for transfers could be used to
   prevent violations of the water quality standard. Perceived
   inequities could arise if similar dischargers are not allowed to
   make similar market transactions. Cost inefficiencies could also
   arise if transfers are evaluated independently.

6. The supply of permits could be reduced to ensure that a given
   standard would be achieved even if the worst possible set of
   discharge locations results from future exchanges of permits. In
   the Willamette case, the supply of BOD permits could be determined
   in this way with a very small increase in cost for the static
   market solution for the dischargers in the case study.

7. A set of rules that restricts transfers of BOD permits could be
   used to reduce or possibly prevent violations of a standard. The
   restrictions considered may be viewed as equitable since they
   would apply uniformly to all dischargers or to groups of dischargers. For example, in the Willamette case, the application of
   a uniform revaluation factor (to reduce the discharge allowed by a
   BOD permit if it is exchanged) was shown to prevent a violation of
   the water quality standard under any possible set of future permit
   exchanges.

8. In the Delaware case study, three sets of rules governing BOD
   permits were considered: specifying limits on the aggregate
   discharge in sections of the river, restricting transfers of
   permits to geographical zones, and applying revaluation factors.
   While all of these approaches would reduce somewhat the magnitude
   of possible violations, none would prevent all violations. The
   use of all three approaches in combination would ensure that a
   given standard would be violated by no more than 0.1 mg/L. There
   is a tradeoff with cost, however, as indicated by simulations of
   the BOD permit market with these rules for the dischargers in the
   case study.

9. It is theoretically possible to design auctions that will prevent
   market manipulation by individual dischargers (even for a small
   total number of participants), but these schemes will usually
   force the dischargers to bear the full financial burden of the
   payments under a government sale of permits. Also, these schemes
   would require different dischargers to pay different prices for

permits. Any procedure to refund auction revenue (except in lump sums) or to distribute free permits to the dischargers will have a theoretical potential for manipulation by strategic bidding. Strategic behavior may lead to inefficiencies and may be perceived by other dischargers as inequitable. The practical significance of these problems may depend on the number of dischargers participating in the program and on their cost characteristics.

10. If the geographic zone of free trade for BOD permits is too small, the number of dischargers may be small, and market manipulation by a few of them may lead to an inefficient and inequitable alloca-tion of rights. If the zone of free trade is too large, there is a greater risk that water quality may be seriously impaired by transfers of discharges to locations with greater impacts on the water quality at critical checkpoints.


## ACKNOWLEDGEMENTS

The authors wish to express their gratitude to the three research assistants -- Sudhir R. Kshirsagar, Barbara J. Lence and Daniel L. Guttman -- whose computer programming efforts were the quantitative backbone for this project. Some of the insights and ideas expressed in this document were developed during discussions with these individuals; some were enhanced by discussions with participants in the 1982 UW Sea Grant conference "Regulatory Reform, Transferable Permits and Enhancement of Environmental Quality" held in Madison, Wis., June 23-25, 1982. We also wish to thank Prof. Jon C. Liebman, whose perspectives played such an important role during the formative stages of this research. The support of the National Science Foundation under award No. PRA 79-13131 is gratefully acknowledged.


## REFERENCES

Atkinson, S.E., and Tietenberg, T.H. 1982. The empirical properties of two classes of designs for transferable discharge permit markets. Journal of Environmental Economics and Management 9:101-121.

Brill, E.D., Jr. 1972. "Economic efficiency and equity in water quality management." Ph.D. dissertation, Johns Hopkins University.

Brill, E.D., Jr.; Eheart, J.W.; Kshirsagar, S.R., and Lence, B.J. (In manuscript). Water quality impacts of biochemical oxygen demand under transferable discharge permit programs. Report No. 2, NSF Award PRA 79-13131, December 1981.

Brill, E.D., Jr.; ReVelle, C.S., and Liebman, J.C. 1979. Alternative effluent charge functions: Cost, financial burden and punitive effects. Water Resources Research 15:993-1000.

Buchanan, J.M., and Tullock, G.  1975.  Polluters' profits and
   political response: Direct controls vs. taxes.
   American Economic Review 65:139-47.

Clarke, E.H.  1971.  Multipart pricing of public goods.
   Public Choice 11:17-33.

Dales, J.H.  1968.  Pollution, Property and Prices.
   Toronto: University of Toronto Press.

Dasgupta, P.; Hammond, P., and Maskin, E.  1979.  The implementation
   of social choice rules: Some general results on incentive
   compatibility.  Review of Economic Studies 46:185-216.

David, E.  1980.  Cost-Effective Management Options for Attaining
   Water Quality.  Madison: Wisconsin Department of Natural
   Resources, Bureau of Planning.

David, M.; Eheart, W.; Joeres, E., and David, E.  1980.  Marketable
   permits for the control of phosphorus effluent into Lake
   Michigan.  Water Resources Research 16:263-70.

Eheart, J.W.  1980.  Cost efficiency of transferable discharge permits
   for the control of BOD discharges.  Water Resources Research
   16:980-89.

Eheart, J.W.; Joeres, E.F., and David, M.H.  1980.  Distribution
   methods for transferable discharge permits.  Water Resources
   Research 16:833-43.

Eheart, J.W.; Brill, E.D., Jr., and Lyon, R.M.  1982.  Methods of
   analysis and assessment of transferable discharge permits for
   control of biochemical oxygen demand.  Research Report No. 3, NSF
   Award No. PRA 79-13131.

Graves, G.W.; Whinston, A.B., and Hatfield, G.B.  1970.  Mathematical
   programming for regional water quality management.  U.S. Dept. of
   the Interior Water Pollution Control Research Series Program No.
   16610 FPX.

Green, J., and Laffont, J-J.  1977.  Characterization of satisfactory
   mechanisms for the revelation of preferences for public goods.
   Econometrica 45:427-38.

Groves, T.  1973.  Incentives in teams.  Econometrica 41:617-31.

Hurwicz, L.  1972.  On informationally decentralized systems.  IN:
   Decision and Organization, C.B. McGuire and R. Radner, eds.
   Amsterdam: North-Holland.

Hurwicz, L.  1973.  The design of mechanisms for resource allocation.
   American Economic Review 63:1-30.

Krupnick, A.J.; Oates, W.E., and Van de Verg, E.  1982.  On marketable
    air  pollution  permits:  The  case  for  a  system  of  pollution
    offsets.  Presented at the Sea Grant Symposium "Regulatory Reform,
    Transferable  Permits  and  Enhancement  of  Environmental  Quality,"
    June 23-25, 1982, Madison, Wis.

Kshirsagar, S.R., and Eheart, J.W.  1982.  Grouped markets for
    transferable  discharge  permits  for  water  quality  management.
    Working Paper No. 4, NSF Award PRA 79-13131.

Liebman, J.C., and Lynn, W.R.  1966.  The optimal allocation of stream
    dissolved oxygen resources.  Water Resources Research 2:581-91.

Luce, R.D., and Raiffa, H.  1957.  Games and Decisions.
    New York: Wiley.

Lyon, R.M.  1981.  "Auctions and alternative procedures for public
    allocation  with  application  to  the  distribution  of  pollution
    rights."   Ph.D.  dissertation,  University  of  Illinois.   (Also,
    Report No. 1, NSF Award PRA 79-13131.)

Lyon, R.M.  1982.  Auctions and alternative procedures for allocating
    pollution rights.  Land Economics 58:16-32.

Montgomery, W.D.  1972.  Markets in licenses and efficient pollution
    control programs.  Journal of Economic Theory 5:395-418.

Moore, C.  1980.  "Implementation of transferable discharge permits
    when  permit  levels  vary  according  to  flow  and  temperature:   A
    study  of  the  Fox  River,  Wisconsin."   M.S.  report,  University  of
    Wisconsin-Madison.

Noll, R.G.  1982.  Implementing marketable emmissions permits.  Papers
    and Proceedings, American Economic Review 72(2):120-24.

Oates, W.E.  1981.  Corrective taxes and auctions of rights in the
    control  of  externalities:  Some  further  thoughts.   Public  Finance
    Quarterly 9(4):471-78.

O'Neil, W.B.  1980.  "Pollution permits and markets for water
    quality."  Ph.D. dissertation, University of Wisconsin-Madison.

Palmer, A.R., and Quinn, T.H.  1982.  Allocating chloroflourocarbon
    permits: Who gains, who loses, and what is the cost?  Report No.
    R-2806-EPA.  Santa Monica, Calif.: Rand Corp.

ReVelle, C.S.; Loucks, D.P., and Lynn, W.R.  1968.  Linear programming
    applied  to  water  quality  management.   Water  Resources  Research
    4:1-9.

Samuelson, W.  1980.  The object distribution problem revisited.
    Quarterly Journal of Economics 94:85-89.

Smith, V.L.  1976.  Bidding and auctioning institutions: Experimental results.  IN:  Bidding and Auctioning for Procurement and Allocation, Yakov Amihud, ed., pp. 43-64.  New York: New York University Press.

Smith, V.L.; Williams, A.W.; Bratton, W.K., and Vannoni, M.G.  1982. Competitive market institutions: Double auctions vs. sealed-bid-offer auctions.  American Economic Review 72(1):58-77.

Thomann, R.V.  1972.  Systems Analysis and Water Quality Management. New York: McGraw-Hill.

Tietenberg, T.H.  1974.  The design of property rights for air pollution control.  Public Policy 22:275-92.

Tietenberg, T.H.  1980.  Transferable discharge permits and the control of stationary-source air pollution: A survey and synthesis.  Land Economics 56:391-416.

Tomasini, L.M.  1976.  A note on the fair division of pollution rights.  Journal of Public Economics 6:313-17.

U.S. Environmental Protection Agency.  1980.  Emission reduction banking and trading project: Annotated bibliography, 5th edition. Washington: USEPA Office of Planning and Evaluation.

Vickrey, W.  1961.  Counterspeculation, auctions and competitive sealed tenders.  Journal of Finance 16:8-37.

# Alternative Policy Instruments under Uncertainty: A Programming Model of Toxic Pollution Control

Peter J. Morgan

Meta Systems, Inc.
Cambridge, Mass.

## INTRODUCTION

A large body of economic literature has developed which advocates pricing mechanisms as relatively efficient ways to regulate environmental pollution by firms. A number of empirical studies have obtained results showing that price-based regulatory schemes may attain a particular goal at considerably less cost than so-called direct regulation, technology-based regulation, etc. (e.g., see Johnson [1967] and Kneese and Bower [1968]). However, some have argued that this presumption in favor of prices rests on an over-simplified analysis of the problem. Weitzman (1974) has shown that if a regulatory authority is uncertain about firms' treatment costs, the slopes of the benefit-and-cost curves of pollution control may significantly affect the comparative advantage of pricing mechanisms. Rose-Ackerman (1973) has pointed out that environmental marginal damage functions often exhibit significant discontinuities due to threshold effects. In such cases, the expected costs of a price scheme may be high because of the high penalty of exceeding the threshold if the price is mistakenly set too low.

Such a discontinuity characterizes upsets of a biological treatment plant by discharges of heavy metals into the sewer system by industrial dischargers. A relatively small increase in the concentration of heavy metals can cause a drastic loss in removal efficiency at the threshold level, whereas further increases in concentration beyond the threshold have less effect.[1]

This paper presents the results of a programming model that examines the relative performance of different regulatory regimes in controlling toxic wastes in the presence of a threshold effect. Four regulatory regimes are examined: nonmarket quantity, price, marketable permit and mixed price-quantity. The model depicts a situation where both households and firms discharge wastes to a joint treatment plant (JTP), which uses a biological treatment process. The wastes discharged by the firms are toxic heavy metals, which can upset the performance of the JTP. The JTP removes some pollutants and discharges the rest, which has negative impacts on the environment.

Having uncertain information about the firms' treatment costs, the pollution control authority wishes to regulate the firms' discharges to maximize expected net benefits of the overall system. The theoretical framework of the model is based on the analysis of the relative performance of price and quantity regulation in Weitzman (1974) and its extension to the case of a discontinuous threshold effect in Morgan (1979). Uncertainty is characterized by the results of an econometric study of the firms' treatment costs and is simulated using random-number techniques. The specific data of the model depict -- with some modification -- the situation of Bridgeport, Conn., which has a number of metal finishing firms. All the market policies perform much better than the nonmarket quantity policy. The differences in performance among the market policies are not great, but can be explained in terms of the framework developed in Weitzman (1974), even though the structure of the model and the specification of uncertainty used here are a good deal more complex.

This paper has four main parts. First, the Weitzman model and its extension to the case of a threshold effect are discussed. Next, we describe the elements and structure of the programming model, including the specification of uncertainty. Then we present the results and finally offer some conclusions.


THEORETICAL FRAMEWORK

Basic Result for Price and Quantity Rules under Uncertainty
In the basic Weitzman framework, a pollution authority has uncertain estimates of the firms' treatment costs (benefits of discharge) and wishes to induce firms to discharge the level of pollutants which maximizes expected net benefits. The firms are assumed to know their own costs exactly. Weitzman shows that different policy instruments that might be chosen by the authority (e.g., price or quantity) will lead to outcomes with different levels of expected net benefits. In a simple case with a single firm, quadratic benefit-and-cost functions, and uncertainty about the coefficients of the linear terms of those functions, Weitzman shows that the relative performance of price or quantity regimes depends on the relative slopes of the marginal benefit and marginal cost curves. In addition, the difference in expected net benefits between the two regimes varies with the degree of uncertainty about the firms' treatment costs (benefits of discharge).

Figure 1 shows units of toxic pollutant H discharged by the firm to the JTP on the horizontal axis. The ES' curve represents the pollution control authority's estimate of the expected marginal benefit to the firm of being able to discharge amount H to the JTP.[2] (The firm benefits from being able to discharge added pollutants because this reduces its treatment costs.) The negative slope of ES' reflects the assumption that firms face increasing marginal costs of removal, and hence decreasing benefits of discharge. The M' curve represents marginal costs of joint treatment and residual discharges. (To simplify the figure, marginal costs are assumed to be known with certainty.[3]) For each regulatory scheme,

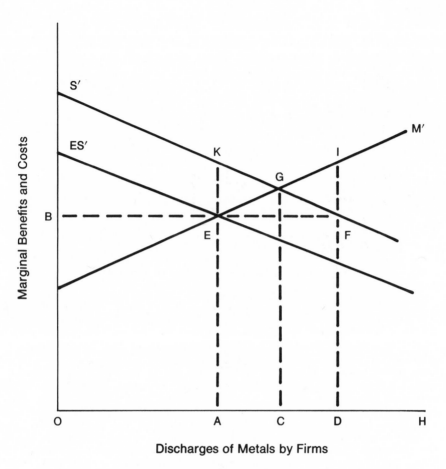

FIGURE 1
Marginal Costs and Benefits of Toxic Pollutant Discharge

the authority sets the level of the instrument to equalize expected
marginal benefits and costs (ES' and M' in Figure 1). Ths implies
optimal policies of price p = OB or quantity standard H = OA.

However, because the authority does not know benefits exactly, it is
unlikely that either policy will equate ex post marginal benefits and
costs, and hence each policy will entail some efficiency loss.
Suppose that actual marginal benefits of discharge are represented by
the curve S' in Figure 1. Optimal output of H is OC, but under the
quantity order the firm will produce OA, leading to an efficiency loss
equal to the area of triangle EGK. Under the price p = OB, the firm
will produce OD, yielding an efficiency loss of triangle IGF. An
expected efficiency loss for each instrument can be computed by taking

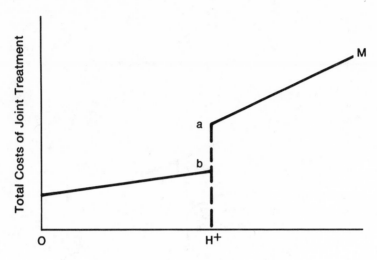

Discharges of Metals by Firms

FIGURE 2a
Total Cost Function

a weighted sum of the respective triangle losses over all possible
realizations of S'. The authority is assumed to choose that policy
instrument which yields the lower expected loss, or, equivalently,
maximizes expected net benefits. This is the basic result of
Weitzman's paper.

To be sure, the basic model is not very realistic. For example, the
general result is more complicated than that shown in Figure 1 if
there is more than one firm. However, Roberts and Spence (1976) have
shown that if the quantity rule is allocated efficiently ex post among
the firms, say, by using marketable permits, and if firms behave
competitively, the regulated firms will behave just as though they
were a single firm. In that case, the comparative results for the
single-firm case carry over to the multiple-firm case. Just such a
marketable permit scheme is examined in this study.

Threshold Effect
Empirical studies of biological treatment plants suggest that these
plants have a threshold-like reaction to some toxic pollutants, among
them heavy metals. Up to a certain concentration, heavy metals have
little effect on the treatment performance of the plant. Once the
threshold concentration is reached, however, the plant suffers a
fairly sharp and significant loss in removal efficiency. Further
discharges of metals over a broad range of concentrations have little
further effect on the removal efficiency of the plant (see fn. 1).

Figure 2a shows the total cost function and Figure 2b the marginal
cost function implied by a very simplified description of this kind of

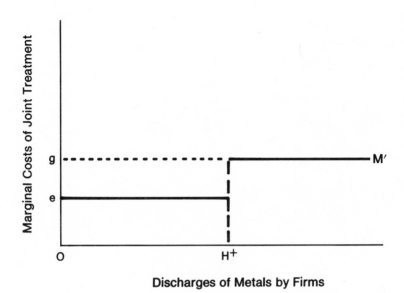

FIGURE 2b
Marginal Cost Function

behavior of costs at the JTP. The horizontal axis shows the discharge of metals by the firms, $H_1$, to the JTP, and the vertical axis total or marginal costs of the joint treatment plant plus environmental impacts of the remaining pollutants (metal and biological) discharged by the plant. Up to $H^+$, the threshold level, marginal costs of removing $H_1$ are assumed constant (equal to e in Figure 2b). However, at the threshold level, the plant suffers a loss in removal efficiency of both metals and BOD. Because the loss in removal efficiency affects every unit of metals and BOD treated, not just the marginal one, discharges of metals and BOD by the JTP -- and hence costs of residual impacts -- rise discontinuously. This discontinuity implies that marginal costs are not defined at $H_1 = H^+$. Once the threshold level of metals is exceeded, further increases in $H_1$ do not affect the removal rates at the JTP. Therefore, marginal costs of $H_1$ above the threshold are again constant, but higher (= g in Figure 2b), due to the impaired ability of the JTP to remove metals and BOD. This "spike" effect is of course a simplification of the actual process, but captures the basic behavior. Ths discontinuous jump at $H_1 = H^+$ implies that the cost function is not convex.

The presence of this nonconvex threshold effect has a number of policy implications. Three different solutions for the optimal level of discharges by firms may exist: an interior solution below the threshold level, a corner solution at the threshold or an interior solution above the threshold.[4] These possibilities are shown in Figure 3. S' and S'* are two possible realizations of the marginal

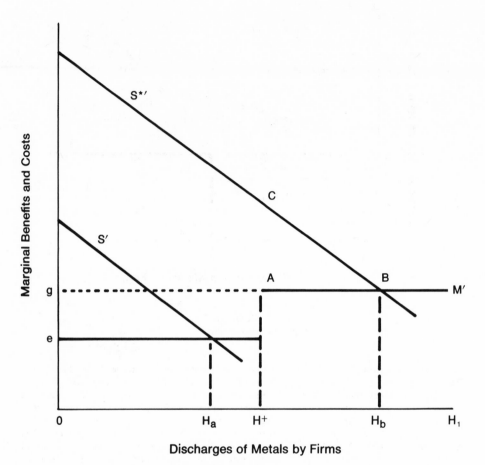

FIGURE 3
Three Possible Solutions for the Optimal Level of Discharges

benefit of discharge function. M' is the marginal cost of joint treatment function from Figure 2b. The intersection of the marginal benefit-and-cost curves yields an interior solution of $H_1 = H_a$ or $H_b$, depending on whether the marginal benefit-and-cost curves intersect to the left or the right of the threshold point. However, a corner solution of $H_1 = H^+$ may be superior to the solution $H_1 = H_b$ if the loss from exceeding the threshold (ab in Figure 2a) is greater than the added benefits defined by the area of triangle ABC.


DESCRIPTION OF THE PROGRAMMING MODEL

This section describes the elements and structure of a model of a system wherein metal finishing firms discharge water and toxic metal

wastes into a sewer network after treating those wastes to some
extent, and a joint treatment plant further treats those wastes
together with biological wastes (BOD) from households before final
release of the residual wastes to the receiving waters.[5] Both the
treatment processes of the individual firms and the JTP produce solid
wastes (sludge), which must be disposed of as well. All residual
charges, solid or liquid, have negative impacts on the environment
whose costs must be included. Using the convention that firms obtain
benefits (reductions in cost) from being able to discharge greater
amounts of pollutants, the object is to maximize the sum of separate
benefits of firms less the costs of sewer transport, joint treatment
and residual impacts. The definitions of the variables are given in
Table 1.

## Elements of the Model

The firms' treatment possibilities are represented by a benefit of
discharge function as described above. Benefits for the $i^{th}$ firm
are specified as:

$$S^i = S^i(Q_{1i}, H_{1i}, H_{si}) \tag{1}$$

where $Q_{1i}$, $H_{1i}$ and $H_{si}$ are amounts of water, waterborne metal
wastes and metallic sludges, respectively, discharged by the firm.[6]
In general, the specification of $S^i$ assumes that the firm faces
constant prices for all inputs and its normal outputs, and varies all
its inputs and its normal outputs to achieve a certain level of
discharge of pollutants and water in the least-cost way. However, it
was not possible to model the production of the firm's normal
outputs. Therefore, the firm's output of normal goods is assumed to
be fixed. This procedure probably overestimates costs (or benefts of
discharge) of the firm, because it might be able to achieve a certain
level of pollution reduction more cheaply by altering its normal
output in some way.

Households discharge water, $Q_B$, and biological wastes, $B_1$, to the
sewer system. These amounts are assumed to be fixed. This is
reasonable because in urban areas it is generally much more economical
to treat sewage wastes centrally. Therefore, it is not necessary to
count explicitly the benefits that households obtain from being able
to discharge to the sewer rather than treat them at home, because
these benefits are constant as well. Data on $Q_B$ and $B_1$ are taken
from Teetor and Dobbins (1967) and Watermation, Inc. (1978, pp. 5-23).

Sewer network costs are a function of total discharges by firms and
households, specified as:

$$C_T = C_T(Q_1 + Q_B) \tag{2}$$

Estimates of sewer costs are very difficult to obtain, because they
depend on the nature of the terrain, the size of the flow, the density
of the population, etc. Some very rough estimates were made on the
basis of information available in U.S. Environmental Protection Agency
(USEPA 1968, pp.63-65) and Downing (1969).

## TABLE 1
### Definition of Variables

The model has the following variables for the $i^{th}$ firm:

$Q_{oi}$ = original discharge[a] rate of water (liters (L)/day)
$Q_{1i}$ = final discharge[a] rate of water (L/day)
$QR_i$ = flow rate of recycling system (L/day)
$H_{oi}$ = original discharge[a] of metals to sewer (kg/day)
$H_{1i}$ = final discharge[a] of metals to sewer (kg/day)
$H_{si}$ = metals disposed of as sludge (kg/day)
$H_{ri}$ = metals recycled (kg/day)
$P_w$ = input cost of water ([\$/yr.]/[kg/day])
$P_Q$ = price of discharging water to sewer ([\$/yr.]/[kg/day])
$P_H$ = price of discharging metals to sewer ([\$/yr.]/[kg/day])
$P_{Hs}$ = cost of sludge disposal ([\$/yr.]/[kg/day])
        (excluding environmental impacts)
$P_S$ = price of environmental impacts of sludge ([\$/yr.]/[kg/day])
$P_{Hr}$ = value of metals recycled ([\$/yr.]/[kg/day])

For the sewer, joint treatment plant and impact functions:

$B_1$ = discharge of BOD from households (kg/day)
$H_1$ = total load of metals[b] reaching JTP (kg/day)

$$= \sum_{i=1}^{n} H_{1i}$$

$Q_B$ = discharge of water by households (L/day)
$Q_1$ = total flow of water reaching JTP (L/day)

$$= \sum_{i=1}^{n} Q_{1i} + Q_B$$

$\delta_H$ = percentage removal of $H_1$ at JTP
$\delta_B$ = percentage removal of $B_1$ at JTP
$H_2$ = discharge of H from JTP (= $(1- \delta_H)H_1$)    (kg/day)
$B_2$ = discharge of B from JTP (= $(1- \delta_B)B_1$)    (kg/day)

Notes:

[a]  By "original": we mean the amounts that the firms would discharge
     in the absence of pollution regulation. "Final" refers to the
     amounts discharged under regulation. Original discharge rates
     $Q_{oi}$ and $H_{oi}$ are assumed to be exogenous to the model.
[b]  $H_r$, $H_s$, and $H_o$ are defined in a similar manner, i.e., they
     are the sum over all firms of their respective quantities.

The joint treatment plant receives the water and waste discharges of
firms and households, removes a certain fraction of the domestic and
toxic wastes (which becomes solid sludge) and discharges the remainder
to the receiving waters. The analysis was performed for a system with

conventional secondary treatment with primary settling and activated
sludge (the system used in Bridgeport). The rate of removal of metals
by this process has been studied fairly extensively.[7] The removal
rates of the activated sludge process are assumed to depend on whether
the concentration of heavy metals, $H_1/Q_1$, exceeds the threshold
level.

Because of the above assumptions, the joint treatment cost function,
M, is assumed to take the form:

$$M = M(Q_1 + Q_B, \delta_H, \delta_B) \tag{3}$$

where $\delta_H$ and $\delta_B$ are constant removal rates of metals and BOD,
respectively, which depend on whether the threshold level is exceeded,
and $Q_1 + Q_B$ the total flow entering the JTP. M is assumed to
include the cost of disposing of sludges, but not any environmental
impacts associated with those sludges. Costs of joint treatment
plants were taken from cost equations for various treatment processes
given in USEPA (1975), and then adjusted to January 1976 levels using
the USEPA Sewage Treatment Construction Cost Index.

Residual discharges of metals and BOD from the JTP to the receiving
waters, as well as sludges produced by treatment processes at the
individual firms and the JTP, impose costs on the environment that are
registered in the model by a set of three environmental impact
functions. These are:

$C_s(H_s)$                 -- Impacts of solid sludge produced by firms

$C_m(H_1-H_2, B_1-B_2)$    -- Impacts of sludge produced by JTP

$C_e(H_2, B_2)$            -- Impacts of discharges to receiving waters

Costs of metallic sludges produced at the JTP ($H_1-H_2$) can be
expected to be greater than those of the sludges produced by firms
($H_s$), because the former interfere with the disposal of the
biological sludge, $B_1-B_2$, that they are mixed with. In the
programming model, the impact functions are assumed to be linear.

It is very difficult to determine the marginal costs of the environmental impacts of discharges of BOD and metals. For BOD, the
following, rather arbitrary, approach is taken. The original
investment of the joint plant is assumed to be beneficial (i.e., the
environmental impacts of the discharge of BOD removed by the plant
exceed the costs of the plant).[8] No specific assumption is made
about the marginal impact of metals discharge $C_{el}$, because data
simply are not available. Instead, a range of values of $C_{el}$ is used
to drive the model and obtain the effect of its value on the solution. The solutions of the model give some insight into what various
assumptions about impacts imply about the desirable level of control.

## The Complete Model

Combining the various elements of the model yields the expression for
expected net benefits that the authority seeks to maximize. As
mentioned above, the authority is uncertain about the costs (benefits

of discharge) of the firms, but is assumed to know costs of joint treatment and residual impacts. Therefore the authority maximizes expected net benefits:

$$G(Q_{1i}, H_{1i}, H_{si}) \qquad\qquad i = 1, \ldots, n.$$

$$= E \sum_{i=1}^{n} S^i(Q_{1i}, H_{1i}, H_{si}) - C_T(Q_1 + Q_B) \qquad\qquad\qquad (4)$$

$$- M(Q_1 + Q_B,\ \delta_H,\ \delta_B)$$

$$- C_s(H_s) - C_m(\ \delta_H H_1,\ \delta_B B_1) - C_e((1 - \delta_H)H_1, (1 - \delta_B)B_1)$$

where:

$$Q_1 \equiv \sum_{i=1}^{n} Q_{1i},\ H_1 \equiv \sum_{i=1}^{n} H_{1i} \qquad , \text{ etc.}$$

with respect to $Q_{1i}$, $H_{1i}$ and $H_{si}$, $i=1,\ldots,n$ and $\delta_H$ and $\delta_B$.

The interpretation of the first-order conditions is straightforward and is not given here. The removal rates, $\delta_H$ and $\delta_B$, depend on whether the threshold is exceeded. The sum of the sewer, JTP and environmental impact functions, $C_T + M + C_s + C_m + C_e$, is equivalent to the joint cost function M shown in Figures 2 and 3.

## Modeling of Policies under Uncertainty

This section describes the way the pollution control authority's uncertainty about the firms' treatment costs is modeled and the methods used to determine the optimal value of each policy instrument under uncertainty.

The cost function for separate treatment by the firms in this model has been derived econometrically (see fn. 6). The variance-covariance matrix of the coefficients yielded by the regression results naturally suggests itself as a way to specify the authority's uncertainty about the firms' treatment costs. (However, this estimate must be consider- ed a lower bound on the actual level of uncertainty, because using it assumes that the regression model was correctly specified.) In the programming model, uncertainty is modeled by using a computer subroutine to make repeated draws of pseudo-random numbers for each coefficient, because explicit derivation of the distribution of the coefficients is quite difficult.

To model the effect of uncertainty, each policy being considered (e.g., a particular overall level of discharge under a tradeable discharge permit regime) is simulated under a set of different possible "states of the world" with regard to a firm's treatment costs, each one yielding a resulting allocation of treatment effort and overall level of net benefits. Averaging the results over all such "states of the world" (assuming each one is equally likely) yields the expected net benefits of that value for that policy instrument.

Each state of the world consists of a specification of the values of the coefficients for each firm's cost function.[9] These coefficients, together with the base values of each firms' flow and discharge levels (assumed constant), define the firm's costs of attaining various levels of treatment in that state of the world. To construct a single state of the world, the coefficients for each firm's cost function are generated separately by a random number generating program that uses the variance–covariance matrix described above to specify the underlying distribution of the coefficients, assuming that the coefficients are normally distributed. For the results given here, the firms' costs are assumed to be uncorrelated. (Some effects of correlation are investigated in Morgan [1979].) Uncertainty about the constant term (the unexplained residual in the regression equation) is not modeled, since this uncertainty does not affect the marginal decisions of firms.

Four different regulatory regimes are examined:
1. Pure quantity (nonmarket);
2. Pure price;
3. Pure quantity (TDPs); and
4. Mixed strategy (TDPs plus minimum price).


RESULTS

Before discussing the comparative performances of the different regulatory regimes, it should be helpful to discuss some of the behavioral properties of the model. The first subsection examines characteristics of the model under uncertainty. Finally, the different regimes are compared.

Effect of Uncertainty of Benefits of Discharge
An important aspect of the model is the distribution of the benefit-of-discharge function of the firms under uncertainty. An examination of this aspect allows us to see how the behavior of our model compares with that of the basic Weitzman model. Figures 4 and 5 show aggregate total and marginal benefits of discharge of metals by the 21 firms in the model for five sample states of the world. (Benefits across firms are assumed to be uncorrelated.) As described above, the coefficients of each firm's treatment cost function are generated separately under each state of the world. The benefit function represents the sum of the firms' treatment costs, given an efficient allocation of treatment effort to meet the overall discharge level shown. Figure 4 shows that the total benefit curves differ mainly by a vertical shift term, and that the slopes of the different realizations for a given discharge of metals are fairly similar. Figure 5 confirms this impression. It also shows that the marginal benefit curves can be divided into three regions in terms of the effect of uncertainty. For discharges of metals in the range of 14 to 31 kg/day, the curve is almost vertical, so that small horizontal displacements imply very large changes in the marginal benefit of a particular discharge level. The variability of marginal benefits for a particular discharge level is fairly large compared to the magnitude of the discharges in this region of the

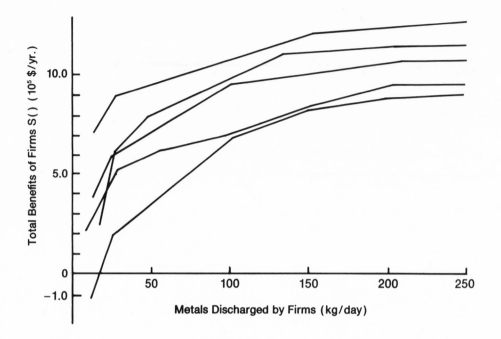

FIGURE 4
Effect of Metals Discharge Rate
on Total Benefits of Discharge of Firms

curve. According to the Weitzman framework, price regulation is preferable in this region because the slope of the marginal benefit curve is likely to be steeper than most plausible marginal cost curves (except for a threshold effect!)

In the second region (31-140 kg/day), the marginal benefit curve flattens out somewhat. Though the curve seems to show the greatest variability in this region, the change in slope implies that the variance of margial benefits for a given discharge level is less than in the first region. The reduction in (absolute value of) slope also means that the presumption in favor of price regulation is lessened.

In the third region (140 kg/day and above), marginal benefits are almost horizontal, and the variability of marginal benefits for a given discharge level is quite small. In this region, quantity regulation is preferable, unless marginal costs are relatively constant as well. Lastly, note that in all three regions the different realizations are not simply horizontal shifts of each other (as is assumed in the Weitzman mode), but have varying slopes as well, which sometimes causes them to overlap.

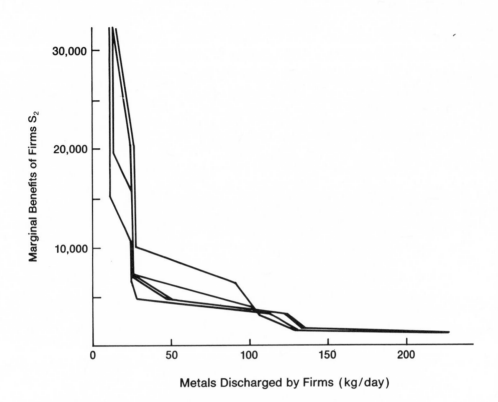

FIGURE 5
Effect of Metals Discharge Rate
on Marginal Benefits of Discharge of Firms

The threshold level at the JTP is about 46 kg/day.  This level has no effect on the benefit of discharge function because it is a characteristic of the JTP, not of the individual firm.

Comparison of Different Regulatory Regimes Under Uncertainty

As described previously, four regimes are compared:  pure quantity (nonmarket);  pure  price;  pure  quantity  (transferable  discharge permits);  and  mixed  (transferable  discharge  permits  plus  minimum price).  The performance of the regimes is compared using a base case and several deviations from it in assumptions about the severity of the threshold effect, the degree of uncertainty.  The assumptions of the base case are shown in Table 2.

Figure 6 shows expected net benefits of the four regimes as a function of the marginal impact of discharges $C_{e1}$ under the assumptions of the base case.  Though the optimal mixed strategy for values of $C_{e1}$

TABLE 2
Base Case Assumptions

===================================================================

Flow of water from households $Q_B$:            19,563 $10^3$L/day

Number of firms:                                21

Threshold concentration:                        2.0 mg/L total metals

Removal rates for activated sludge:

| | below threshold | above threshold |
|---|---|---|
| $\delta_H$ | .56 | .40 |
| $\delta_B$ | .71 | .60 |

Flow of water from households $Q_B$:            19,563 $10^3$ L/day

Loading of BOD from households $B_1$:           2,331 kg/day

Environmental impact of BOD:                    338 ($/yr.)/(kg/day)
(impact coefficient of $C_{e2}$; see fn. 8.)

Environmental impact of sludge, $C_{s1}$, $C_{m1}$, $C_{m2}$:     0 (zero)

Environmental impact of metals discharge $C_{e1}$:     A range of values
                                                       is considered.

All costs are total annual costs in 1st quarter-1976 dollars (i.e.,
operating and maintenance costs plus capital costs multiplied by a
capital recovery factor (= .163) reflecting a cost of capital of 10
percent and a 10-year equipment life.

-------------------------------------------------------------------

less than 4,500 ($/year)/(kg/day) is actually identical to the pure
price strategy (with the standard set at $H_1$ = oo), the below-the-
threshold mixed strategy is shown for the sake of comparison. The
diagram is remarkable mainly for the closeness of the results of the
price and quantity regimes at all levels of $C_{e1}$ and the closeness of
all three market regimes for values of $C_{e1}$ greater than 4,500. The
similarity of results for the pure price and quantity (market) regimes
in the range of $C_{e1}$ of (0, 4,500) occurs because the optimal
discharge of metals by firms in this region (124-180 kg/day) is high,
and hence both marginal cost and benefit curves are nearly horizontal
in that region. (For the marginal benefit curve, see Figure 5;
marginal joint treatment costs are constant because with metals
discharges of these magnitudes, the threshold is exceeded with 100
percent probability). The difference in the (absolute) slopes is near
zero, so the Weitzman framework implies little comparative advantage
for either regime.

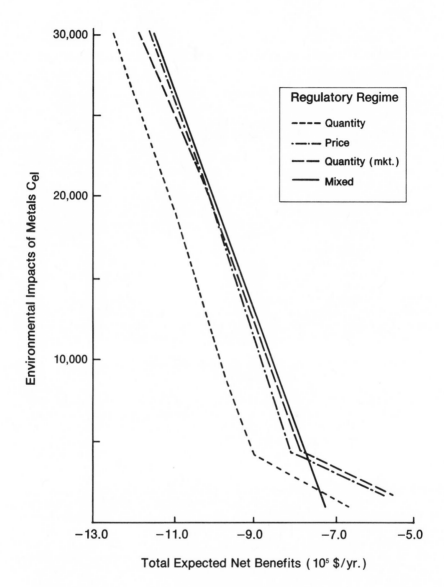

FIGURE 6
Performance of Differenct Regulatory Regimes:  Base Case


In the range of values of $C_{el}$ of (4,500, 19,000) the mixed regime
and the pure quantity regimes perform a shade better than the pure
price regime.  In this region, it becomes optimal even under the price
regime to set the price on metals discharges so high that they never

exceed the threshold. However, the mixed and pure quantity regimes perform better than the price regimes in this region because a standard allows greater average discharges of metals by firms (and hence lower treatment costs) while still keeping discharges below the threshold level.

For values of $C_{el}$ greater than 19,000, the performances of the mixed and pure price schemes converge, while that of the quantity regime lags increasingly. In this region, costs even below the threshold level are so high, and hence discharges are so low, that the threshold level ceases to be a binding constraint. Therefore, the premium required by the pure price regime to keep discharges below the threshold declines. Because the threshold effect no longer plays a role, marginal treatment costs are constant while marginal benefits are almost vertical. According to the Weitzman framework, this situation clearly favors price over quantity regulation.

The small variation in terms of costs among the various policies probably results from two effects. First, since all firms in the model are metal finishing firms, their treatment costs are roughly similar, so great gains from a reallocation of treatment effort should not be expected. If firms from different industries were represented, the effects would likely be greater. Second, the uncertainty about the concentration of heavy mtals depends on the total discharge of metals by firms. Given that the uncertainty of firms' discharges is uncorrelated, the variance of the total discharge is relatively small.

Figure 6 shows one thing clearly, namely that all the market regimes do much better than the nonmarket quantity regimes. Though total metals removal is almost the same under all four regimes, the market regimes allow large cost-savings (about \$100,000 in annual costs at all levels of $C_{el}$) by reallocating treatment effort to lower-cost plants.

Case 2 has the same assumptions as the base case, except that the post-threshold removal rates of both BOD and metals ( $\delta_B$ and $\delta_H$) are assumed to be 0.1 — considerably less than in the base case. This assumption implies that post-threshold environmental impacts are higher, and hence it is equivalent to a higher value for $g$ in Figure 2b. The results for the regimes are shown in Figure 7.

Unlike the base case, both the pure quantity (market) and pure price regimes stay below the threshold for the entire range of values of $C_{el}$. As before, lacking an upper limit on discharges, the pure price regime must enforce a lower average value of discharges to stay below the threshold with 100 percent probability. This results in higher treatment costs for firms, so the pure price regime performs less well than the mixed and pure quantity regimes for $C_{el}$ less than 13,000. However, the average discharge under the mixed regime falls increasingly below the threshold level, and the quantity regimes performs relatively more poorly as the value of $C_{el}$ increases. For values of $C_{el}$ greater than 9,500, the results are identical to those of the base case, because the threshold is not exceeded in any of the regimes in either case.

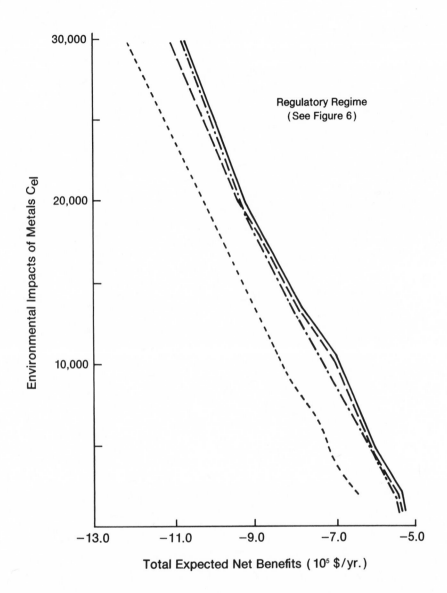

FIGURE 7
Performance of Different Regulatory Regimes:   Case 2

Note that under Case 2 it is never optimal to exceed the threshold even with very low impacts of metals discharges; whereas in the base case, discharges remain above the threshold level under at least some regimes until the marginal impact $C_{el}$ reaches 9,000.   The results for Case 2 are quite powerful, because they are unaffected by any assumptions about post-threshold costs worse than those that were made. Thus, the corner solution of $H_1 = H^+$ may be regarded as being robust with respect to a large range of assumptions about impact costs and the severity of the threshold effect.


CONCLUSIONS

All three market regimes perform much better than the nonmarket quantity regimes if discharge benefits are uncorrelated across firms. The differences in performance among the three market regimes are surprisingly small, even when a good deal of uncertainty is assumed. This results from only analyzing firms in one industry and the effect of averging of discharges of all firms. Even though the specification of uncertainty and the slopes of the marginal benefit-and-cost curves differ significantly from those of the Weitzman model, that framework proves quite useful in explaining the differences in performance, or lack thereof, that occur. Also, there is a combination of a level of marginal environmental impacts and treatment efficiency loss that implies a "risk-averse" policy of always keeping discharges below the threshold level. This strategy proves to be quite robust, because any worse set of assumptions than this combination would lead to the same policy.


ACKNOWLEDGEMENTS

This paper is taken from my 1979 Ph.D. thesis, Yale University (Morgan 1979). I wish to thank my committee members, Profs. Susan Rose-Ackerman, Guy Orcutt and William Nordhaus. In addition, I would like to thank Prof. Donald Brown for theoretical help, Prof. Charles Walker for initiation into the world of water pollution, an anonymous reference, and Robert Moore, deputy assistant commissioner, and other members of the Water Compliance Unit of the Connecticut Department of Environmental Protection for their cooperation in making their files available and their toleration of my frequent visits. Of course, all errors are my own. The simulation model was written in Fortran IV and run on the Yale Computer Center IBM 360/70 system.


FOOTNOTES

[1]    For example, see Barth et al. (1965b).

[2]    To avoid confusion over terms, it should be noted that our definitions of the cost and benefit functions are the reverse of those used in Weitzman (1974). In his usage, the firms to be regulated have cost function, and the benefit function shows the external effects of their activities. In our terminology, firms have "benefit of discharge" functions, and the authority has a cost function for joint treatment and residual impacts.

3     In fact, uncertainty about joint treatment costs (benefits in Weitzman's original formulation) does not affect the basic results of the Weitzman model (see Weitzman 1974, p. 485).

4     These are analyzed more thoroughly in Chap. V, Part I, of Morgan (1979).

5     The source of this framework is Bohm (1972).

6     The benefit function has two components: (1) an econometrically estimated cost function, $C^i$, relating costs to the extent of flow reduction, degree of pollution control and recycling practiced by the firm, and (2) credits for recycling or other reduction of water or metals together with sludge disposal costs resulting from the pollution control effort. (These credits do not include effluent charges, which are modelled separately.) This can be represented mathematically as:

$$S^i(Q_{1i}, H_{1i}, H_{si}) = -C^i(Q_{oi}, Q_{1i}, H_{si}, H_{ri}, H_{oi}H_{1i})$$

$$\text{(6a)}$$

$$+ P_w(Q_{oi} - Q_{1i}) + P_{Hr}H_{ri} - P_{Hs}H_{si}, \qquad\qquad i = 1, \ldots, n.$$

For a description of the general characteristics of $S^i$, see Morgan (1979, Chap. 3). The outputs of metals by the firm are assumed to obey the materials balance relation:

$$H_{oi} = H_{1i} + H_{si} + H_{ri}, \quad i = 1, \ldots, n. \qquad\qquad \text{(6b)}$$

Firms' treatment options are assumed to be limited to three discrete options: (1) flow reduction only; (2) flow reduction plus end-of-pipe treatment (chemical precipitation); and (3) flow reduction, end-of-pipe treatment and recycling (e.g., reverse osmosis, ion exchange). Firms can vary their flow rates continuously. Though a continuous specification of costs might be more tractable computationally, (a) the data are not available, and (b) this specification is a fair first approximation of the set of choices facing a metal finishing firm.

7     Information on removal rates of the activated sludge process was obtained from Daniels (1975), Roberts et al. (1977), Oliver and Cosgrove (1974), Barth et al. (1965a), Argaman and Weddle (1974), Watermation, Inc. (1978) and USEPA (1977, 1975). Estimated removal rates of BOD and metals are .71 and .56, respectively. The relatively low rates of removal of BOD are due to excessive flow. See Watermation (1978). In Morgan (1979), the alternative of a JTP using physical-chemical treatment was also examined.

8     Let $\delta_B B_1$ be the amount of BOD removed by the JTP per day and M be the annual cost of the JTP. We then have:

$$C_{e2} = M/ \delta_B B_1, \text{ or}$$

$$338 \ (\$/yr.)/(kg/day) = 2.23 \times 10^6 \ (\$/yr)/(.71 \times 9{,}323) \ kg/day.$$

The sensitivity of the model to this assumption was tested using a range of values of $C_{e2}$ from \$50 to \$400. Using the other assumptions of the base case, it was found that higher values of $C_{e2}$ lowered the value of $C_{e1}$, at which it became optimal to keep firms' discharges of metals below the threshold from \$4,400 to \$7,700. The results of the model are unaffected for values of $C_{e2}$ outside this range. Therefore we conclude that the model is not overly senstivive to the base assumption about $C_{e2}$.

9   Because of computer time costs, only a limited number of realizations of the benefit of discharge function simulated by these random draws can be tried for any set of assumptions. This raises the possibility that using different sets of random numbers for, say, different values of the impact function or different regulatory regimes could obscure the relative performance of different cases in unpredictable ways. Therefore, the same set of random numbers is used for all alternative cases investigated. This should greatly increase the reliability of the estimates of the relative behavior of the model under different assumptions. In practice, 20 diffferent realizations of the benefit of discharge function were generated for each firm. With 21 firms in the model and four coefficients to be generated, 1,680 random numbers are generated for each candidate value of the policy instrument.

BIBLIOGRAPHY

Argaman, Y., and Weddle, C.L. 1974. Fate of heavy metals in physico-chemical treatment processes. American Institute of Chemical Engineering: Chemical Engineering Progress Symposium Series 70(136):400-414.

Barth, E.F., et al. 1965a. Field survey of four municipal wastewater treatment plants receiving metallic wastes. Journal WPCF 37(8):1101-16.

Barth, E.F., et al. 1965b. Summary report on the effects of heavy metals on the biological treatment processes. Journal WPCF 37(1):86-96.

Bohm, P. 1972. Pollution: taxation or purification. Kyklos 25(3):501-517.

Daniels, S.L. 1975. Removal of heavy metals by iron salts and polyelectrolyte coagulants. AIChE Symposium Series 71(151):265-71.

Downing, P.C. 1969. Extension of sewer service at the urban-rural fringe. Land Economics 45(2):103-110.

Johnson, E.L. 1967. A study in the economics of water quality management. Water Res. Res. 3(2):291-305.

Kneese, A.V., and Bower, B.T. 1968. Managing water quality.
    Resources for the Future, Johns-Hopkins University Press.

Morgan, P.J. 1979. "The economics of joint vs. separate treatment of
    domestic and industrial wastewaters." Ph.D. dissertation, Yale
    University (unpublished).

Oliver, B.G., and Cosgrove, E.G. 1974. The efficiency of heavy metal
    removal by a conventional activated sludge treatment plant.
    Water Research 8(11):869-74, November.

Roberts, M.J., and Spence, A.M. 1976. Effluent charges and licenses
    under uncertainty. Journal of Public Economics, 5(3,4):193-208.

Roberts, P., et al. 1977. Metals in municipal wastewater and their
    elimination in sewage treatment. Prog. Water Tech., 8(6):301-306.

Rose-Ackerman, S. 1973. Effluent charges: A critique.
    Canad. Journal of Economics VI(4):512-28, November.

Teetor and Dobbins, Consulting Engineers. 1967. Water pollution
    control facilities for Bridgeport, Conn.: West Side Plant.
    Islip, L.I., N.Y.

Teetor and Dobbins, Consulting Engineers. 1971. Preliminary report
    on combined sewerage system. Islip, L.I., N.Y.

U.S. Environmental Protection Agency. 1968. Cost of clean water to
    the consumer. Washington: USEPA.

USEPA Office of Water Program Operations. 1975. A guide to the
    selection of cost-effective wastewater treatment systems:
    Technical report. Washington: USEPA.

USEPA Office of Research and Development. 1977. Industrial waste and
    pretreatment in the Buffalo municipal system. Ada, Okla.: USEPA
    (600/2-77-018).

Watermation, Inc. 1978. Wastewater treatment in Bridgeport, Conn.

Weitzmann, M.L. 1974. Prices versus quantities.
    Rev. Econ. Studies 41(4):477-92.

# The Regulation of Water Pollution Permit Trading under Conditions of Varying Streamflow and Temperature

**William B. O'Neil**

**Department of Economics
Colby College**

## INTRODUCTION

Though the idea of creating markets for the exchange of pollution permits has been discussed widely in the theoretical literature, the State of Wisconsin has only recently begun one of the first experiments in this area. Administrative rule N.R. 212, Wisconsin Administrative Code, forms the legal basis for the operation of a market in biochemical oxygen demand (BOD) effluent permits on the Fox River. The rule specifies an allocation of allowable effluent levels for individual dischargers that is intended to maintain a target level of dissolved oxygen (DO) under a variety of flow and temperature conditions. In addition, the rule allows the "flow/temperature" permits to be traded among the dischargers in quantities that preserve the DO target.

This paper is an evaluation of certain aspects of the Wisconsin permit market system. The permits are generally referred to as Transferable Discharge Permits (TDPs). Two issues are addressed in particular. First, it is observed that prospective contracts for the exchange of permits over a multiperiod planning horizon require advance knowledge of the expected stream conditions. Assuming such perfect foresight, we estimate the potential cost savings associated with operation of the permit market in comparison with the cost of traditional regulatory rules. The second part of the paper is a preliminary attempt to assess the implications of uncertainty in the knowledge of stream conditions.

## WATER QUALITY REGULATION WITH KNOWN STREAM CONDITIONS

The rate of streamflow and water temperature are the most important physical parameters that affect the capacity of a stream to assimilate BOD effluent. In this section, it is assumed that flow and temperature vary in a predictable sequence over the course of an annual cycle. For control purposes, the year is divided into several "periods," each exhibiting constant stream conditions. Polluters are assumed to have complete control over the level of their discharges. These assumptions are embodied in the following linear model.

Suppose along the river there are n dischargers of BOD effluent and m monitoring points for the measurement of DO. The following vector notation describes the system:

$Q_t$       DO levels during period t (in mg/L)
m x 1

$Q_t^o$      Maximum availability of DO during period t (mg/L)
m x 1

$E_t$       Daily BOD5 discharges during period t (pounds per day)
n x 1

$\overline{E}$       Maximum BOD5 discharges as specified by BPT rules
n x 1    (pounds per day)

$H_t$       BOD5-DO impact matrix, where $h_{ijt} = \Delta DO_{jt} / \Delta BOD5_{it}$
m x n    with i = 1, 2, ..., n
         j = 1, 2, ..., m
         t = 1, 2, ..., T

If any plant undertakes post-BPT abatement, this can be denoted as $X_{it} = \overline{E}_i - E_{it}$. We can now define a wasteload allocation in terms of the implied vector of post-BPT abatement activities:

$X_t$       Abatement levels during period t (pounds of BOD5 per day)
n x 1

The DO profile resulting from compliance with BPT limits during period t is given by:

$$Q_t = Q_t^o - H_t \overline{E}$$
m x 1

where the DO demand vector, $H_t \overline{E}$, at time t, can be written:

$$\sum_{i=1}^{n} h_{ijt} \overline{E}_i$$

for all m monitoring points.

If the regulatory authority specifies a DO target, Q*, which is expected to be maintained at all times, the excess demand for DO at time t under BPT compliance is:

$$\Delta Q_t = H_t \overline{E} - (Q_t^o - Q^*).$$
m x 1

The values of $\Delta Q_t$ are the quantities of DO that must be released from BPT levels of assimilative use at the various monitoring points in order to achieve the target DO profile. The economic problem faced by the authority is to determine an allocation of post-BPT abatement requirements across the n polluters which "supplies" the needed quantitites of DO, $\Delta Q_t^o$, in an equitable and cost-effective manner.

Before discussing cost, it is appropriate to note that the authority
has at least two basic options for writing permits. Assuming
knowledge of $Q_t$ and $H_t$, the authority can solve the following $\underline{m}$
equations for each time period:

$$H_t\ X_t\ =\ \Delta Q_t$$

to obtain time-dated sets of water quality-feasible abatement
activities.[1] For example, during period $\underline{t}$, a traditional method
would be to calculate the individual abatement requirements based on
equal percentage reductions from BPT, denoted:

$$X_t\ =\ (\hat{X}_{12},\ \hat{X}_{2t},\ \ldots,\ \hat{X}_{nt})$$

Having generated feasible abatement sets for each period, the
authority can impose either a "worst case" permit plan or a time-
varying permit plan, "flow-temperature permits." Under the worst-case
plan, the authority observes the sequence of flows and temperatures
over the year and chooses the values of $Q_t^0$ and $H_t$ that are
associated with a high-temperature, low-flow period. Using these
parameters, the authority can solve for feasible abatement requirements that are to be enforced at all times. From the polluter's
perspective, the result is a steady-state control plan. The alternative is to write each agent's permit as a function of time, thus
allowing the possibility of conserving on operating expenses during
periods when polluters' full abatement capacity is not needed to
protect the DO target.

Having described two basic permit-writing options, "time varying" and
"steady state," the regulatory authority then has four plans from
which to choose. It may (1) allocate BOD permits according to an
equal percentage reduction from BPT based on worst-case $Q_t^0$ and $H_t$
values and not allow permit trading, or (2) allocate BOD permits as in
the first plan but allow DO-preserving trades, or (3) issue a sequence
of time-dated BOD permits according to the percentage reduction rule
based on the appropriate $Q_t^0$ and $H_t$ values and not allow trading,
or (4) issue permits as in the third plan but allow trading. To
compare these four plans requires consideration of the costs of
abatement.


A MULTIPERIOD ECONOMIC MODEL

In a multiperiod setting, each polluter faces two decisions regarding
abatement expenditures. First, it must decide how much abatement
capacity to construct, and then it must choose how intensively to
operate its plant in each time period.

Let:     $CK_i(XK_i)$ = the annualized expense of constructing
                  abatement capacity of $XK_i$ pounds of
                  BOD5 per day at plant $\underline{i}$ (\$/year).
         $C_i(X_{it})$ = the cost per period of operating the abatement
                  plant $\underline{i}$ at the removal rate $X_{it}$ pounds of BOD5
                  per day (\$/period).

In this context, a cost-effective abatement plan would be one which solves the following streamwide cost minimization problem:

$$\text{Min:} \quad \sum_{i=1}^{n} \left[ CK_i(XK_i) + \sum_{t=1}^{T} C_i(X_{it}) \right] \qquad (1.1)$$
$$XK, X$$

subject to:

$$X_t \leq XK \qquad\qquad \forall\, t \qquad\qquad (1.2)$$

$$H_t X_t \geq \triangle\, Q_t \qquad\qquad \forall\, t \qquad\qquad (1.3)$$

$$X_t \geq 0 \qquad\qquad \forall\, t \qquad\qquad (1.4)$$

The solution to this problem consists of a set of abatement capacities across the polluters and a sequence of abatement activity levels for each polluter. These solution vectors, denoted $XK^*$ and $X_t^*$, respectively, represent the efficient allocation of abatement requirements.

Inspection of this problem yields two conclusions. First, an arbitrary rule for assigning abatement requirements, such as proportionate reductions, would only by chance coincide with the least-cost solution. Second, the time invariant permit plan would be more expensive than the time-varying plan as long as it is possible for plant operators to reduce operating expenses in slack periods. The last assumption is important, because some types of abatement plants cannot be operated much below design capacity without damaging the biological processes involved.[2] However, in the present case study, it is assumed that it is possible to operate plants below design capacity.

A less obvious implication of the problem is that a worst-case plan is not necessarily more costly than a time-varying permit plan. Suppose the year is divided into three control periods, one of which is characterized by lowest flow and highest temperature. A time-invariant permit would require a constant level of abatement activity equal to that necessary to achieve the DO target in that single worst period. But the constraining period is chosen by reference to flow and temperature, not by reference to individual plant capacity requirements. Consequently, it is possible that when other periods are included in the plan, a least-cost DO preservation strategy may imply larger capacity requirements for some plants than were needed in the worst period. In other words, flow and temperature are imperfect proxies for abatement requirements and do not lead to a true economic worst case. This possibility is illustrated in the Fox River simulations.


T.D.P. MARKETS AND COST MINIMIZATION

It has been shown (Montgomery 1972) that a properly defined competitive market for trading effluent permits can yield an equilibrium allocation of permits that is identical to the least-cost solution.

The conditions necessary for this outcome are that (1) a sufficient quantity of permits be issued initially to allow full use of the available DO and (2) subsequent trades of BOD permits are restricted to those which preserve aggregate DO demand levels. The first condition is met if the central authority solves the water quality constraint equations (1.3) exactly and writes the resulting effluent quantities in individual permits. The proportionate reduction rule is a suitable method of solution in many cases if it is applied to each DO constraint and adjusted for multiple constraints. This method of determining initial permit allocations is referred to as the "cluster rule," since it treats polluters that affect a single DO monitoring point as a group. The second condition is met by requiring that if one agent sells TDPs to another agent, the quantity sold is multiplied by the ratio of the two agents' impact coefficients to determine the quantity received by the buyer. In the event of multiple monitoring points, the most restrictive ratio regulates the trade. This procedure ensures that the DO released from use by the seller is exactly offset by the extra DO demand embodied in the permits received by the buyer.

In the case of steady-state, or time-invariant, permits, polluters could be granted permits based on the proportionate reduction rule, and they would have an incentive to trade away from this initial allocation as long as the marginal cost of supplying DO varied across the polluters. Consequently, one set of trades would be expected to occur in which the initial permit allocation is replaced by the least-cost allocation. The new allocation would dictate all plants' capacity requirements, and all plants would then be operated at design capacity in all periods.

In the case of a flow-temperature, or time-varying, plan, polluters would initially be allocated a sequence of time-dated permits (one set for each control period), and then they could contract with one another for a sequence of permit trades. Specifically, the permit is defined as the right to discharge a certain quantity of BOD per day at location $i$ during period $t$. Polluters could agree to sell or lease permits for the duration of a control period. Since $Q^O$ and $H_t$ are assumed to be constant during a control period, any exchanges made for a period are governed by the ratios of impact coefficients from the appropriate impact matrix. Thus, each period generates a new market equilibrium of temporary permit holdings.

The result of this market operation is that trades made during a polluter's most constrained period would dictate that plant's abatement capacity. Trades made during other periods would affect the polluter's abatement activity levels in the slack periods and so would be motivated by the desire to reduce operating expenses. In this way, polluters as a group can minimize construction costs as well as operating costs and achieve an efficient, streamwide abatement plan. In addition, the plan can be considered equitable if the initial allocation of permits is equitable. Fairness is achieved because any agent that performs more abatement in the least-cost solution than would be required in the initial allocation is compensated by revenues from permit sales or leases.

FOX RIVER SIMULATION OF T.D.P. MARKET PERFORMANCE

To simulate the operation of TDP markets on the Fox River, four annual scenarios of stream conditions were constructed from data on $H_t$ and $Q_t$ provided by the Wisconsin Department of Natural Resources. This data set was generated by use of the water quality simulation model, QUAL-3, as adapted for the Fox River. Each of the four scenarios represents a stylized "year" on the stream that is assumed to be replicated every year. Each scenario or "year" consists of three control periods (spring, summer, fall) defined by the appropriate $Q_t$ and $H_t$ values. The flows and temperatures of the scenarios are shown in Table 1.

Since there are two critical "sag points" in the DO profile of the Fox River, two linear constraints reflect post-BPT DO requirements in each of the three control periods. The TDP market solution is estimated as the solution to the resulting linear program.

Scenario A represents minimum flows and maximum temperatures normally observed in each of the three periods. This case is of primary interest because it includes the "worst case" period for which abatement planning will be carried out. The flow/temperature combination of 950 cfs and 80°F has been considered a "worst case" for the Fox River and so it is included in Scenario A as well as in Scenario S, the steady-state scenario.

Scenario B represents average flow/temperature conditions occurring in each period, and Scenario C represents the actual conditions observed during 1978. Scenarios B and C are analyzed to provide some insight into the comparison of the alternative regulatory strategies under a variety of potential river conditions. For the purpose of actual planning for the Fox River, though, Scenario A is the most realistic.

TABLE 1

Multiperiod Simulation Scenarios

| Scenario | Flow (cfs) | | | Temperature (°F) | | |
|----------|-----------|-----|-----|----|----|----|
| Period: | 1 | 2 | 3 | 1 | 2 | 3 |
| A | 1,500 | 950 | 950 | 80 | 80 | 72 |
| B | 2,500 | 1,500 | 1,500 | 72 | 72 | 64 |
| C | 2,500 | 2,500 | 1,500 | 64 | 72 | 72 |
| S | 950 | 950 | 950 | 80 | 80 | 80 |

TABLE 2

Abatement Cost Summary: Fox River

| Scenario | Transferable Discharge Permits | | Cluster Rule Allocation | |
|---|---|---|---|---|
| | Annual Expense[a] | Abatement Capacity[b] | Annual Expense[a] | Abatement Capacity[b] |
| A | 16,821 | 42,938 | 23,069 | 48,827 |
| B | 9,761 | 30,710 | 16,615 | 35,471 |
| C | 8,658 | 28,361 | 15,210 | 31,984 |
| S | 16,747 | 38,573 | 22,168 | 46,756 |

[a]Thousands of 1978 dollars.          [b]Pounds of BOD5 per day.

Permit allocations based on proportionate effluent reductions within clusters are used to generate alternative allocations for comparison with the allocation expected from TDP market operation. In addition, the "cluster" rule allocation is used as an initial allocation from which trading may occur. The abatement capacity and total annual expense results are summarized in Table 2.

Focusing on the nonsteady-state scenarios, Table 2 contains several useful pieces of information. First, it is clear that the TDP market solution potentially allows substantial cost savings in all three scenarios. For example, in Scenario A, the TDP allocation costs approximately $16 million annually, while the cluster allocation costs about $23 million. The cluster rule implies total annual expenditures about 42 percent greater than the potential TDP solution. Consequently, an authority and polluters could spend up to $7 million annually on the supervision of a market and still save money by its use.

Another interesting observation is that Scenario A does represent the most costly set of river conditions among the four scenarios. It was expected that Scenario A would be more costly than B or C because it included the apparent worst case based on flow/temperature information alone. But as was discussed previously, it was not clear whether Scenario A would be more costly than S. Since the minimum cost solution of Scenario A exceeds that of S, it is apparent that the other flow/temperature conditions included in A did generate increased capacity requirements for some polluters. This illustrates the previous conclusion that no single flow/temperature condition can be thought of, a priori, as an economic worst case.

TABLE 3

Abatement Requirements and DO Supplies TDP Solution:  Scenario A

| Agent | Period 1 | | | Period 2 | | | Period 3 | | |
|---|---|---|---|---|---|---|---|---|---|
| | BOD5 | DO 1 | DO 2 | BOD5 | DO 1 | DO 2 | BOD5 | DO 1 | DO 2 |
| 1 | 0 | .000 | .000 | 0 | .000 | .000 | 0 | .000 | .000 |
| 2 | 0 | .000 | .000 | 0 | .000 | .000 | 0 | .000 | .000 |
| 3 | 1269 | .269 | .150 | 2239 | .842 | .309 | 2239 | .775 | .363 |
| 4 | 7703 | 1.171 | .354 | 7703 | 1.750 | .354 | 7703 | 1.725 | .462 |
| 5 | 0 | .000 | .000 | 1999 | .356 | .076 | 1999 | .352 | .100 |
| 6 | 3042 | .365 | .183 | 3042 | .651 | .219 | 3042 | .602 | .262 |
| 7 | 0 | .000 | .000 | 0 | .000 | .000 | 0 | .000 | .000 |
| 8 | 0 | .000 | .000 | 1191 | .000 | .169 | 2258 | .000 | .361 |
| 9 | 9905 | .000 | 1.545 | 9905 | .000 | 2.694 | 9905 | .000 | 2.635 |
| 10 | 0 | .000 | .000 | 0 | .000 | .000 | 0 | .000 | .000 |
| 11 | 2394 | .000 | .249 | 5722 | .000 | .973 | 5722 | .000 | .996 |
| 12 | 7410 | .000 | 1.793 | 7410 | .000 | 3.275 | 7410 | .000 | 3.112 |
| 13 | 0 | .000 | .000 | 1468 | .000 | .713 | 1468 | .000 | .666 |
| 14 | 0 | .000 | .000 | 1193 | .000 | .377 | 1193 | .000 | .329 |
| Totals: | | | | | | | | | |
| | 31723 | 1.805 | 4.274 | 41872 | 3.605 | 9.160 | 42939 | 3.454 | 9.286 |

Abatement is measured in pounds BOD5 per day.
DO increase is measured in mg/L.


For brevity, detailed information is presented only for Scenario A.
The results are organized in Tables 3, 4, and 5.  Table 3 presents the
least-cost results expected from the TDP market.  Column 1 lists the
14 polluters in the order of their location on the Fox River, running
downstream.  Subsequent columns show the efficient allocation of
abatement requirements and the quantitites of DO supplied or released
from assimilative use through abatement.  For example, Agent 1 would
not be required to perform any post-BPT abatement in an efficient plan
and so would not supply DO at either critical sag, "DO1" or "DO2."

Table 4 shows all agents' abatement capacities and annual capital
expenses for the two allocation rules.  For example, after trading,

Agent 5 must construct a plant capable of removing 1,999 pounds of BOD5 per day at an annual capital cost of $313,000. If Agent 5 had not been allowed to buy permits, it would have had to comply with its cluster allocation by investing in 2,742 pounds of abatement capacity at an annual cost of $552,000.

Table 5 shows permit trades for all periods. A trade is defined as the difference between a post-trade abatement level and an initial abatement level for a given polluter. Hence, a negative entry indicates a sale (or leasing out) of permits for the duration of the control period. Agent 1, for example, is a net buyer of permits in each period. As shown in Tables 4 and 5, Agent 1 avoids the necessity of constructing abatement capacity of 244 pounds per day by purchasing

TABLE 4

Abatement Plant Capacity Requirements

| | TDP Equilibrium | | Cluster Reduction | |
|---|---|---|---|---|
| Agent | Abatement Capacity[a] | Capital Costs[b] | Abatement Capacity[a] | Capital Costs[b] |
| 1 | 0 | 0 | 244 | 615 |
| 2 | 0 | 0 | 3646 | 2105 |
| 3 | 2239 | 309 | 1557 | 98 |
| 4 | 7703 | 1320 | 5881 | 1008 |
| 5 | 1999 | 313 | 2742 | 552 |
| 6 | 3042 | 1011 | 2140 | 711 |
| 7 | 0 | 0 | 439 | 323 |
| 8 | 2258 | 601 | 1733 | 461 |
| 9 | 9905 | 6237 | 6784 | 4272 |
| 10 | 0 | 0 | 3618 | 2101 |
| 11 | 5722 | 2302 | 5441 | 2189 |
| 12 | 7410 | 2333 | 5425 | 1708 |
| 13 | 1468 | 1040 | 954 | 648 |
| 14 | 1192 | 717 | 8222 | 4947 |
| TOTALS: | 42938 | 16183 | 48827 | 21736 |

[a]Abatement capacity is measured in pounds of BOD5 per day.
[b]Cost is measured in thousands of 1978 dollars per year.

permits worth 244 pounds per day in Period 2, and lesser quantities of
permits in Periods 1 and 3. Clearly, the "capacity" relief is
determined at the margin by the Period 2 trade. The agent's willingness to pay for permits in Period 2 is based on the total costs
avoided, including capital costs.


PERMIT MARKET OPERATION WITH UNCERTAIN STREAM CONDITIONS

A crucial assumption maintained in the analysis so far is that the
parameters of the system are known in advance, even though they vary
across seasons. In reality, the underlying sources of variability —


TABLE 5

Permit Trades:    Scenario A

| Agent | Cluster | | |
|---|---|---|---|
|  | Period 1 | Period 2 | Period 3 |
| 1 | 192 | 244 | 189 |
| 2 | 2866 | 3646 | 2819 |
| 3 | −45 | −682 | −1035 |
| 4 | −3081 | −1822 | −3156 |
| 5 | 2155 | 743 | 121 |
| 6 | −1360 | −902 | −1388 |
| 7 | 345 | 439 | 340 |
| 8 | 1316 | 430 | −525 |
| 9 | −4750 | −3558 | −3121 |
| 10 | 2749 | 3385 | 3618 |
| 11 | 1740 | −632 | −281 |
| 12 | −3288 | −2334 | −1985 |
| 13 | 725 | −575 | −514 |
| 14 | 6247 | 6500 | 7029 |

Trades are measured in pounds of BOD5 per day.
Negative entries reflect effluent permit sales.
Positive entries reflect effuent permit purchases.

flow and temperature -- are difficult to predict. In this section we assume that $Q_t$ and $H_t$ are stochastic and examine the implications for the permit market. The problem can be described simply by focusing on a single monitoring location and by omitting time subscripts.

Suppose initially that only $Q^o$ is a normal random variable. In this case the regulatory authority cannot expect to achieve a deterministic DO target, but instead may impose a probablistic or "chance" constraint, such as:

$$Pr \{ Q \geq Q* \} \geq B$$

where B is the desired frequency of achieving the target.

In the context of the abatement model developed earlier, this new rule implies that the $\Delta Q$ vector in equation (1.3) consists of random variables and the typical constraint is written as:

$$PR \{ \Sigma h_i X_i \geq \Delta q \} \geq B \qquad (1.5)$$

If $\Delta q$ is distributed normally with mean $u$ and standard deviation $\sigma$, then equation (1.5) can be converted into the deterministic constraint, (1.6):

$$\Sigma h_i X_i \geq u + Z_B \sigma \qquad (1.6)$$

where $Z_B$ is the value of the standard normal variable corresponding to the B probability level.

Using the deterministic constraint (1.6), the authority can calculate a feasible initial allocation of permits and allow trading to proceed as in the fully deterministic case. Permit trading will not change the probability of a violation, since the DO "supply" term, $\Sigma h_i X_i$, remains constant.

But suppose instead that the impact coefficients, $h_i$, are stochastic. Then it can be shown that permit trading is not consistent with maintenance of even a probablistic water quality constraint. To see this, imagine the simplest case in which the impact coefficients are normally and independently distributed with means $u_i$ and standard deviations $\sigma_i$. Then the DO supply term in equation (1.5) is:

$$\Sigma h_i X_i \sim N (\Sigma u_i X_i, \Sigma X_i^2 \sigma_i^2)$$

Given the appropriate information, the authority could calculate an initial allocation of permits that would satisfy (1.5) in the same way as in the case of a stochastic $\Delta q$ term. But the relation would hold only for initial set of permits. Seeing that the variance of $h_i X_i$ is a weighted sum of the $\sigma_i$'s with the weights being $X_i^2$, clearly the variance of $\Sigma h_i X_i$ will change as a result of any reallocation of permits. Consequently, permit trading in this case would lead to a violation of the prescribed probability target.

This implication for permit trading deserves further examination, including an assessment of the damage of violating the DO target and of the potential frequency of violation under various assumptions regarding the distribution and correlation of the impact coefficients.


SUMMARY AND CONCLUSIONS

This paper has presented an evaluation of the potential performance of a BOD permit market on Wisconsin's Fox River in a multi-season setting. The empirical results include cost-effectiveness information as well as information on the probable pattern of permit trading. In addition, the paper presented a preliminary analysis of the problem of uncertainty in the regulation of the market.

The cost-effectiveness analysis suggested that the traditional rules for abatement allocation imply total system costs about 40 percent greater than the minimum-cost potential market solution. Under the worst-case flow/temperature scenario, it appears that up to $7 million could be spent annually on the management of a permit market before the market would become a less-preferred strategy.

The uncertainty analysis suggested that some types of uncertainty are more damaging to the market strategy than others. Specifically, if the impact coefficients that form the basis of the trading rules are stochastic, then it may not be possible to use the market to maintain a DO target with a desired frequency of violation.

In conclusion, the empirical analysis of the Fox River provides strong support for further consideration of the permit market idea. The cost differential between the market solution and alternate strategies appears to be so large that even serious operational difficulties may be unlikely to erase the advantage of the market. On the other hand, questions still remain regarding the stochastic nature of the system and the associated enforcement problem.


FOOTNOTES

[1]   In cases with several monitoring points, exact solutions may not exist, and some underutilization of available DO may result.

[2]   Such biological processes use microorganisms that "eat" BOD waste. When such an abatement plant is shut down, these organisms must be fed some BOD nutrient, such as molasses.


REFERENCES

Dales, J.H.  1968.  Pollution, property and prices.
    Toronto: University of Toronto Press.

David, M., et al. 1980. Marketable effluent permits for the control
    of phosphorus effluent into Lake Michigan.
    Water Resources Research 16:263-70.

de Lucia, R.J. 1974. An evaluation of marketable effluent permit
    systems. Socioeconomic Environmental Studies Service.
    Washington: USEPA (6005-74-030).

de Lucia, R.; McBean, E., and Harrington, J. 1978. A water quality
    planning model with multiple time, pollutant and source capabili-
    ties. Water Resources Research 14:9-14.

Eheart, J.W. 1980. Cost efficiency of transferable discharge permits
    for the control of BOD discharges.
    Water Resources Research 16:980-86.

Gale, D. 1960. The Theory of Linear Economic Models.
    New York: McGraw-Hill Book Company, Inc.

Hass, J.E. 1970. Optimal taxing for the abatement of water
    pollution. Water Resources Research 6:353-65.

Jordan, E.C. 1979. Preliminary data base for review of BATEA
    effluent limitations guidelines, NSPS, and pretreatment standards
    for the pulp, paper, and paperboard point source category.
    Washington: USEPA (68-01-4624).

Kneese, A.V., and Bower, B.T. 1968. Managing Water Quality:
    Economics, Technology, Institutions.
    Baltimore: Resources for the Future.

Montgomery, W.D. 1972. Markets in licenses and efficient pollution
    control program. Journal of Economic Theory 5:395-418.

O'Neil, W.B. 1980. "Pollution permits and markets for water
    quality." Ph.D. dissertation, University of Wisconsin-Madison.

Rose-Ackerman, S. 1977. Market models for water pollution control:
    Their strengths and weaknesses. Public Policy (Summer).

Tietenberg, T.H. 1979. Transferable discharge permits and the
    control of air pollution. Berlin: Institute for Environment and
    Society.

U.S. Environmental Protection Agency. 1978. Analysis of operations
    and maintenance costs for municipal wastewater treatment
    systems. Washington: USEPA (430/9-77-015).

USEPA. 1978. Construction costs for municipal wastewater treatment
    plants: 1973. Washington: USEPA (430/9-77-013).

Yaron, D. 1979. A model for the analysis of seasonal aspects of
    water quality control. Journal of Environmental Economics and
    Management 6:140-51.

# Is a Viable Implementation of TDPs Transferable?

**Martin H. David**

**Department of Economics**
**University of Wisconsin-Madison**

**Erhard F. Joeres**

**Environmental Studies and**
**Dept. of Civil & Environmental Engineering**
**University of Wisconsin-Madison**

WASTELOAD ALLOCATION REGULATIONS FOR WISCONSIN

In September 1981, the Wisconsin Legislature gave final approval to administrative regulations that provide the possibility for trading permits to discharge BOD on water quality-limited stream segments. The regulations represent the creative application of trading to deal with water quality problems in Wisconsin.

The administrative code enacted (N.R. 212) can be characterized as an APS with one pollutant -- BOD. The assimilative capacity at each receptor is determined by daily river flow and temperature as well as adjustments for monthly variables related to insolation. In its application to the Fox River, the system relates to two receptors.

Initial distribution of rights on the Fox River was based on 1972 maximum production levels at the paper mills on the river and 1976-77 average wastewater generation for the municipalities. (The share of rights will change over time as the municipalities have first claim on use of reserve capacity as their population rises. Initially, reserve capacity was distributed to all dischargers to avoid an excessive requirement for abatement.) The State of Wisconsin used a free initial distribution of permits; it did not consider selling off rights because the revenues thus earned appeared to present a constitutional problem, which we discuss here in greater detail later.

The administrative code adopted was permissive. Permits can be adjusted, subject to approval from the Wisconsin Department of Natural Resources (WDNR), which will scrutinize each proposed trade for consistency with the preservation of desired dissolved oxygen levels at the receptor points. No mechanism was proposed for establishing prices, for facilitating the flow of information between potential traders, or for brokering trades. This leaves the dischargers in the position of individualistic entrepreneurs who can seek to contract with any other dischargers for the sale or purchase of discharge rights. The period for which rights can be traded is limited by the five-year cycle on which permits are issued under the Wisconsin Pollution Discharge Elimination System.

Presently, only the Fox and Wisconsin rivers have multiple dischargers on water quality-limited stream segments, so only those stream segments are governed by a model of assimilative capacity for verifying the consistency of alternative discharge patterns with environmental standards. But other stream segments are potential candidates as the number of water-using dischargers increases.

The system is administered in three ways. Responsibility for monitoring river flow and temperature is in the hands of an operational agency; responsibility for operation of abatement plant, self-monitoring and locating trading partners lies with the dischargers; responsibility for enforcement, granting economic variances, the initial permit distribution, permit reissuance and modification of the administrative regulation rests with the WDNR. While this capsule summary of NR212 is incomplete and impressionistic, it will do until we are better able to put this trading system in perspective.


CONCLUSIONS

Four years' experience in the development of a set of regulations that enable the contracting of transfers of discharge permits has led us to four principal conclusions. Two arise out of the experience of what has already happened; two represent an agenda for what must be done to preserve the value of TDPs in future years. We believe that these conclusions offer convincing strategies for the development of TDPs in other geographic settings and an agenda for the continued development of TDPs in Wisconsin. Failure to understand these conclusions may account for the lack of implementation of TDPs in water pollution abatement. The delays in the implementation of TDPs in Wisconsin were certainly associated with our failure to appreciate these points.

These four conclusions must be dealt with in implementing TDPs:

1.  The financial incentives for systems of marketable permits are limited.

2.  TDPs constitute a small part of the regulatory structure; the implmentation of TDPs must be incorporated into policy decisions on much broader problems.

3.  Institutional adjustments that incorporate improved environmental modelling and changing concepts of equity will be required; a TDP system cannot generate those adjustments.

4.  Existing enforcement institutions and penalties do not provide incentives to use TDPs for short-term adjustments in discharge limits.

Each of these conclusions requires some elaboration. The first can be understood only when the participants in regulatory changes and their roles have been discussed. The second requires an understanding of the regulatory setting. (We deal with both of these in the next section.)  The third and fourth conclusions evolve from our discussion of ambiguity in the development of regulations and historical regulatory practices.

Recognizing that our perspective is limited, that we are privy neither to the day-to-day workings of the regulatory bureaucracy nor to the internal workings of industry, we offer our observations about the implementation of TDPs in Wisconsin as a set of "stylized facts" that we hope will encourage critical comment and elaboration from the parties involved.


OBSERVATIONS SUPPORTING THE CONCLUSIONS

The Participants
A superficial view of the regulatory problem posed by a need for cleaner water would suggest two participants -- the regulatory authority and the regulated dischargers.  Implementation of wasteload allocation regulations in Wisconsin (NR212) involved a considerably more complex roster of participants.[1]

The regulators include both the WDNR and the U.S. Environmental Protection Agency (USEPA).  Relationships between the two are not strictly hierarchical, as the WDNR has powers independent of the USEPA and its legislative mandates.  Yet it is clear that the principal drive for improved water quality derived from the 1972 amendments to the Clean Waters Act of 1965 (PL 92-500).  Wisconsin's primary response to that legislation was to pass the necessary enabling legislation to become the administrator for this federal law.[2]

The regulated include two extremely different groups -- the municipalities and the paper industry.  (A varied private industrial structure would be present in other settings, but in Wisconsin the paper industry dominates BOD discharges.)  They differ in motivation and in methods for financing wastewater treatment facilities.  The paper industry is an oligopoly in which many firms have a national, multiplant production operation.  Though the industry is tied to the resource base of pulpwood supplies, it has some flexibility in the location of those plants.

The availability of pulpwood in northern Wisconsin has prompted 14 firms to locate on the river, making Wisconsin's Fox River valley the site of the largest concentration of paper mills anywhere in the world.  They compete in varying degrees for the paper market, and they make use of the same common property resource -- dissolved oxygen for the disposal of BOD.[3]

The municipalities clearly differ from the paper industry in the nonprofit character of their wastewater treatment operations.  They also have access to federal subsidies for the construction of wastewater treatment plants -- a financial characteristic different from the financial incentive created for industry in the amortization provisions of the U.S. tax laws.

Several actors besides the regulators and the regulated made significant impacts on the regulatory framework. Section 208 of the 1972 ammendments to the Clean Water Act mandates that the development of a management plan for each river basin be the task of a designated regional agency. On the Fox River, the Fox Valley Water Quality Planning Agency (FVWQPA) was so designated. In the case of the Fox River, the FVWQPA was not directly responsible to the state government.

The "public" is a term loosely used to cover the remaining participants in the development of environmental regulation. Citizens, environmental lobbyists and academics might all play a role in the formation of regulations because of the mandate that new regulations be developed with public participation. In fact, as we will discuss later, the public contributed little to the development of TDPs through the legally mandated channels for public participation. The principal role of our research group was as an adjunct to the activities of the WDNR.


The Agenda
The task facing the participants was that of devising a regulatory scheme for maintaining ambient water quality standards. The means available included (1) those which reduced loading to the environment and (2) those which increased the assimilative capacity of the environment.[4]

Choosing among the feasible means entailed reaching a consensus on a scheme that was viewed as "equitable" from the perspectives of the various participants. Clearly, value judgements, differences in information and the objectives of the participants affected the way they ranked feasible alternatives. Technical judgements also affected the rankings, as different participants held different views on the impact of particular discharges on water quality.

Another way of describing this agenda is to stress that the task of the new regulation was to reduce demand for the assimilative level of the environment below the available supply. Demand results from emission of BOD wastes. Supply is generated by natural processes, augmented by in-stream aeration or the regulation of dams.[4] The additional factor introduced into this situation by TDPs is that demand may be conceptualized as an aggregate whose component parts may vary according to the contributions of individual dischargers. For a transfer to be feasible, it is necessary that the environmental impact of discharges be identical before and after the transfer.[5] Each of these concepts -- demand, supply and identity of environmental impact -- had to be precisely defined as part of the agenda for designing the new regulation.

Some sense of the difficulty attached to reaching a consensus may be gleaned by reviewing the ambiguities inherent in the task of implementing revised water quality regulations. This will be done in the next section, but first we digress to mention briefly the advantages of TDPs.

The availability of a market in permits relaxes a fixed constraint on dischargers. A percentage reduction from federally mandated categorical standards would prevail in the absence of TDPs. TDPs offer dischargers the alternative of purchasing a substitute for abatement. Entering the market is not coercive and will only be done when it appears profitable. In the short run, permits can be purchased to cover the excess discharges associated with plant failure or production overruns. On a seasonal basis, TDPs can be purchased to cover deficient abatement capacity during a period of exceptionally limited assimilative capacity in the river. On a long-term basis, TDPs may be used to provide for a substantial part of abatement during periods where one firm is deficient in abatement capacity while another has excess capacity. Sales would be arranged for an obverse set of motivations.

The estimated cost savings for the Fox River are significant. Several methodologies were used to estimate the savings, each leading to somewhat different valuations. O'Neil's programming model calculated costs for the long term in which all abatement plant is replaced; he found savings of 30 to 40 percent in comparison the the percentage allocation proposed without TDPs.[5] The savings calculated on the basis of existing abatement capacity and the projected need for additional facilities to meet federal categorical standards were somewhat lower, but between TDPs and other abatement alternatives it was estimated that little or no new construction would be required on the Fox River to meet ambient water quality standards.[4]

On the Fox and Wisconsin rivers, it appears likely that TDPs will be used to arrange both long and short-run adjustments.


AMBIGUITIES

One of the major obstacles to establishing a system of TDPs in this setting was the ambiguity associated with the regulatory task. Each of the elements in the agenda specified above is open to alternative interpretations, judgements and technical specifications. The water quality standard, the roster of feasible management alternatives, the concept of equity and the nature of environmental impacts associated with discharges -- none of these was well defined, yet each of them must be precisely defined before TDPs can be implemented.

The ambient water quality standard was not fully defined at the time that implementation of a new regulatory system began. Agreement had to be reached on both the minimum tolerable level of DO in the stream and the period over which the level had to be observed (the longer the period, the greater the opportunity for averaging peaks and pulses in discharges).

A second ambiguity surfaced when the dischargers pointed out that regulations were being designed to maintain ambient water quality for a "worst case" of simultaneous low flow and high temperature that had never occurred in 44 years of Fox River flow and temperature records. Dischargers argued that it was unreasonable to design regulations to meet such highly improbable conditions. Once this position had been accepted by the regulators, the question became one of what level of risk was tolerable to society and, conversely, what conditions must the dischargers anticipate in their plans for abatement? These questions had not clearly surfaced in the design of categorical standards for pollution abatement.

Other ambiguities were introduced by the model of the environment that relates discharges to environmental quality. Discharges clearly vary in their effect on levels of water quality. The location of the discharge, the nature of the process creating the discharge and measurable characteristics of the discharge each affect its impact at particular stream locations. The nature of the impact is modified by exogenous variables -- sunlight, temperature and flow -- which affect the assimilative capacity of the stream. The modelling of environmental impact entailed agreement on an abstract model of these variables and quantitative measures of its parameters. When a particular estimate of the model had been accepted by both the regulators and the regulated as a reasonable representation of environmental impact, equivalent environmental impacts could be calculated.[6]

Ambiguities in management strategy also confused the agenda for developing regulations. As long as the possibility of enhancing assimilative capacity remained, less need was felt for the exchange of discharge permits to accommodate real constraints at the plant level.

The ambiguity of the basis for allocating discharge permits also created difficulties. This was clearly a distributional issue in which the dischargers (and the public) were involved in an apparent zero-sum game. Dischargers winning a larger share of the initial allocation of permits would have less abatement problems. It was only after the model of the environmental impact was estimated that it became clear that allocation of abatement is a nonzero-sum game, since abatement by those dischargers with greatest impact on the critical points in the stream would permit an additional quantity of waste to be discharged elsewhere.[7] In any case, the principles for the initial allocation of permits were unclear while the regulation was being developed.

Another ambiguity involved the enforcement of environmental regulations. Historically, the WDNR had been vigorous in citing violators and pursuing informal remedies. At the same time, those with the most eggregious problems had been able to apply for variances. Such variances were granted to accommodate the gestation period of new facilities, local planning and delays encountered in receiving federal grants.

Few violations were transmitted to the state attorney general for prosecution. (The WDNR made it clear that it would not tolerate scofflaws in the Scott Paper case.[8]) As a consequence, dischargers worked in an environment in which penalties for violations were small, the probabilities of being fined were even smaller, and great potential existed for delaying the process of adjudicating a penalty.

The last ambiguity surrounding the development of NR212 concerned USEPA approval of the wasteload management plan. As WDNR was the administrator for USEPA's national system of discharge permits, any regulations issued through WDNR required USEPA approval.[9] Region V USEPA did not endorse many of the innovative approaches embodied in NR212, and the WDNR was forced into a position of challenging the USEPA to implement the system agreed upon by the participants.

From these examples we can infer that the broad agenda for increased pollution abatement encompassed a large number of poorly defined problems. Each problem had to be resolved before a workable scheme for TDPs could be put in place.


CONSTRAINTS ON THE PARTICIPANTS

Achieving the objectives of improved water quality in a regulatory system that incorporated TDPs was constrained by the roles of the participants and the information available. As these constraints imply a narrow scope for trading and limited financial gains from trading, it is useful to review them in some detail.

Constraints on the Regulators
The primary mission of the WDNR is to secure protection for the environment. The mandate to the WDNR is to promulgate regulations and enforce those regulations. The objectives of the national permit system for waterborne discharges and the state-designated ambient water quality standards for stream segments must be met. Nothing in the mission statement asserts a need for the WDNR to consider the private or social cost of abatement.

The other mandate on the WDNR is constitutional and affects the distributional consequences of uses of the natural resources of the state. Under the Public Trust Doctrine, the Wisconsin Constitution reserves the water resources of the state for the benefit of the general public.[10] The government may not act to convey rights to these water resources to particular individuals. Nonetheless, it is clear that the issuance of any form of permit to discharge wastes allocates the assimilative capacity of the state's waters.

These constraints create tensions for the implementation of TDPs. At a minimum, the constitutional doctrine implies that a monopoly right to discharge wastes cannot be granted to particular corporations. Some have argued that the Public Trust Doctrine also implies that the state cannot sell permits (e.g., by auction). The distribution of revocable (limited-term) permits was not viewed as a compromise of the public trust by the WDNR.

A third constraint on TDP implementation is that federal law maintains a minimum abatement requirement for each discharger. Limits are placed both on the daily maximum discharge and the monthly average

discharge.  Thus the scope for the trading of permits relates to the
excess  abatement  beyond  federal  categorical  standards  required  to
maintain  water  quality  on  water  quality-limited  stream  segments.
(Even on such segments, under favorable conditions of low temperature
and high flow, this excess requirement is zero.)

The  last  constraint  on  the  WDNR  was  procedural,  and  it  is  not  clear
how  significant  that  procedural  requirement  may  have  been.   As  the
FVWQPA was charged with developing a management plan for the Fox River
valley, it had the initiative, and the WDNR had the role of approving
a management plan.  (In the case of the Wisconsin River, the Section
208 agency was part of the WDNR, so this problem did not arise.)

If (as proved to be the case) the FVWQPA had few incentives to propose
TDPs,  it  would  be  difficult  to  incorporate  TDPs  as  an  option  for
managing environmental quality.

Constraints on the FVWQPA
The  principal  constraint  on  the  FVWQPA  was  its  funding.   It  had  been
created  and  funded  through  federal  legislation.   Upon  implementation
of  a  management  plan  for  the  Fox  River  valley,  the  FVWQPA  no  longer
had a clear mandate for continuing its existence.  Cuts in funding for
Section  208-related  activity  in  fiscal  1982  and  1983  have  made  this
constraint  binding.   As  a  consequence  of  its  limited  mandate  and
funding,  the  staff  of  FVWQPA  favored  those  management  alternatives
that require a public utility to deliver a public-good product, and
they favored the alternative of reregulating flow to gain increased
assimilative  capacity.   TDPs  did  not  require  this  type  of  public
utility and provided a substitute option.  The FVWQPA staff chose not
to  discuss  TDPs  in  its  report  to  the  WDNR,  though  the  WDNR  had
requested comments.[11]

Constraints on the Paper Industry
Four  factors  constrained  the  role  of  the  paper  industry  in  supporting
TDPs: (1) cost structure, (2) plant organization, (3) structure of the
industry  and  (4)  strategic  problems.   For  the  paper  industry  in
Wisconsin, pollution abatement costs have been estimated to be less
than one percent of the cost of the product.[12]  The potential gain
to  dischargers  from  trading  permits  is  a  small  fraction  of  that
abatement cost.  Thus, the scale of the financial rewards that TDPs
represent was far below the magnitude that would attract attention
from corporate officers concerned with the long-run financial picture.

As a consequence, decisions on pollution abatement fall on engineering
staff  at  the  plant  level.   These  technicians  have  little  direct
interest in the financial gains to be made from short-term trading of
permits.   Rather,  it  is  the  responsibility  of  the  technicians  to
assure  that  the  treatment  operation  is  maintained  in  good  working
order and that permit levels are not violated despite random shocks
and aberrations in the biological treatment system.  It appears that a
high premium was placed on a safety margin of treatment beyond that
required  to  meet  even  the  federal  categorical  levels  of  discharge.
(In  part,  such  margins  arose  out  of  long-term  planning  to  meet
increased  production  levels  and  the  legislated  targets  of  "zero

discharge by 1984.")   A decrease in the margin of safety for the plant
would make the operational decisions of the wastewater engineer more
difficult.

At plants with insufficient treatment capacity, one presumes that the
problems of negotiating variances and settlements for violations of
permits is handled by a legal staff, not the engineers.   Yet it was
the engineers who were involved in discussions of the management
alternatives for the wasteload allocation.   Hence, a curious situation
resulted -- those likely to be able to sell TDPs had little incentive
to do so, while those who might be interested in purchasing TDPs were
not involved in formulation of the regulations.

The foregoing argument stresses the facts that gains from trading TDPs
are small by comparison to any measure of the industry's financial
activity and that the managers in charge of the treatment plants would
be likely to find safety margins reduced by trades without seeing
compensating gains.

The remaining arguments are more strategic in character.   The
oligopolistic character of the paper industry implied asymmetric
interests in trading permits among the several firms with plants in
Wisconsin.   Historically, capital requirements and access to pulpwood
sources have kept new firms from entering production.   With a
relatively small number of producers, each realizes that its share of
the market is dependent on the actions of others.   At various times,
groups of Fox River firms have been prosecuted under federal antitrust
laws for colluding to set prices.   It is clear that each of the firms
knows they are competing for overlapping markets and that an increase
in marketed production at one plant potentially reduces the market
share of a (nearby) competitor.

Regulatory control of waste discharge affects this picture in two
ways.   First, each firm is directly affected, since the regulatory
control raises the cost of production, albeit to a different degree
for different firms.   Second, relative cost levels are altered by the
sale and purchase of TDPs.   Thus, the transferability of discharge
permits implies that firms compete for a cost determinant as well as a
share of the market.

Firms whose corporate financial policy has been to finance more-than-
adequate pollution abatement capacity will be the sellers under the
TDP system.   Managers of firms whose costs are high and whose
financial position limits the installation of new abatement capacity
are likely to be the buyers of TDPs.   Since participation in the TDP
market is (and must be) voluntary, the leaders of the successful firms
may prefer to forego short-run gains from the transfer of permits to
accelerate the failure of marginal firms.   A long-run profit to other
firms could result from the disappearance of the marginal firm.
Clearly, the various firms in the paper industry need not share a
common interest in TDPs.

Constraints on the Municipalities
The principal limitations on municipalities have already been

mentioned.  Wastewater treatment is a cost-recovery operation.  Fees
for sewage treatment are set in such a way as to cover the expense of
the operation.  Taken by itself, this does not imply less interest in
cost reductions than in profit-making enterprises.  However, the fees
that may be charged are reviewed by the Wisconsin Public Service
Commisssion.  Faced with the need to justify rate changes to that body
and considerable inertia in the process of reviewing rates (i.e.,
regulatory lag), the plant manager is likely to discount both the
value of revenues that might follow from the sale of TDPs and savings
in abatement costs that result from purchase of TDPs.

The second factor constraining municipal interest in TDPs is that
financing for new construction is heavily subsidized by federal
grants.  Such subsidies reduce the perceived costs of excess capacity
and direct the attention of managers towards the regulations that
accompany federal participation in construction projects.  Stipula-
tions accompanying federal grants that a municipality may not "profit"
from its use of such funds cause some uncertainty.  Would earnings
from the sale of TDPs be construed as a profit?  Would that endanger
the subsidy?  The answers are not clear, and we surmise that a
cautious manager would not want to jeopardize grant funds through the
sale or lease of TDPs.

The foregoing argument indicates why managers of municipalities might
not be interested in revenues from TDPs.  Why would a manager fail to
be interested in the opportunity to purchase TDPs?  Existing regulatory practice is to grant variances to municipalities that do not have
sufficient abatement capacity.  This practice undercuts demand for
TDPs.  Were the WDNR to insist that variances be granted only after
the possiblity of purchasing sufficient TDPs was proven to be
infeasible, two of the four municipal dischargers on the Fox River
could be expected to investigate the purchase of TDPs.  With a TDP
purchase, one community could avoid substantial capital outlay.  For
the other, advantages arise from the timing of the investment relative
to its population growth.

## Constraints on Public Involvement

To the extent that the beneficiaries of TDPs -- consumer users of the
environment and shareholders -- recognize the value of TDPs, these
consumers might provide a political force for the adoption of a TDP
system.  Unfortunately, mobilization of the public is unlikely.
Little public involvement was evident in the promulgation of
NR212.[13]  In the first place, comprehending the details of an actual
system for trading permits requires understanding of the numerical
model of the environment, of economics and industrial organization,
and of the interactions among the dischargers and between the
dischargers and the environment.  None of the information needed for
such an understanding was easily accessible to the general public.
Secondly, the use of TDPs implies the relocation rather than the
elimination of discharge.  This is not a comforting fact for the
environmentalists who may be lobbying for zero discharge.

The principal means for mobilizing general public support for TDPs
appears to be through demonstrated cost savings, and as we suggested

earlier, even substantial savings are not likely to appear large because prices of consumer goods are negligibly affected and because federal subsidies to municipalities insulate taxpayers from the full capital cost of a new abatement plant.

The gist of this argument is that none of the participants have strong incentives to support TDPs. Neither financial nor political incentives appear to move TDPs to the center of regulatory reform. (Some ways in which incentives can be made more apparent to the beneficiaries of a TDP system are discussed at the end of this paper.)


LIMITATIONS OF T.D.P.s

Some advocates of TDPs suggest that they cure all regulatory difficulties. Overselling the system is of no help. TDPs can provide flexibility for new water-using industries. They can be devised in a way that a reduction in discharge can be achieved through purchases in the marketplace. Three aspects of the system in which TDPs are embedded will require continuing review outside of the market mechanism : (1) the environmental model, (2) the equity of principles for allocating permits (whether temporary or permanent property rights) and (3) synergisms in the regulation of different pollutants.

It was clear in the development of TDPs in Wisconsin that a consensus on NR212 depended on the willingness of both dischargers and regulators to accept a model of the environment. The model was not perfect, yet consensus was reached on a model for the upper reaches of the river. But wasteload allocation for the remaining dischargers on the Fox River requires a more elaborate model to conform to observed conditions. As environmental modelling becomes more precise, there will be a future need to review the basis on which different dischargers can trade permits. This activity must be done outside of the marketplace.

A second problem lies in the perception of equity involved in the rights to permits. If growth in some industries occurs while others decline, it may not be perceived as equitable to award the first users of discharge rights the perpetual ownership of those rights. The institutional framework for TDPs must contemplate this problem. The federal permit system assures that rights must be reissued periodically. What is required in addition is some formula for the continuing reallocation (or auction) of those rights. As we have indicated, in Wisconsin, allocation appears to be constitutionally preferred to auctioning.

The third area where the marketplace will not be sufficient results from the dynamic agenda for environmental regulation. At present, we have reasonably well-formulated principles for the regulation of BOD. Principles for the regulation of other pollutants have yet to be established. Since pollutants generally interact, the market in one pollutant will need to be re-examined as others are brought under control.

CONSEQUENCES

The constraints we list imply that few financial incentives exist for setting TDPs in place — for either the regulators or the regulated. The regulators also had little political incentive to incorporate the transferability feature because so few of the participants (and almost none of the public) understood their implications. Furthermore, industrial structure and the dependency of municipalities on federal grants assure that neither buyers nor sellers would wish to reveal clearly their demands (supplies) of permits.

Hence, Conclusion 1:  The financial incentives for TDPs are limited.

Ambiguity implied that the assimilative capacity of the environment was unknown and the nature of the constraint on demand for its use was therefore unclear.  Ambiguity also implied that the setting of a standard for ambient water quality required a consensus, not an arbitrary declaration.  Uncertainties surround the modelling of environmental impact.  All of these imply that TDPs could only be understood in relation to a broad discussion of regulatory structure through which participants reach consensus on parameters and the dimensions of the environmental standard.

Hence, Conclusion 2:  TDPs are a small part of the regulatory agenda; implmentation must be embedded in that agenda.

The same need for an understanding of environmental impact implies that continued investigation of environmental models will be required to assure their accuracy and admit the modelling of additional dimensions of emissions.

Hence, Conclusion 3:  The marketplace does not substitute for institutional adjustments that incorporate improved environmental modelling and changing concepts of equity.

Demands for TDPs may be short-term, covering emergency needs.  The availability of TDPs on a short-term basis encourages plant managers to reduce their safety margins and allow more of the assimilative capacity to be utilized.  These behavioral responses are wanted to avoid the building of excess abatement plant.  At the same time, they change the need for effective enforcement.  Penalties for violations must be immediate and large in relation to marginal treatment costs. Otherwise, dischargers operating near their permitted limits have no incentive to purchase permits.

Hence, Conclusion 4:  Existing enforcement institutions and penalties are inappropriate for a regulatory environment in which TDPs permit short-term adjustments in discharge limits.


SUCCESSFUL IMPLEMENTATION OF T.D.P.s ELSEWHERE

The foregoing conclusions may appear to have a negative tone, but we feel that they offer positive direction to those who wish to develop TDPs in other settings and those who wish to maintain existing systems.

## Embed TDPs in Regulatory Reform

We have pointed out that, for the principal participants, financial incentives are not significant for establishing a TDP system. This lack of incentive is further compounded by the ambiguities described as well as the limitation of the use of TDPs on water quality-limited streams only: since all dischargers must meet the federally prescribed categorical treatment levels, discharges are bounded. The opportunity for trading is available only when ambient water quality conditions dictate further treatment.

It is consequently difficult to establish a forum where TDPs receive serious consideration and discussion. Such a forum can best be created by embedding discussion of TDPs in broader regulatory reform. The willingness of the regulator to allow the dischargers to partici- pate from the outset in discussions for new regulations is essential. The dischargers must feel that they are part of the reform process so that a general dialogue and consensus mode can develop.

It is difficult to engender the feeling among dischargers that real policy innovation is possible. Past regulatory policy development has put them on the defensive. They expect to be faced with fully defined policy options to which they can react only in self-defense. This feeling of impotence can be countered only through a slow and tedious process: dischargers must be able, through technical advisory committees or similar instruments, to confront regulatory staff personnel -- the planners and modelers themselves -- directly at the outset.

Each group will initially be suspicious, even hostile, of the other. The process of questioning contemplated control actions does not eliminate the adversarial climate, but it does allow for emerging consensus that policy options should be examined for their effective- ness in achieving improved environmental quality. The feeling that real regulatory innovation is possible can develop from dialogue.

## Create Incentives

Once a dialogue has been established, incentives must be provided for the participants to advocate TDPs. The secondary role of financial incentives requires that others must be found to take their place. For the dischargers, the important incentive is that TDPs allow flexibility in operation. Industries can then more readily vary production and operate closer to the margin without always having to consider long-range capital investment planning. While it is hard to value flexibility in dollars, flexibility can be stressed as an advantage.

Municipalities can gain from improved timing of wastewater treatment plants. Delays in construction can be handled with the purchase of permits, rather than requests for variances. And the delay in construction may allow refinement of population service demand projections. This creates potential for improved plant designs.

Incentive for the regulator derives from the fact that TDPs support the environmental mission of the agency. TDPs enhance the likelihood of meeting environmental goals. Requiring dischargers to fully explore TDPs prior to requesting variances will reduce the number of such requests to the agency, thus reducing the need for difficult social welfare decisions.

With the identification of these incentives, it remains to find ways to inform the participants to see TDPs as being in their own best interest. Here the public advocacy of unaffiliated researchers can play a major role. It can be hoped that public discussion and understanding of TDPs through wider use will provide the public advocacy climate.

## MAINTENANCE OF T.D.P.s IN THE FUTURE

The incorporation of TDPs into the administrative rules of the WDNR is no guarantee that the benefits available under such a permit system will be sustained. We see two issues that must be addressed to make the system work:

### 1. Create Institutional Capability for Future Adjustments

We have pointed to the hurdles and ambiguities that confound creation of a TDP system. Models of the environmental response to pollution will change and be refined; societal attitudes will shift, causing redefinition of acceptable water quality; the mix of dischargers will be altered in number and capacity; and concepts of equity will be modified. All of these changes indicate that an institutional capability for making changes in the permit system must be maintained. This can perhaps best be accomplished by maintaining the Technical Advisory Committees (TAC) as permanent forums. Prior to any permit re-issue cycle, the TAC can engage in periodic review of the permit system.

### 2. Modify Enforcement

The present enforcement approach -- or rather, experience -- undermines demand for TDPs in Wisconsin. Financial penalties for violations must exceed the cost of purchasing permits; otherwise, no inducement for permit trading exists. One change that may have merit is the "parking ticket" (stipulated forfeitures) approach. Dischargers agree to a schedule of penalties in advance of permit trading. Violations become automatic grounds for assessment of the penalty. Protracted adjudicative proceedings are eliminated. Whenever a discharger exceeds the allowable permit level, the fine that results is known a priori. Research is needed to set the fine schedule sufficiently high to provide inducement for dischargers to seek permit trades to remain in compliance, yet reasonable enough that treatment plant failure does not threaten the existence of the enterprise.

In summary, we return to the rhetorical question in the title of our paper: "Is a viable implementation of TDPs transferable?" Our answer is a qualified yes. We have summarized a number of observations and conclusions. All of them are generic to policy evolution in the

public institutional setting. Once the major hurdle -- the resistance
to change -- is accepted, recognition of the factors that must be
dealt with and positive efforts towards their resolution should give
TDPs a reasonable chance of success.


NOTES

1    Chapter NR212, Wisconsin Administrative Code, modified NR102 and
     NR104(a) creating permits that vary by flow and temperature
     (Sections 40 and 60), (b) establishing a legal framework for
     in-stream aeration and flow reregulations (Sections 12 and 13)
     and (c) allowing for modifications of point source allocations
     (Section 11). This last section provides:
     "(2) For stream segments where the reserve capacity is zero, new
         or increased point source discharges may be allowable
         through the permit issuance or modification process under
         the following conditions:
         (a) The person applying for the new or increased permit
             source discharge secures a legally binding agreement
             that one or more existing point source allocations shall
             be reduced by an amount sufficient to prevent the total
             maximum load from being exceeded; and
         (b) The amounts by which the existing point source alloca-
             tions are reduced account for the differences in waste
             characteristics and locations of the affected point
             sources; or
         (c) The new or increased discharge shall only occur during
             stream conditions where that discharge will not cause
             the total maximum load to be exceeded."

2    Waltraud Arts and James L. Arts. 1980. The legal standing of
     TDPs. IN: Market Flexibility with Regulatory Control: Imple-
     mentation of Transferable Discharge Permits on the Fox River,
     Wisconsin, eds. Martin David and Erhard Joeres (forthcoming).

3    Jack Day, William Ellman, Donald Theiler and Roy Christenson.
     March 1980. River cleanup plan developed with citizens and
     industry. Civil Engineering (ASCE), pp. 78-81.

4    Elizabeth David and Martin David (forthcoming.) Implementing
     the clean water act: Cost-effective options. Water Resources
     Bulletin.

5    William O'Neil, Martin David, Christina Moore and Erhard Joeres
     May 1981. Transferable discharge permits and economic effici-
     ency. Madison, Wis.: Social Systems Research Insitute (DP8107).

6    Christina Moore. 1980. Implementation of transferable discharge
     permits when permit levels vary according to flow and tempera-
     ture. Madison, Wis.: Department of Civil and Environmental
     Engineering.

[7]    William B. O'Neil.   1980.   "Pollution permits and markets for
       water quality."  Ph.D. dissertation (unpublished), University of
       Wisconsin-Madison.

[8]    State of Wisconsin vs. Scott Paper Company.

[9]    See Arts and Arts, note #2.

[10]   See Arts and Arts, note #2.

[11]   Fox   Valley   Water   Quality   Planning   Agency.   March,   1981.
       Management  structure  to  implement  wasteload  allocations  for  the
       Lower Fox River.   Appleton: FVWQPA, September 1980.

[12]   Russell Pittman.   1979.   "The costs of water pollution control to
       the   Wisconsin   paper   industry:   Estimation   of   a   production
       frontier."    Ph.D.    dissertation    (unpublished),    University    of
       Wisconsin-Madison.

[13]   At hearings held by the Citizen Board of the WDNR in March 1981,
       only   one   public   witness   commented   on   the   marketable   permit
       option.    The representative of Citizens for a Better Environment
       (David Bartell) discussed the value of management options that
       would maintain clean water at low cost.

[14]   While   public   involvement   in   the   process   of   formulating   new
       environmental regulations was assured by PL 92-500, the limited
       information available to most of the public and the complexities
       of the decisions that were required to implemented TDPs implied
       that  few  beyond  those  with  direct  interests  would  be  able  to
       understand, much less advocate, TDPs.

# Economics and Public Policy on Pollution: Some General Observations

**Daniel W. Bromley**

**Chairman, Department of Agricultural Economics**
**University of Wisconsin-Madison**

In presenting some general observations on the public policy problem of transferable discharge permits, I would like to comment on several specific aspects of a few of the preceding papers and also comment on the institutional environment in which such permits must function.

In general, I was encouraged by the tenor of the discussions I heard at the conference in June 1982. There has been little talk of the "optimal" level of environmental quality; instead, there has been a search for efficiency within a policy context, where the objective function has been specified by the political process. Foster said it well when he noted the reluctance of politicians to rush into a market for TDPs out of recognition that it was a form of market failure that led us into our current problem [p. 71]. The recognition of the political climate pervaded the conference, and it is a healthy sign that we can accept the world as it is yet still attempt to improve upon obvious inefficiencies when we can locate them.

Indeed, recall that a major social choice is that of deciding which subset of human interactions is to be decided on the basis of bargained exchange and which will remain outside of the market. Given the immense political costs of removing an activity from the domain of individual choice, I find the reluctance of politicians to introduce markets in pollution permits quite explicable. Just consider the intense struggle over land use controls and the perceived threat to individual sovereignty from any public action. Once a domain of choice is given to private individuals, the state faces a difficult task in reclaiming that authority if antisocial outcomes persist. Economists are not the only ones who worry about irreversibilities.

One of the speakers at the conference referred to institutions as "anything that impedes the application of a viable theory." I was most unhappy to see institutions relegated to the general class of constraints. Institutions liberate as well as constrain; accelerated depreciation, investment tax credits and tax-deductable interest on home mortgages are all examples of facilitating institutions. If TDPs are accepted as a policy instrument, it will be because of facilitating institutions; moreover, if they are rejected in the political process, it will be because certain influential individuals or groups were opposed to them. To refer to this opposition and subsequent absence of facilitating institutional arrangements as mere constraints sweeps too much under the rug.

It was interesting to be reminded that the offset policy opened the door to a discussion of TDPs; in this instance economists were ahead of the politicians and responded quickly to the opening. In effect, a legislative mandate created a demand for economic models. I find an interesting parallel in the Flood Control Act of 1936, which stimulated the development of benefit-cost analysis.

In the public works field, there was the legislative mandate to the agencies that they could build anything they wished if the benefits exceeded the costs. Of course, the interesting problem was one of how to determine benefits and costs. In the public works area, the construction agencies had the budgets and the powerful constituencies; economics became the handmaiden of what they wished to accomplish. And an entire generation of economists spent considerable time both perfecting benefit-cost techniques for the agencies, as well as criticizing the agencies when proper methods were not followed.

In the case at hand, the Clean Air Act created a policy objective that was unattainable, so a concerned agency sought professional help. But from what I have seen of the work on TDPs both at the conference and in the literature, I am encouraged by the absence of condescension toward the particular agencies responsible for implementing pollution control programs.

Turning to another matter, I should like now to talk of property arrangements, politics and Pareto. One author raised the issue of compensation to the "victims" of regulation and proposed an interesting mechanism whereby this might be achieved. I am not prepared to provide critical comments on the particular mechanism chosen, but the paper raises the essential institutional questions that most of the other authors simply ignored.

As one who is fascinated by the constant struggle between the state and the private sector, I believe it is appropriate to remind you of the difference between eminent domain and the exercise of the policy power. As you know, eminent domain protects owners of real property from uncompensated losses when that economic value is taken for the creation of public benefits. On the other hand, the police power is exercised to preclude the creation of public harm. With this in mind, I ask you to ponder momentarily the issue of the "victims" of environmental regulation. Few of us would give serious thought to the compensation of the "victims" of speed limits, drug laws or prohibitions against molesting small children. These too are regulations, enacted for the simple reason that the world will be a more civilized place with such rules than without them.

While I appreciate the fact that the current government in Washington is much concerned with "overregulation" -- and I defy an economist to define that apart from his/her political views -- we must be careful not to be drawn into a trap. Indeed, talk of mechanisms to compensate the victims of environmental regulations overlooks the logically prior question of what sort of world we wish to live in and who will bear the costs of attaining that world.

The neo-Wicksellians are apparently attracted to the compensation rule because it recognizes the special position of the status quo ante; indeed, good Wicksellians seem especially concerned with the activist state. But what sanctity ought we to accord the status quo? There is no compelling logic to sustain an argument that firms caught by changing tastes and preferences ought to be compensated. We know that discipline comes through the market: he who makes lousy hamburgers will soon be back at his former occupation. But when changing tastes come through the political arena rather than a leftward shift in the demand curve, some economists start to worry about compensation. I understand the conventional efficiency/equity arguments but suggest that we reconsider this conventional wisdom in light of a world of pervasive market/state interactions. Obviously, the state cannot continuously change institutional arrangements without some compensation to those harmed, but few can argue that environmental regulations represent some recent whim on the part of the state.

Moreover, it is incorrect to invoke Pareto in a discussion of the compensation of those adversely affected by regulation. Pareto optimality is only defined within a particular structure of property entitlements (called "resource endowments" in our texts). One goes beyond our science to say that one property structure (and consequent wealth position) is Pareto superior to another property structure (and attendant wealth position). In point of fact, the policy options are Pareto-noncomparable.

Reference is often made to the property values destroyed by regulation. In environmental control, what has been taken is not a recognized property right but usually a presumptive right on the part of the erstwhile polluter. I know that the state regularly indemnifies all manner of ill-gotten gains, but let us be clear that polluters never possessed "rights" to anything. What they exercised was "privilege" and others had "no rights" in the terminology of John R. Commons. That legal setting is in the process of being transformed into one where the air and water are being converted from open-access resources, where dischargers enjoy privilege, to the common property of all citizens, where "rights" over quality must now be recognized, with which dischargers have a "duty" to comply.

In sum, I see an impressive account here of relatively solid conceptual and empirical work, virtually all of it concerned with the questions: (1) could permit markets function? (2) what would those markets look like? and (3) would those markets be stable? I hope that future work on TDPs will be directed toward the political and institutional environment within which such markets would operate.

There was some discussion at the conference about the possibility of environmental groups as potential bidders for permits. I wish someone had asked why it is that such groups ought to be required to purchase

clean air and water?  If we are so serious about the sanctity of the
status quo, then it becomes crucial to establish which time period is
recognized as the real status quo.  Some could argue that the relevant
status quo is prior to all discharges of pollutants.  Now that's a
real initial condition for the Wicksellians!  Let us ask why it is
that the state should now compensate the "victims" of environmental
regulation, or require those who simply want clean air and water to
buy out those currently using the natural environment as a refuse dump.

The prevailing institutional structure has an important affect on the
nature   of   so-called   efficient   bargains   —   not   to   mention
distributional matters.  We might ask those who want clean air and
clean water what level of compensation would be required for them to
acquiesce in the continued discharge of pollutants (thus preventing
the attainment of the initial status quo).

Hence, I am impressed both by the sophistication of the economic
models  and  by  the  naivete  of  the  political  and  institutional
analysis.  But then that is the case with virtually all political
economy these days.  My hope is that someday soon we will start to
work on the naive part.

# Transferable Discharge Permits: An Implementor's View

**Donald Theiler**

**Director, Bureau of Air Management
Wisconsin Department of Natural Resources**

I would like to take this opportunity to discuss some problems I have encountered with the concept of transferable discharge permits in the field of environmental regulation. Many papers at the conference dealt with transferable discharge permits as though they were a purely hypothetical concept that may or may not actually be adopted in the future. Transferable discharge permits are not theory. They exist today. The Clean Air Act provides for the transfer of emission rights between existing and prospective facilities in nonattainment areas. These transfers are known as "offsets." They are built into the regulatory structure of each state's State Implementation Plan for nonattainment areas. They embody nearly all of the characteristics of transferable discharge permits as discussed at the conference. We also have the "internal offset," or "bubble," which allows a transfer of emission reduction credits between emission units within a facility. Bubbles do not involve transfers between firms but are otherwise interchangeable in the classic sense. In water, the transferable discharge permit idea is not as fully developed, but it does exist in a limited form here in Wisconsin.

What has been the experience of the state regulatory agencies in implementing these concepts? In my view, it is mixed at best. Some of the advantages often credited to the transferable discharge permit have been realized in providing cost savings and flexibility to some members of the regulated community, but problems have already developed. I would like to list some of these problems to give you an idea why bureaucrats like myself have reservations about the wholesale, unquestioning adoption of the concept. I will focus on air emission offsets and bubbles, because this is where we have the most experience.

Two major philosophical problems present themselves. First is the creation of a "property right" in the use of the assimilative capacity of the environment, and the second is the apparent move away from the "technology-forcing" aspects of the Clean Air Act.

Should the assimilative capacity of the environment to accept waste be turned into a property right? If so, on what basis should these property rights be distributed? With regulatory developments like offsets, bubbles and banking, we are rapidly turning the assimilative capacity of the environment into what very closely resembles a "property right." This is happening without really answering the questions posed above. The exact legal status of this "property right" is not well defined at this time. The general public currently has little cognizance of the significance of these developments. We are moving toward a situation where a few private entities could hold the economic future of an area in their hands because of their control of the assimilative capacity of the environment for various emissions. This control is currently being given away on a first-come, first-serve basis. The country has already gone through giveaways of this type in the distribution of water rights in the West and grazing rights on public lands. It would seem that we should learn from these lessons; this does not appear to be happening.

The second philosophical problem is the apparent movement away from the concept of forcing new pollution control technology during the modernization process at existing facilities and during the construction of new emission sources. Both the Clean Air Act and the Clean Water Act recognized that it was much easier and more economical to utilize the latest in pollution control technology during the process of making major capital investments at a facility than to try to retrofit old equipment. As old equipment turns over, the entire universe of emission points would eventually be controlled with the latest pollution control technology. This would result in continued improvement in air quality and increased assimilative capacity to accommodate new growth.

The development of the ability to credit emission reductions from existing facilities against new development (internal offsets, or bubbling) has begun to undercut this concept. Facilities are making increasing use of this technique to escape various technology-forcing requirements. What appears to be happening in some cases is that the emission reductions which receive credit are reductions which would result regardless of the new development occurring. Examples are facility shutdowns, paving and highly efficient retrofit technology, like baghouses. These reductions are then used as a justification for not putting the latest control technology on new and modified existing sources. The Reagan administration appears to be considering the expansion of this concept under the rubric of "regulatory reform." Such action will slow the improvement in air quality that has occurred across the nation. This may be warranted when measured against the cost savings, but again I do not believe that adequate attention has been focused on the philosophical question.

A number of practical problems also have arisen with the development of transferable discharge permits. They include trading of non-equivalent pollutants, paper offsets, increased administrative burden and the inefficiencies resulting from a poorly developed market.

The trading of nonequivalent pollutants is a problem that is often ignored. For example, within the category of volatile organic compounds, some compounds are listed as being considerably more toxic

than others. Should they be traded equally, regardless of potential
health hazard? Another example results from the trading of particulate emissions that are not inhalable against the fine particulates
that do present a health hazard. The larger particles are much more
amenable to control than fine particulates and therefore provide an
attractive alternative for reduction to offset against the difficult-
to-control fine particulates. This problem may be overcome with more
refined definitions, but this redefinition will considerably reduce
the size of the markets. Also, the present administration at USEPA
appears to be going in just the opposite direction.

"Paper offsets" are occurring that may result in actual increases in
pollution because the emission reductions claimed for credit exist on
paper only. This situation may arise when a facility can claim credit
for emissions that do not exist. A common example is a facility that
receives credit in their permit for theoretical emissions occurring at
a constant rate over a 24-hour period, when in fact the facility never
operates at that level. This is a very troublesome problem for which
no adequate resolution has been developed. In the development of
permit conditions it is nearly impossible to limit the emissions from
a facility to its recent actual level when that level differs
significantly from its potential. Such action would severely limit
the flexibility of existing establishments to use their facilities.
On the other hand, crediting the facility with its legal allowable
(potential) can result in paper offsets. The paper offset occurs when
that potential is sold by the company because it decides it does not
need the flexibility to operate at its allowable level.

A very practical problem for an administrator like myself is the
additional administrative burden that reforms such as transferable
discharge permits entail. It is frequently stated that regulatory
reforms like liberalized offset requirements and bubbles will reduce
the administrative burden. Not true! Offsets and bubbles increase
the administrative burden on regulatory agencies. There is no
comparison between the administrative simplicity and ease of enforce-
ability of a generic single-source, single-emission limit program to a
uniquely devised multiple-source bubble option. Each bubble must be
developed and evaluated as a unique entity, and individually tailored
compliance programs must also be developed. Offsets also provide
increased tracking problems for the administering agency in addition
to the fact that each facility must be treated on a unique basis
rather than generically. Adequate resources should be provided to the
regulatory agencies to run these increasingly complex programs. This
does not appear to be the direction in which we are heading; in fact,
our administrative resources are rapidly diminishing. Therefore, I
fear that we will end up with a monumental administrative mess on our
hands.

The last problem I would like to touch on is the lack of trading in
the marketplace. Many potential offsets exist, but very few trades
actually occur. Every study of which I am aware confirms this fact.
This is due to a number of interrelated factors, but I believe the
basic cause of this lack of trading is a very poorly developed and
poorly understood market. Companies that have already generated

offsets have a very difficult time estimating their worth and are reluctant to part with the offset because it may be needed in the uncertain future, either as a buffer against enforcement action for violations of existing source emission limits, or to accommodate new growth at the existing plant site. Facilities that might generate offsets have little or no incentive to do so because of this poorly developed market. There is also a very real fear that, if offsets are generated, they will be "confiscated" by the regulatory agencies in their efforts to reduce emissions. As long as the market is not well developed, the need to obtain an offset may be viewed as an insurmountable barrier to development at certain locations.

I appreciate this opportunity to discuss this fascinating development in the field of environmental regulation. Though my comments may not reflect it, I am actually in favor of transferable discharge permits. However, we must be realistic and not expect that they are a great panacea, that they will be easily implemented, or that they will be widely and quickly accepted. They are useful in certain situations and may provide a very useful regulatory tool to obtain and maintain a cleaner environment, which is really what the environmental protection program is all about.

When economists undertake post-mortem studies on the concept of transferable discharge permits and "discover" some of the problems I have outlined here, don't be surprised.

# Summary

**Pixie A.B. Newman**

Dept. of Civil & Environmental Engineering
University of Wisconsin-Madison

**Stuart S. Rosenthal**

Department of Economics
University of Wisconsin-Madison

In these times of growing economic costs, regulatory reforms like transferable discharge permits (TDPs), which can achieve environmental goals at comparatively low costs, are becoming increasingly popular. Once promoted solely by economists (theoreticians), TDPs are now being formally recognized as legitimate regulatory options by state and federal agencies. So great is the potential role of TDPs in environmental pollution control that the administrator of USEPA has proclaimed TDPs "the most important innovation in environmental policy for the next decade" (Theiler). TDPs are being implemented in noncompliance air quality management areas across the country and have been written into water quality management law in at least one state (Wisconsin's NR212 for water quality-limited streams).

TDPs will have an impact on the vested interests of all groups affected by environmental regulations. To safeguard their interests, environmental organizations and industry as well as regulatory agencies should become familiar with the details of potential market-oriented reforms. Through the political process, these groups may express their views and, in turn, may help to develop TDP systems that are best-suited to a particular pollutant, watershed or airshed.

Held at a time when many state agencies are beginning to seriously consider implementation of TDPs, this conference brought together individuals from four distinct groups: state and federal regulators, economists, scientists and engineers, and industrial and municipal dischargers. Conference presentations highlighted a myriad of economic, political and scientific questions related to the development and implementation of TDP systems. The broad range of issues analyzed to date reflects the interdisciplinary character of environmental management.

The views of conference participants, as presented in their papers during formal and informal discussions, on the issues surrounding the implementation of TDPs are summarized below. The principal issues and concerns are grouped into three sections, covering (1) the political and institutional barriers to incorporating market emission/discharge permits (i.e., TDPs) into regulatory reform, (2) the technical (scientific and economic) problems of designing market and institutions for implementing TDPs and (3) implications of using marketable permits for enhancing environmental quality. These are followed by some concluding comments.


## INCORPORATING T.D.P.s INTO REGULATORY REFORM

Before market-mechanisms for pollution control can be incorporated into state and federal regulatory reform, advocates for this reform must recognize certain political and institutional realities that may retard the adoption of TDPs. Where possible, advocates of these reforms should modify their approach to counteract or balance the influence of these realities. This section discusses political inertia, characteristics of regulatory personnel and existing regulations, the lack of industrial support for TDPs, ambiguities, and political controversies that must be resolved before a viable TDP system can be established.

It was asserted during the conference that "the best prediction of what a regulator will do today is what he or she did yesterday." Such a statement attests to the difficulty of regulatory reform. In light of this inertia, "incrementalism" rather than sudden, dramatic change was suggested as the most realistic approach to regulatory reform (Foster).

But whether or not this approach is successful, environmental regulation vitally needs reform. Past legislation -- in part a consequence of the attitudes and perspectives of regulatory personnel -- has tended to support regulatory policies that are not cost-effective. This added unnecessary costs to pollution control, but it was not perceived to be a problem by regulatory personnel, whose training has been skewed toward law and the physical sciences with only minor emphasis on economics. As regulators become better informed about the potential cost-savings of market mechanisms for pollution control, they will be more likely to actively support TDP systems.

Ironically, the group that stands to benefit most directly from market-oriented regulatory reform -- industry -- may not be a proponent of such reform. Why? Information regarding market-mechanisms and other innovative regulatory reform is not rapidly disseminated to industry engineers. The incentive-and-reward structure within industry often does not promote adoption of innovative regulatory reform policies (David and Joeres). The engineers responsible for plant operation do not receive the direct benefits of more efficient environmental pollution control strategies like TDPs and therefore do not have a strong incentive to promote or use TDPs. Reform that appears to increase the risk of permit violations is not readily embraced by risk-averse treatment facility managers. In addition, the cost of pollution control, as a minor portion of the total costs of production, attracts a correspondingly small interest from higher management. Furthermore, incentives to promote and use TDPs may be undercut when industrial managers believe other regulatory options -- such as rolling averages and flow/temperature permits in water pollution control -- provide sufficient flexibility and savings (Earl; David and Joeres). Clearly, these perceptions and attitudes may change as the details of TDP systems are more precisely defined and articulated to industrial emitters and dischargers.

Ambiguities in the regulatory process have also frustrated the adoption of market-based reforms and aggravate the barriers to implementation outlined above. Due to insufficient scientific knowledge, the environmental impact of pollutants is rarely fully specified. The "optimal" pollution control level is difficult or impossible to quantify precisely. Difficulties arise from uncertainty in assessing industry's aggregate marginal cost function for pollution abatement and in estimating the social benefits of pollution control. Jurisdictional uncertainties may also plague the adoption of TDPs. Existing, nationwide federal regulations may restrict states from implementing more cost-effective measures tailored to the specific characteristics of the region.

Two additional politically controversial questions that must be resolved are: (1) what are the minimum "acceptable" ambient conditions or environmental "standards" and (2) how should a fixed number of transferable permits initially be allocated? In the absence of well-defined social benefits, standards must be prescribed as proxies. Surely, a concensus on these standards will not be obtained easily because of the conflicting vested interests of the regulators, emitters/dischargers, and environmental groups. These interests will also be affected by the initial allocation of permits, because the allocation influences the distribution of control costs among dischargers, consumers and taxpayers. Grandfathering, government permit sales, various kinds of auctions and the "final product formula" were all discussed at the conference (Quinn; Eheart et al.). The different impact each proposed allocation scheme has on who bears the costs has yet to be assessed. This question and other equity issues require additional research (Bromley). As information on the impacts of decisions on these points becomes available to different interest groups, the controversy over them will doubtlessly intensify.

To date, only a few of the political and institutional realities have been identified and discussed formally. Many aspects of how TDP systems fit into regulatory reform have yet to be discovered. Nonetheless, the prevailing attitude conveyed by the conference participants was that these impediments to regulatory reform are, indeed, surmountable.


## MARKETS AND INSTITUTIONS FOR IMPLEMENTING T.D.P.s

Assuming the political and institutional barriers to market-based regulatory reform will be overcome, careful consideration must also be given to numerous technical and theoretical questions about the design of permit markets and institutions before TDP systems can be implemented. These questions include the form, or the unit of measure, in which the permits to be traded are written; the method of permit exchange; the potential for strategic behavior of traders within the market; the size of the markets for various pollutants, and the groups that may participate in the permit market. Issues of this sort represent the nuts-and-bolts decisions that policymakers must make before TDPs can be successfully implemented. Failure to anticipate relevant technical issues may lead to economic inefficiencies and environmental damage.

Two general forms of permit systems have been debated: the emissions-based permit system (EPS) and the ambient-based permit system (APS) (Foster; Oates; Eheart et al.). EPS permits are written in terms of maximum permissible mass-loading rates for air emissions or water discharges. The EPS allows one-for-one trades of discharges and ignores differences in geographic environmental impacts. Total mass loadings of pollutants are fixed in time, but their spatial distribution will vary depending on the location of existing and new dischargers. Unlike the EPS, the APS allows trades that maintain or improve ambient environmental impact at the predetermined control point or receptor. Hence, APS rules are written in terms of maximum permissible use of the environment's available assimilative capacity. An early formulation of the APS incorporated an additional "non-degradation" constraint: any affected receptors could not show increased pollution concentrations after the trade. This constraint may be relaxed as long as ambient quality standards are not exceeded at any receptor. This latter form of the APS system is referred to as the pollution-offset system (POS, Oates).

To use an APS, geographic or type-of-waste specific differentials in environmental impact are defined by a physical model of environmental quality. Where these differentials exist, trades are not on a one-for-one basis, but instead take these differentials into account. If permits are designed to reflect the stochastic nature of the environment's assimilative capacity (as in flow/temperature permits in water), then trading coefficients vary according to physical conditions. It is also important to recognize that although the total mass loading of pollutants may increase through trading under APS, the ambient environmental quality goal is maintained or improved.

A special kind of APS is the prioritized permit system. Under such a system, permitted emission levels depend on the period's available assimilative capacity. Junior rights would yield to senior rights in a predetermined order during periods of reduced assimilative capacity (Howe).

Once the form of the permit is determined, a method of exchange must be established. While they are appealing to theorists, auctions are viewed with skepticism by many regulators and considered impractical by most industries (Quinn). An informal market with a predominance of bilateral trades, overseen by a regulatory agency, seems more tractable, given the incentives and constraints affecting all agents.

Other points also related to permit exchange received brief attention at the conference: the importance of controlling coalitions of buyers and sellers to prevent strategic behavior in trades (Eheart et al.);

the need to design the market so to ensure a stable solution (Hahn), and the need to take advantage of benefits from economies of scale in coalitions (Heaney).

The size of the market must also be considered. The more finely pollutants are differentiated, the greater are the number of markets created and the higher are the transactions and management costs (Mendelsohn). Long-range as well as local impacts of pollutants must be studied, and the implications these impacts have for market size and permit form must be considered. For instance, a firm that builds a tall smokestack to meet local APS standards for $SO_2$ may find itself in violation of long-range $SO_x$ standards that may later be imposed to control acid rain (Atkinson). Permit violations could also occur if a short-range EPS were subsequently imposed. Natural features like multiple or moving critical points along a river system will also affect the size of a permit market. The shifting of constraining control points or receptors present special difficulties for APS (Eheart et al.).

While the principal actors in the market will be the regulatory agency and local industry, special interest groups like environmental organizations or competing firms may also choose to buy permits. Such participation would be beneficial as a vehicle for the valuation of societal preferences. Where the size of the market is small, the additional competition may help to reduce strategic behavior by dominant sellers or buyers. Initial investigations, however, indicate such participation to be very unlikely (Oppenheimer).

ENHANCEMENT OF ENVIRONMENTAL QUALITY

The effect of marketable permit mechanisms on environmental quality was the area least discussed during the conference. Market mechanisms offer the potential for enhancing environmental quality; but if not carefully defined and implemented, they could cause environmental degradation as well.

Static cost-savings from TDPs, as estimated by several people at this conference, significantly reduce the costs of control in a number of situations (O'Neil; Eheart et al.). But perhaps the greatest enviromental benefit induced by market mechanisms will be derived from long-run technological change. Under a market-based permit system, firms that adopt new, more cost-efficient abatement facilities will likely be sellers in the permit market. These firms will be rewarded for their technological innovations in two ways: by lower control costs for their wastes, and by revenues from permit trades. Over time, technological improvements from one firm will be adopted and improved by other firms, since each firm has the same two incentives to improve its control technology. The lower long-run costs of control make pollution abatement less expensive and improved ambient environmental quality a more realistic goal.

In contrast to the above benefits, improper management of market-based permit systems could increase environmental degradation. "Paper

offsets" are one example where environmental degradation has resulted
from implementation of a poorly defined trading system. The USEPA's
offset policy is an EPS where it is assumed that the total allowable,
or total actual, emission loading is fixed. If a firm trades a
portion of its permit that it never used, then the new pollution
resulting from this market transfer is not offset by reductions in
pollution levels elsewhere. For this reason, it is referred to as a
"paper offset." Contrary to the intent of the policy, the actual
pollution loading increases (Foster). Such unanticipated inconsis-
tencies in environmental regulations will require continual regulatory
review and flexibility.


CONCLUSIONS

In the final session of the conference, the observation was made that
TDPs are not simply an academic policy to be studied for possible
future use, but a real regulatory strategy being used right now.
Consequently, it is imperative for individuals concerned with
environmental control to understand the many institutional and
technical issues addressed at this conference. If such understanding
does not develop, it is unlikely that TDPs will lead to lower-cost
environmental quality. Instead, "paper offsets" and other, as-yet-
unknown problems may arise.

The fundamental issues surrounding environmental management are
inherently normative in nature. This characteristic complicates the
entire regulatory reform process. It has been noted that the
definition of the "rights" to pollute, compensation for the "victims"
of regulation vs. compensation for the "victims" of pollution, the
benefit to society from improved environmental quality, and the
baseline for environmental quality are normative distinctions
(Bromley). While the theorist can talk in terms of maximizing social
welfare based on a social welfare "function," in our society that
function is defined and continually redefined through the political
process. Engineers and economists have the responsibility of clearly
identifying the implications of different regulatory strategies for
meeting environmental goals, for determining costs and benefits, and
for showing the distribution of these costs and benefits among
societal groups. It behooves us to make this analysis and share this
information with policymakers early in the regulatory reform process.

Providing environmental protection at reduced cost is a formidable
challenge. Our conference was one step toward implementing regulatory
reform that will achieve that goal. The groups represented by
participants at the conference are those responsible for addressing
the issues presented and for establishing TDP systems. We believe
this monograph will assist others in this joint endeavor.

# Appendix A
## List of Conference Participants

Scott Atkinson
Department of Economics
University of Wyoming
P.O. Box 3985
Laramie, WY 82071

William Bateson
Department of Economics
University of Wisconsin
Madison, WI 53706

John J. Boland
Department of Geography and
  Environmental Engineering
The Johns Hopkins University
Baltimore, MD 21218

E. Downey Brill, Jr.
Dept. of Civil Engineering
University of Illinois
Urbana, IL 61801

Daniel W. Bromley
Department of Ag. Economics
University of Wisconsin
Madison, WI 53706

Martin David
Department of Economics
University of Wisconsin
Madison, WI 53706

Peter DeRossi
Green Bay Packaging, Inc.
P.O. Box 1107
Green Bay, WI 54305

Donna Downing
SRI International
Menlo Park, CA 94025

Wayland Eheart
Dept. of Civil Engineering
University of Illinois
Urbana, IL 61801

Virgil Endres
Wisconsin Power & Light
P.O. Box 192
Madison, WI 53701

John Flickinger
Wisconsin Power & Light
P.O. Box 192
Madison, WI 53701

David Foster
U.S. Environmental
  Protection Agency (USEPA)
202 M Street, S.W.
Washington, DC 20460

Robert Hahn
Dept. of Engineering & Public Policy
Carnegie-Mellon University
Pittsburgh, PA 15213

Robert Haveman
Department of Economics
University of Wisconsin
Madison, WI 53706

Diane Heaney
Water Resources Research Cntr.
University of Florida
Gainesville, FL 32611

James Heaney
Water Resources Research Cntr.
University of Florida
Gainesville, FL 32611

Gregory D. Hedden
Sea Grant Advisory Services
University of Wisconsin
1815 University Avenue
Madison, WI 53705

Charles Howe
Department of Economics
University of Colorado
Boulder, CO 80309

Erhard Joeres
Department of Civil and
  Environmental Engineering
University of Wisconsin
Madison, WI 53706

Gary V. Johnson
Institute for
  Environmental Studies
University of Illinois
Urbana, IL 61801

Clifford Kraft
Sea Grant Advisory Services
E.S. Building, #105
University of Wisconsin
Green Bay, WI 54302

Randolph Lyon
Department of Economics
University of Texas
Austin, TX 78712

James MacDonald
Law School
University of Wisconsin
Madison, WI 53706

Robert Mendelsohn
Department of Economics
University of Washington
Seattle, WA 98195

Shirley Mitchell
USEPA - Region V
230 South Dearborn
Chicago, IL 60604

Peter Morgan
Meta Systems, Inc.
10 Holworthy Street
Cambridge, MA 02138

Pixie A.B. Newman
Department of Civil and
  Environmental Engineering
University of Wisconsin
Madison, WI 53706

Richard Noss
Dept. of Civil Engineering
University of Massachusetts
Amherst, MA 01003

Wallace Oates
Department of Economics
University of Maryland
College Park, MD 20742

William O'Neil
Department of Economics
Colby College
Waterville, ME 04901

Joe Oppenheimer
Resources for the Future
1755 Massachusetts Avenue
Washington, DC 20036

Lori Parsons
Wisconsin Department of
  Natural Resources
P.O. Box 7921
Madison, WI 53707

John P. Perrecone
USEPA - Region V
230 South Dearborn
Chicago, IL 60604

Michael Quigley
USEPA - Region V
230 South Dearborn
Chicago, IL 60604

Timothy Quinn
Rand Corporation
1700 Main Street
Santa Monica, CA 90406

Sharon Reinders
USEPA - Region V
230 South Dearborn
Chicago, IL 60604

Stuart Rosenthal
Department of Economics
University of Wisconsin
Madison, WI 53706

Clifford Russell
Resources for the Future
1755 Massachusetts Avenue
Washington, DC 20036

John Stolzenberg
Wisconsin Legislative Council
Capitol Building
Madison, WI 53707

Kshersagar Sudhir
Dept. of Civil Engineering
University of Illinois
Urbana, IL 61801

Don Theiler
Wisconsin Department of
   Natural Resources
P.O. Box 7921
Madison, WI 53707

Alan Weinstein
Department of Urban Planning
University of Wisconsin
P.O. Box 413
Milwaukee, WI 53201

# Appendix B
# Glossary

## Ambient-based Permit System (APS)

A system whereby permits written in terms of a proportion or quantity of the environment's assimilative capacity, not in terms of the absolute level of discharge, are traded. Trades under this system preserve or improve existing ambient environmental quality at all critical points or receptors. (Applies to both air and water markets.)

## Asset Utilization Model

A model designed to estimate the benefits from waste discharge abatement. The environment is viewed as asset-like resource, capable of sustaining many different service flows. The service flows are interactive; the use of one service affects the availability or quality of others. Society's objective is taken as the maximization of some measure of satisfaction received from the environment as a whole.

## Banking

A USEPA provision that allows firms to accumulate credit for past emission reductions. A firm that permanently reduces its emission loading rate by a given amount may sell that amount or loading rate to another firm at any time after the original reduction. Through this belated "trade," the total loading rate of emissions is maintained or reduced. (Sales or trades are permitted so long as they do not result in new violations of ambient environmental quality standards or prevent the planned removal of an ambient environmental quality violation.)

## Biochemical Oxygen Demand (BOD)

A measure of the demand for oxygen generated by organic waste discharged into a water system.

BOD5 is BOD that takes five days to decompose.

Best Practicable Control Treatment (BPT)

> The treatment levels specified for industrial and municipal discharges as a result of PL 92-500 federal Water Pollution Control Amendments of 1972. (Applies to water markets.)

Bubble

> A USEPA provision that allows "swaps" of emissions of a particular pollutant within plants, across plants and even across firms, provided pollution is not made worse. (Usually applies to air market.)

Chemical Oxygen Demand (COD)

> Measure of chemical oxygen demand generated by waste discharged into a water system.

Dissolved Oxygen (DO)

> A measure of ambient water quality (expressed in parts per million [ppm] or milligrams per liter [mg/L]).

Emission-based Permit System (EPS)

> A system whereby permits written in terms of absolute levels of discharge or emission are traded. Trades under this system preserve the total discharge or emission loading within the market. (Applies to air and water markets.)

Final product formula

> The initial allocation of pollution-based distribution of final product output. (Hypothesized for air market.)

Gaussian plume model

> The dispersion model used for examining the spatial/temporal change of pollutant concentration. Model assumes that the spread form is Gaussian, or normally distributed.

Grandfathering

> Distribution of permits or other rights based on their historical share of that market or waste proportion.

Minimum Costs, Remaining Savings (MCRS)

A method of apportioning project costs among groups whereby a
minimum charge is allocated to all users. Options include
(1) MC = 0, (2) MC = separable costs (see SCRS), (3) MC =
activity unique charge. The remaining costs are prorated in one
of six ways: (1) equally, (2) proportionally to physical measure
of use, (3) entirely to highest priority group up to limits of
their benefit, (4) proportionally to benefit in excess of
assigned separable cost, (5) proportionally to excess cost to
provide service by some alternative means and (6) using remaining
benefits method in (5).

Offsets

A USEPA provision that allows a firm to increase its emission
loading rate if another firm offsets this increase by a simultaneous, equivalent reduction in its loading rate. (For comments
on restrictions and total loadings, see Banking.)

Pareto optimality

An allocation of resources is Pareto optimal, or Pareto efficient, when every other allocation that makes one agent better
off necessarily makes at least one other agent worse off.

Pollution Offsets System (POS)

A system whereby permits written in terms of a proportion or
quantity of the environment's assimilative capacity are traded.
Trades may reduce environmental quality at some receptors so long
as the ambient quality standard is not exceeded at any critical
receptor or point. (Applies to air and water markets.)

Priority Pollution Rights System (PPRS)

A system whereby prioritized permits are traded. Junior rights
yield to senior rights in a predetermined order during periods of
reduced assimilative capacity.

Separable Costs, Remaining Benefits (SCRB)

A method of apportioning project costs among various groups
whereby separable costs are allocated to each group, and the
remaining costs, or nonseparable costs, are allocated based on
the proration ratio of their remaining benefits. The separable
cost is defined as the difference between costs of the

multiple-group project and cost of the project with the group
omitted (i.e., the direct and incremental cost of changing size
of multigroup cost elements). The remaining benefits are defined
as the benefits of independent action less the separable costs,
so that:

$$x(i) = sc(i) + (i) (nsc)$$

where $x(i)$ = group $\underline{i}$'s cost;
$sc(i)$ = separable cost;
$(i)$ = proration ratio;
$nsc$ = nonseparable costs.

## Trading coefficient

The rate at which emissions/discharges from one firm can
substitute for those from another firm with no change in ambient
conditions at the mutually affected critical point or receptor.
(Applies to APS in both air and water markets.)

## Transfer coefficient

Measure of the environmental quality impact of a particular
source on a specific receptor. (Applies to air and water
markets.)

# Keyword Index